Congressional Reform

Congressional Reform

Leroy N. Rieselbach
Indiana University

PRESS

A division of Congressional Quarterly Inc.
1414 22nd Street, N.W., Washington, D.C. 20037

Printed in the United States of America

Library of Congress Cataloging in Publication Data

Rieselbach, Leroy N.
  Congressional reform.

  Bibliography: p. 159.
  Includes index.
  1. United States. Congress — Reform. I. Title.
JK1061.R485 1986   328'.3042'0973   86-2333
ISBN 0-87187-385-0

*To my mother
and the memory
of my father*

Preface

"Congress is a much maligned institution." So I wrote in the preface to an earlier (1977) work on congressional reform. Although much has changed in the national legislature, at least one thing remains the same: Congress continues to be the object of much scorn and derision. It is an easy target in many ways. Its members regularly behave idiosyncratically. They often seem more interested in their own reelection, or in attaining higher office, than in crafting effective legislation. The assembly frequently appears to be excessively deferential to the president, especially in foreign policy, but the chief executive castigates it as uncooperative, "taxers and spenders," narrowly parochial. The complicated congressional process baffles all but the most dedicated observers. Constituents may appreciate their own senators and representatives, who cater to their concerns, but most of the time they hold Congress, the institution, in "minimum high regard."

During the 1960s and 1970s members of the legislature recognized Congress's shortcomings. They acknowledged that the oft-quoted aphorism "the president proposes and Congress disposes" had a ring of truth. Congress was often slow to act, and when it did bestir itself it did not always effectively resolve the nation's policy problems. They admitted that they, as members, did not always do their jobs in ways that allayed fears about their ethics and integrity. As a result, they launched a major campaign, beginning with the Legislative Reorganization Act of 1970, to reform and revitalize their institution. This book addresses the causes and character of these reforms and their consequences in the 1980s.

Such an assessment is difficult. Reform is a tricky business. First, it implies change for the better, but what one person sees as improvement may appear deleterious to another. Second, to put it baldly, Americans have spent little time thinking about, much less deciding, what ideally Congress should be, what it should do in national politics. Matters of the moment color evaluations deeply: when Congress behaves "properly"— whether that entails supporting or opposing the president, passing or rejecting favored legislation, or focusing on constituency service and oversight rather than on policy making—the observer approves; when its acts seem "inappropriate," the same observer finds Congress wanting. In the absence of widely shared standards of judgment, definitive conclusions about reform and its consequences are virtually impossible.

Nonetheless, despite the subjectivity of reform evaluations, a close look at the institutional changes during the past two and one-half decades may sharpen our thinking and enable us to face up to the real-world and normative implications of congressional reform. Can the nation afford to permit the executive and his administrative apparatus to dominate the formulation of public policy? Are there reasonable ways to harness administrative expertise to the "public good" or to equip Congress to assert more forcefully its own conception of the "national interest"? From the legislative vantage point, are there clear channels through which the voices of individuals, alone or in organized groups, can be heard? Are there structural mechanisms that can permit Congress, representing the citizenry, to exert policy influence? Can the public be motivated to hold its elected lawmakers to strict account for the ways they conduct the country's business? Finally, is there some way to create a governmental system capable of both solving problems and responding to the needs and preferences of the people?

To set the framework for exploring these questions, Chapter 1 outlines Congress's place in the larger context of national politics and introduces broad evaluative criteria—executive force and congressional supremacy perspectives—and narrower standards—responsiveness (representativeness), responsibility (policy-making efficiency), and accountability (opportunity for citizen control)—with which to assess Congress and its performance. Chapter 2 details the critics' specific charges against Congress. Chapter 3 traces the reform movement that flowered during the 1970s, describing the steps taken to make Congress more effective, and Chapter 4 assesses the impact of these reform initiatives. Finally, Chapter 5 confronts the normative issues directly. It identifies specific visions of what the legislature could or should be, suggests additional reforms to move it toward those particular ends, and proposes one possible picture—majoritarian democracy—that might offer an appropriate blend of desirable values.

All authors incur numerous obligations in the course of their work, and I record mine with pleasure and gratitude. Roderick Bell first offered me the opportunity to write about congressional reform. Bruce Oppenheimer provided an enormously insightful and valuable reading of the manuscript, offering suggestions that required rethinking and rewriting many portions of the text. Over the years, I have learned a great deal, much of which has filtered into these pages, from discussing Congress in general and legislative change in particular with many, too numerous to name here; conversations with my colleague Larry Dodd have been especially rewarding. The Department of Political Science at Indiana University has offered a congenial home that has given me the time and material support needed to continue research and writing. The department's administrative assistant, Doris-Jean Burton, has made my life easier for more than a decade, allowing important things to drive out the trivial. The staff at CQ Press—Joanne Daniels, its director; Nola Lynch; and Barbara de Boinville—were easy to work with, prompt, and efficient. Finally, Roberta Scott prepared a manuscript from my long-hand scrawls with good humor and dispatch. I am more than grateful to all these people for their help.

The book draws on three earlier essays: "Assessing Congressional Change, or What Hath Reform Wrought (or Wreaked)?" in *The United States Congress: Proceedings of the Thomas P. O'Neill, Jr. Symposium*, ed. Dennis Hale (Chestnut Hill, Mass.: Boston College, 1982), 167-207; "Legislative Change, Reform, and Public Policy," in *Encyclopedia of Policy Studies*, ed. Stuart S. Nagel (New York: Marcel Dekker, 1983), 359-94; and "Reforming Congress: Philosophy, Politics, Problems, Prospects," in *Reforming Government and Bureaucracy*, ed. Donald J. Calista, *Public Policy Studies: A Multivolume Treatise*, vol. 9 (Greenwood, Conn.: JAI Press, 1986). The Bibliography is an updated version of a similar effort, "Legislative Change, Reform, and Public Policy," *Policy Studies Review* 2 (1983): 813-21.

This book goes to press as I conclude my twenty-fifth year of university teaching. I use the "occasion" to offer a long overdue thank you to three individuals—Robert E. Lane, Samuel P. Huntington, and Karl W. Deutsch—who have had a profound impact, dating from my student days in Cambridge and New Haven, on my career. Not only did each demonstrate in word and deed what serious scholarship is all about, but their friendship, guidance, and personal kindness to an aspiring academic far exceeded any ordinary expectations about faculty-student relationships. While they bear no responsibility whatsoever for the content of this book, had it not been for their encouragement and support this volume most certainly would never have been written.

Always last but never least comes one's family. The affection, encouragement, and forbearance of Helen Rieselbach and our children—Erik, Kurt, Alice, and (especially over the past few years) Karen—have enriched my life immeasurably. To them goes love and gratitude far deeper than mere words can convey.

Contents

Congressional Reform

Congress and American Politics | 1

No other legislature is quite like the U.S. Congress. Its ability to compete with the executive branch, and to impose its will on national politics when and if it chooses to do so, distinguishes it from most other twentieth-century assemblies. Even its critics acknowledge that Congress continues to pose serious policy-making challenges for the president; what the country does in foreign and domestic affairs often, although not always, bears the stamp of the national legislature. Much of American political history, in fact, has featured a power struggle between the president and the Congress for policy-making primacy. Yet Congress has not always asserted its authority to the fullest extent. The alleged failure of Congress to leave its mark on public policy spawned the reform movement that began in the mid-1960s, the subject of this book.

While dissatisfaction with congressional performance antedated the Vietman War and the Watergate crisis, those two singular events provided the catalyst for the first major reform movement in Congress since the 1940s and the most far-reaching set of changes in congressional procedures and practices since the second decade of this century.[1] These events demonstrated with finality that the modern liberals' faith in the ultimate benevolence of the American president was misplaced: the chief executive was not automatically an engine of progress and sound policy. Vietnam and Watergate, symbolic of the dominant "imperial presidency" of their era,[2] created both the climate and the commitment for a complete reexamination of the relationship between the two elected branches of the national government, a reassessment that led many observers to conclude that the Congress should operate as a more effective check on the executive.

The Indochina conflict illustrated congressional impotence in foreign affairs. American involvement, as John Kennedy and Lyndon Johnson engineered it, and disengagement, as Richard Nixon conducted it, were almost exclusively managed by presidential decision. Only after the Watergate burglary and cover-up swamped Nixon did Congress act to cut off funds for military involvement in Vietnam. Similarly, most other aspects of the nation's foreign policy, especially in the areas of military strategy and defense posture, were formulated beyond the purview of Congress; the president and the Pentagon, the critics of Congress charged, reduced the legislature to a minor role in world politics.

In domestic affairs, the events surrounding Watergate told a similar tale of presidential dominance. A president, without hindrance from Congress (even one controlled by his political opposition), engaged in or condoned numerous illegal activities: obstructing justice by concealing evidence of the break-in at Democratic National Committee headquarters; using federal agencies—the Federal Bureau of Investigation, the Central Intelligence Agency, and the Internal Revenue Service—for political purposes; employing campaign "dirty tricks"; trying to influence the judge in the case of Daniel Ellsberg, the author of the *Pentagon Papers;* and temporarily accepting a surveillance plan that infringed the civil rights of citizens. Moreover, Nixon challenged Congress directly over the federal budget. He tried to force the legislature to limit spending, and in an unprecedented fashion, he began to impound (refuse to spend) money that Congress had duly appropriated.

A more general criticism, which predated Watergate, was that Congress did not respond to national needs. Vested interests within the legislature remained firmly in tune with the status quo: the environmental crisis continued unabated; crime abounded; poverty and unemployment worsened; and inflation eroded the purchasing power of those who did have jobs. Congress did not respond adequately to these crises, its antagonists asserted, because it was not organized to deal effectively with contemporary policy problems. It had abdicated its responsibility, relinquishing to the executive the role of prime mover in public affairs.[3] The aim of the reform movement that flowered in the Vietnam-Watergate era was to repair these deficiencies, to make Congress a "better," "more efficient" legislature.

Congress and the Constitution

Reform was both attractive and possible because the decline of the legislature was neither inevitable nor irreversible. Congress retained the constitutional and statutory means to exert a major impact on the form and content of public policy. The Constitution clearly assigns to Congress, as one of the "separate institutions sharing power," important policy-making responsibilities. The legislature possesses the ability to declare war and to appropriate money to sustain the military. It holds the power to authorize and fund major domestic programs. How Congress employs its constitutional power to meet its obligations at any moment in history goes far to determine what the nation does or does not accomplish. Congress can, when a majority of its members wish to act, impose its collective preferences on the body politic. Not only can it act affirmatively, however. It also is able (and more likely) to block initiatives that others—the public, interest organizations, and the courts, as well as the president—propose. If Congress has not used its powers, it is because most lawmakers have chosen to defer to executive expertise, to permit others to make decisions that they, as elected legislators, can choose to make for themselves.

Congress has other obligations beyond policy making. The Legislative Reorganization Act of 1946 authorizes Congress to exert "continuous watchfulness" over the departments, agencies, and bureaus that comprise the administrative branch of government. In general, this process of congressional oversight of the executive aims to keep bureaucrats, from cabinet secretaries on down, honest and efficient.[4] The Senate, exercising its "advice and consent" prerogative, must approve the president's nominations for the top political posts in any administration. For example, the Senate subjected Ronald Reagan's choice for attorney general, Edwin Meese, to close scrutiny because of a series of charges that Meese had used his position as a White House advisor to the president to reward friends for loans and other favors they had done for him and his family. This Senate consideration forced appointment of a special counsel to investigate the accusations, delayed confirmation for many months, and exacted from the nominee pledges to avoid even the appearance of ethical impropriety in the future. Congress also writes the civil service statutes that specify who works, and under what conditions and with what qualifications, for the federal bureaucracy below the level of the president's political appointees. In so doing, the legislature may entrench individuals who oppose presidential initiatives in the administrative branch as career civil servants. Policing the personnel of the executive may, in short, bring Congress into conflict with the president.

Oversight also entails congressional examination of bureaucratic performance. Legislative committees regularly look to see whether administrators get "a dollar's worth of value for a dollar spent." Members of Congress are predictably outraged when they discover that the government has paid defense contractors $7,622 for a coffee ma-

3

chine, $748 for a pair of pliers, or $640 for a custom-made toilet cover.[5] In the long run the fact or threat of legislative investigation may deter bureaucrats from pushing forcefully for presidential initiatives. As this suggests, oversight may be couched in terms of efficiency, but it has clear programmatic implications. The revelations of defense industry abuses seem to have prompted Congress to cut back sharply on procurement of the MX missile to levels well below those the president favored. Here, too, oversight may exacerbate differences of opinion between the legislature and the executive.

Finally, Congress is the "people's branch": it should speak for and to the citizenry and represent the people. In other words, the members should both listen to and act on behalf of their constituents, informing and educating them about the activities that occur in the nation's capital. Representation takes several forms.[6] Senators and representatives engage in policy representation; they are expected to translate public preferences into practical programs. They are also expected to "deliver the goods" to their constituents—in the form of public projects and contracts for local industries—and to perform for them a variety of "casework" services, such as tracing lost Social Security or income tax refund checks or providing information about how the federal bureaucracy operates. Finally, representation has a symbolic dimension; if for no other reason than to promote their reelection, members feel an obligation to present a favorable image of themselves to the "folks back home." Thus, they develop a "home style," a way of relating to residents through regular attention to their states and districts.[7] By making appropriate gestures to constituents, members of Congress hope to earn trust and confidence and to win at least some freedom to pursue their own policy preferences.

Like oversight, representation is related to lawmaking. What members hear from constituents—the opinions and complaints that reach them—may alert them to policy needs or deficiencies and compel them to respond. Representation also may generate differences with the executive. To the extent that the public favors one set of programs and the president another, legislators will have to choose. The most prudent course politically may be to defer to constituents and to oppose the chief executive. Unpopular positions—raising taxes, committing troops, dealing with abortion—may be avoided; difficult problems may remain unresolved. Constituency relations, then, assume great importance in member's lives for policy making as well as oversight and representation.

In short, whatever Congress does when it legislates (or fails to act), oversees, and represents is likely to bring it into conflict with the executive. Constitutional arrangements virtually guarantee that the legislature will view its work differently than will the president. The latter is chosen by all the people; the president is the focus of national attention, the central actor in the political drama. By contrast, members of Congress are elected by states and local constituencies that vary widely in terms of population characteristics and social and economic conditions. Senators represent large, populous states (California, New York, Texas) and sparsely settled states (Alaska, Utah, Idaho); energy-producing states (in the Southwest) and energy-consuming states (in New England); Farm Belt states and states where urban, inner-city areas dominate; industrial "smokestack" states (the Frost Belt) and service-industry states (the Sun Belt). Differing constituencies give senators varying interests to represent. Districts in the House of Representatives are often more homogeneous. They may be almost pure working-class, farm, suburban, or black constituencies; they may, at least on controversial issues, send their legislators loud and clear messages. In such circumstances, members may well speak for interests that require responses that bring them into conflict with the president.

Moreover, the federal system, which undercuts the possibility of centralized, disciplined, national political parties, provides members with independence. The national organizations, even the president's party, have little leverage with members, who are essentially local candidates. Senators and representatives, running in single-member districts that select winners by plurality vote, control their own electoral fates. They run their own races in response to local conditions; they recruit their own campaign workers, solicit their own campaign funds, plan their own schedules, and select their own campaign issues. They come to office and regularly win reelection as the result of their own efforts, with little if any debt to the national party, which has few sanctions with which to discipline members who defect from nationally established party positions.[8] Electorally entrenched in their constituencies, members are free to oppose the president when that seems to be wise strategy; whether for policy or political purposes, they can pursue their own interests without fear of real reprisals from the chief executive.

In sum, the Constitution, with its checks and balances, separation of powers, and federalist principles, makes Congress independent of the executive. Congress has the constitutional authority to impose its policy preferences; its members have the political freedom to do so. For better or worse, Congress and the president will sooner or later clash over the content of public policy. The Constitution ensures such conflict.

Politics, Values, and the Assessment of Congress _____

Whether this conflict is "good" or "bad" is, of course, a matter of philosophy, of political preference. Some observers profess satisfaction with the status quo, preferring minimal policy change most of the time to a too-powerful, imperial president. Congress, they believe, should serve to restrain the executive. Others, however, want action; they see major problems that need solution, and they deplore the immobilism that, in their view, the executive-legislative balance inevitably entails. Either position may spawn proposals for reform. The former group, believing that after the New Deal of the 1930s Congress gradually relinquished its ability to resist the president, proposes changes to strengthen the legislature's capacity to countervail the executive. The latter group, assessing the same circumstances, ironically sees something quite different: a too-powerful Congress. It suggests reforms intended to reduce the legislature's opportunities to obstruct presidential leadership, to block innovative policy initiatives that the president is most likely to produce.

The adherents of these positions are not consistent, however; as time passes and political circumstances alter they are likely to shift their views, depending on the particular policy at issue. For example, "liberals," those predisposed toward social activism or government intervention in the economy, decried Congress's refusal to embark on new programs during periods other than the New Deal or the Great Society eras. Yet if a president proposes to retrench, to eliminate desirable programs already on the statute books, these same liberals applaud Congress's refusal to repeal these policies. They were more than happy to see the legislature block many conservative proposals that Richard Nixon advanced between 1968 and 1974.[9] Presumably, they are equally content with Congress's resistance to Reagan administration cutbacks in the size and scope of numerous federal programs. Conversely, "conservatives," those enamored of the free market and minimal government, cheer when Congress blocks new federal initiatives and hiss when it fails to heed the bidding of presidents, like Ronald Reagan, who espouse their philosophy. Thus, today's reforms shape tomorrow's performance; the influence of change may outlast the reformers and produce consequences they never considered or intended.

Broad Perspectives

Although evaluations of Congress often reflect political, particularly policy, values, there are larger views of the institution, sweeping visions of what Congress might be like in the best of all possible worlds.

A few observers have set forth broad, comprehensive, and presumably timeless philosophies of Congress's proper political role. These views, in a sense, transcend the politics of the moment and current policy preferences to advance a clear picture of the "good," "ideal," or at least "better" Congress. Four such visions of the national assembly warrant brief discussion: the executive force theory, the responsible parties theory, the "literary" theory, and the congressional supremacy theory.[10]

The Executive Force Theory. Proponents of the executive force theory are pessimistic about Congress's capacity to govern.[11] They stress the need to solve pressing political, economic, and social problems and despair that the legislature can contribute meaningfully to policy formulation. The executive is viewed as the likely catalyst for progress; Congress, given its basic structures and processes, can only impede innovation. As a decentralized, fragmented institution representing multiple interests—especially the rural, small-town, conservative constituencies of Middle America—the legislature is incapable of acting decisively. It is better suited to oppose than to create, to react than to invent.

In consequence, if policy making is to meet the nation's needs, the president must be permitted to lead, unobstructed by a recalcitrant Congress. Executive initiatives must pass and be implemented. Reform should reduce legislative ability to frustrate presidential policy making. Independent sources of power—committees and subcommittees, for instance—should be curbed. Rules of procedure that permit minorities to block action require modification. In general, the path of presidential proposals through Congress should be smoothed. This executive supremacy view, in sum, stresses presidential leadership and reduces Congress's role to legitimizing, perhaps modifying, and reviewing after the fact decisions the president makes.[12] The president proposes, and the legislature disposes according to his wishes.

The Responsible Parties Theory. An alternative way for the executive to escape congressional obstructionism is to make good use of disciplined, cohesive, "responsible" political parties.[13] If the majority party, given its command of the legislative terrain as the chief organizational mechanism of the assembly, marched smartly and decisively in rank, its policy proposals would triumph at each stage of the lawmaking process. Moreover, if the president commanded the party troops, they would advance his programs without risk of rearguard delay or defeat.

Proponents of responsible parties promote reforms to enlist rank-and-file members of Congress in the partisan armies. In general, they empower the national committees of the parties to manage the electoral process by giving them a legal monopoly over campaign finances. By controlling the nomination, the central committees could dictate the actions of the elected representatives: to break ranks would, in effect, end the deserter's political career; the nomination would be given to a new, more loyal, recruit. Inside Congress, the rules would be rewritten to ensure that disciplined majorities could carry the legislative day more easily. In the responsible parties view, the president proposes, and his partisan army loyally obeys his marching orders. Here, too, Congress would eschew policy making, emphasizing instead legitimizing and nonpolicy representation (for example, constituent service) activities.

The "Literary" Theory. What proponents of executive force and responsible parties view as vices are virtues to adherents of the "literary" theory.[14] The latter pay homage to the written tradition of checks and balances and separation of powers under the Constitution. In their view, Congress should restrain the power-seeking executive during both policy formulation and implementation. New policies, departures from the status quo, should come slowly, only after careful deliberation of all alternatives, and only after a genuine national consensus emerges. Thus, a decentralized legislature, which is influenced by multiple interests and can act only cautiously, is highly desirable.

These virtues have been lost in the twentieth century, the so-called age of executives, and reform is required to restore the status quo ante. To that end, literary theorists resist all centralizing mechanisms. They prefer an election system that protects legislators' independence; they fear disciplined political parties that might run roughshod over citizens' sentiments; they distrust executive leadership in any form; and, most important, they favor congressional procedures that protect the power of individual legislators to speak, slow action down, promote deliberation, and oversee the administration. Overall, they want Congress to propose and dispose—make policy, represent citizens, police the bureaucracy—to countervail the executive. They seek to restore Congress to what they see as its rightful place at the center of the political process.

The Congressional Supremacy ("Whig") Theory. Legislative supremacists stress the centrality of Congress to an even greater extent than do the literary theorists.[15] They see Congress as the first branch of government, the prime mover in national affairs, and they favor all the reforms that the literary theorists advocate as well as other changes intended, in effect, to strip the chief executive of the ability to dominate national policy making. This "Whig" view envisages a Congress that proposes and an administration, president, and bureaucracy that disposes in strict accordance with legislative desires. A supreme Congress will make policy—explicitly and on its own terms—as well as oversee the implementation of that policy.

Conclusion. Each of these broad visions of Congress entails its own particular set of structural and procedural reforms and could provide a model against which to evaluate specific reform proposals. Central to any assessment of a reform is a general question about the obligation of government and a narrower issue relating to the role of Congress in policy making. Proponents of executive force and responsible parties stress action; government must find prompt and effective solutions to national problems. In stark contrast, the literary and congressional supremacy views focus on caution and consensus; policy initiatives should come slowly, after due deliberation leads to wide agreement that new programs are needed.

All four visions carry concomitant organizational requisites. Those who desire to foster active policy making (the executive force and responsible parties theorists) seek to centralize congressional structure. Dominant executives, sustained by an accommodating legislature, formulate and implement public policies. Those who prefer inaction look favorably on a decentralized legislature—with numerous, autonomous decision-making centers—that can move only after attending to many points of view and melding them into widely acceptable programs. In other words, the proexecutive visions seek to minimize independent congressional policy influence, whereas prolegislative views seek to maximize it.[16]

Narrower Standards: Responsibility, Responsiveness, and Accountability

These broad visions of the "good" legislature have inspired more talk than action. They are hard to implement; each would in all likelihood require amending the Constitution, a difficult task under any circumstances and more onerous still when it involves altering basic features of the political process such as the electoral system. Needless to say, given the sharp contrasts between the proexecutive and legislative supremacy positions, there is little shared basis for agreement. For every proponent of a particular view, there is an opponent who rejects that position. Furthermore, in the "real world" of practical politics few with the opportunity and authority to change the way Congress operates— the members themselves—have taken a genuine interest in stepping back from day-to-day political pressures to examine Congress and its policy-making role in philosophical terms. Rather, they tend to react pragmatically and to call for reform only if it seems absolutely necessary. Members have tended to evaluate Congress's performance using three criteria: responsibility, responsiveness, and accountability.[17] These three standards relate to the broader visions but do not require the same levels of agreement or pose insuperable obstacles to taking specific reform steps.

Any assessment of the need for congressional reform raises fundamental questions about Congress's place in the national government, an issue that the executive-legislative conflicts over "hot" issues such as Vietnam and Watergate brought to the top of the political agenda. What should Congress's role be? Should it relinquish its claim to participate meaningfully in policy making? Should it focus its attention and resources on overseeing the executive branch, sounding the alarm when presidents move in the wrong direction or when bureaucrats perform unsatisfactorily? Should the legislature be content simply to represent the public—transmitting popular opinion to those who actually make decisions, informing citizens about government programs, or performing nonpolicy casework services for constituents? Or should Congress revitalize its mode of operation and attempt to exercise policy initiative and leadership? The three criteria yield quite different answers to these questions, but each provides a starting place for analysis of the legislative branch.[18]

Responsibility.   The first standard, responsibility, focuses on problem solving. A responsible institution makes reasonably successful policies that resolve the major issues confronting the country. The responsibility criterion emphasizes speed, efficiency, and, of course, success. Can Congress enact policy that deals promptly and effectively with national problems? Can it control inflation or reduce unemployment? Can it pass laws that strengthen the nation's defense, promote international trade, or encourage Third World social and economic development? If, as many critics of Congress have argued, the answer to such queries is "no," then reform to improve the *product* of the legislative process is clearly in order.

A responsible Congress is compatible with both proexecutive and prolegislative visions. To the extent that Congress simply ratifies the president's program without delay or major revision, it acts as the executive force or responsible parties advocates prefer; it concurs with the executive, approving policies that address the major issues of the day. Policy independence, however, is minimal: the legislature merely defers to the initiatives of others. On the other hand, to the degree that Congress imposes its own programmatic priorities, it behaves consistently with the legislative supremacy (literary and "Whig") positions; that is, it will do what it thinks best, regardless of what executives, interest groups, or public opinion may favor. This may entail blocking what seem to be unwise executive initiatives or, a more problematic course, enacting its own priorities. Here, Congress exercises genuine policy autonomy and influence, but it will most certainly encounter difficulty, especially when it seeks to act affirmatively. Other political participants will mobilize to block congressional action. The president may veto legislation, which can be overruled only if Congress musters a two-thirds majority in each chamber. Needless to say, asserting supremacy in the face of determined opposition will prove more challenging than joining a government-wide policy consensus. A policy-oriented legislature may spend more time studying and debating legislation and will probably devote less effort to oversight and representational activities. In any case, the responsibility standard assesses Congress in terms of its ability to enact workable public programs with dispatch.

Responsiveness. The second criterion, responsiveness, emphasizes *process* more than product, the content of policy. This is not to suggest an indifference to policy, but merely to indicate that substance is secondary to the ways that the legislature operates. To be responsive, Congress must listen to and take account of the ideas and sentiments of those who will be affected by its actions: individual citizens, organized groups, local and state governments, and national executives. The lawmakers must provide an open channel of communication to those whom their decisions will influence; those with policy preferences or requests for services must have free and easy access to the legislators. Congress should not act until all who have opinions have had the chance to voice them. In other words, it should heed and respond to the preferences of its clientele.

A responsive Congress tends to be a deliberate, slow-moving institution. Unless it gets unequivocal and forceful messages from the public, an infrequent occurrence, it is likely to restrain rapid, innovative policy making, at least in the short run. Executive force proponents prefer prompt action and consider congressional caution and delay debilitating. They grow impatient if the legislature takes time to listen to all points of view and to negotiate middle-of-the-road compromises that do not, in their opinion, resolve the country's pressing problems. Congressional supremacists, by contrast, tend to appreciate responsiveness. Fearing a too-powerful president, they prefer a legislature that restrains the chief executive; they want Congress to listen, wait, and act only when a true and enduring national consensus emerges. They are not alarmed when Congress stresses oversight and casework at the expense of active policy making. Regardless of the philosophical perspective invoked, however, the responsiveness standard emphasizes the benefits of openness and free communication between ruled and rulers and the need of the latter to react to the former. It plays down the costs of inaction or inefficiency.

Accountability. A third criterion is accountability. Congress should be held accountable for what it does or does not do; that is, its decisions should be evaluated regularly by the citizenry. If the electorate finds the decision makers wanting, they can "turn the rascals out." When voters disapprove of Congress's policy choices (including failure to act) or perceive that members have unethically placed self-interest above the public good, they can use the ballot box to send new, presumably wiser and more honest individuals to Washington. The contrast between Congress and the federal judiciary is sharp. Justices of the Supreme Court, once appointed, serve for life and cannot realistically be removed (they can be impeached but never are); members of Congress must face the voters every two or six years. Thus, the legislators must calculate the popular response, real or potential, to their actions. In short, accountability operates after the fact: decision-making failure may result in the loss of position and power should the voters conclude that new officeholders would perform more successfully.

An accountable Congress is an institution on public display. Interested citizens can discover what the representatives they elect are doing and saying in committee and on the floors of the House and Senate. Citizen scrutiny is likely to promote caution. To avoid alienating blocs of voters, members will take care not to make rash statements or take extreme stands on controversial issues. They may avoid tackling difficult problems by deferring to the president or delegating authority to the bureaucracy. If they do, they eschew policy-making independence and leave program innovation to the president and the administration, to the satisfaction of executive force adherents. If, by contrast, Congress simply refuses to act without permitting others to decide critical questions, policy immobilism may ensue, to the pleasure, in principle, of the congressional supremacists. In short, accountability, whether real or potential, inclines members to avoid risks even as it exposes their behavior and ethics to public examination.

Conclusion. These three criteria of evaluation—responsibility, responsiveness, and accountability—are by no means mutually exclusive; they can be applied simultaneously. This is clear in the case of accountability. Regardless of whether voters judge congressional performance in terms of product or process, they remain capable, in theory, of discovering what their representatives are doing and of sending those whose performance they deem unworthy into early retirement. Similarly, in the abstract at least, decision makers may act both responsibly and responsively; they can move rapidly, on the basis of full consultation, to adopt workable policies. Ronald Reagan, in effect, made such a claim. He argued that his administration, with congressional support, handled the major economic and defense issues during his first term both responsibly (solved problems efficiently) and responsively (represented large majorities of Americans). Reagan believed that his large 1984 reelection margin—he captured 59 percent of the two-party vote— constituted a "mandate" approving his reduction of unemployment and inflation as well as his success in rearming the nation and gave him carte blanche to proceed during his second term.[19]

In practice, however, responsibility and responsiveness are likely to conflict. Responsibility requires rapid and efficient problem solving; responsiveness calls for careful attention to a wide variety of viewpoints. A problem may grow worse or effective solutions may become obsolete if time is spent waiting for numerous sentiments to be expressed. To act quickly while the problem remains tractable may be to prevent those whose views are hard to ascertain or imperfectly formulated from voicing their opinions. In short, it is unlikely that Congress or any other institution can be fully responsible and responsive; there will be tension between the two evaluative standards. Nonetheless, each criterion provides a benchmark—narrower than the broad, philosophic visions— against which to assess Congress's performance.

Summary

The U.S. Constitution involves Congress deeply in the national policy-making process; the legislature shares with other political participants, particularly the president, the authority to authorize and fund public policies. Armed with these powers, it has and will compete for policy-making primacy. If the chief executive sometimes seems "king of the Hill," it is because members of Congress, for their own reasons, have opted to defer to him. The issue underlying periodic efforts to reform Congress is not whether the legislature *can* make policy—it clearly can if it chooses to act—but whether it *should* be central to policy formulation. If Congress undertakes a serious policy-making role, questions about the character of that role, and the organization of the institution to play it, immediately arise. If Congress eschews or minimizes policy activity, presumably it will devote itself to its other roles: oversight and nonpolicy representation.

Discussion of Congress's proper place in national politics, especially its relation to the president, has proceeded along two tracks. At a broad, philosophical level, a few theoreticians have advanced sweeping, comprehensive visions of Congress. Proponents of the executive force and responsible parties theories prefer to see the legislature support the president, the likely source of innovative solutions to fundamental problems. Their vision is of a Congress that poses few impediments to creative executive action. Adherents of the congressional supremacy, literary theory and Whig positions, by contrast, see Congress as an independent policy-making force, free to block excessive or unwise initiatives from a potentially tyrannical president. Each of these proexecutive and prolegislative postures carries its own particular reform agenda.

Most reformers, especially the members of Congress who enact whatever reforms are adopted, find such philosophical views, and the multitude of particulars they entail, impractical. It is too difficult to amend the Constitution; broad visions engender too much controversy. They are inclined instead to propose specific steps to deal with specific problems. Some may focus on executive-legislative relations, others may stress internal congressional procedures. They will ask whether particular reforms, or a series of reforms, will serve to move Congress even a short distance toward some preferred vision of the "good" or "better" legislature. In this book three evaluative criteria are emphasized: Reform may improve legislative policy making (responsibility), enhance the potential for citizen communication with Congress (responsiveness), or open up Congress to public scrutiny (accountability). In the real world of practical politics, all three values are unlikely to be realized simultaneously.

Assessment of Congress's place in the political process depends on which evaluative standard seems most important. Is Congress to be preeminently a responsible policy maker? Should it give up its decision-making functions and concentrate instead on overseeing the executive and serving as a conduit for popular opinion? Or is it more important that the citizenry be able to hold its national legislature accountable? Alternatively, is it more realistic to look for an optimum "mix" of responsibility, responsiveness, and accountability that will permit Congress to survive and work well?[20]

The remainder of this book addresses these basic issues. Chapter 2 examines the complaints about Congress that motivated the reform movement of the 1970s; Chapter 3 outlines the reforms adopted to respond to the critique of the institution; Chapter 4 assesses the accomplishments of those reforms in terms of the reformers' intentions and the results they attained; and Chapter 5 explores the implications, normative and practical, of a decade of reform experience.

NOTES

1. See George B. Galloway, *The History of the House of Representatives,* 2d ed. (New York: Crowell, 1976).
2. Arthur M. Schlesinger, Jr., popularized this phrase and the notion of an excessively powerful presidency. See his *The Imperial Presidency* (Boston: Houghton Mifflin, 1973).
3. This position, of course, is an overstatement. Many legislators continued to be energetic and effective workers for social change. The critics claimed, however, that Congress as an institution had not distinguished itself as a source or proponent of innovative solutions to major policy solutions. Except for the early New Deal (1933-37) and Lyndon B. Johnson's Great Society initiatives of 1964 and 1965, Congress was more often cautious than creative. On this issue see Bruce I. Oppenheimer, "How Legislatures Shape Policy and Budgets," *Legislative Studies Quarterly* 8 (1983): 551-97, and Gerald C. Wright, Jr., Leroy N. Rieselbach, and Lawrence C. Dodd, eds., *Policy Change in Congress* (New York: Agathon, 1986).
4. On oversight see Morris S. Ogul, *Congress Oversees the Bureaucracy: Studies in Legislative Supervision* (Pittsburgh: University of Pittsburgh Press, 1976); Lawrence C. Dodd and Richard L. Schott, *Congress and the Administrative State* (New York: Wiley, 1979); Randall B. Ripley and Grace A. Franklin, *Congress, the Bureaucracy, and Public Policy,* 3d ed. (Homewood, Ill.: Dorsey Press, 1984); Bert A. Rockman, "Legislative-Executive Relations and Executive Oversight," *Legislative Studies Quarterly* 9 (1984): 387-400; and Mathew D. McCubbins and Thomas Schwartz, "Congressional Oversight Overlooked: Police Patrols versus Fire Alarms," *American Journal of Political Science* 28 (1984): 165-79.
5. *Congressional Quarterly Weekly Report,* May 25, 1985, 986-87.
6. See Hanna F. Pitkin, *The Concept of Representation* (Berkeley: University of California Press, 1967); and Heinz Eulau and Paul D. Karps, "The Puzzle of Representation: Specifying the Components of Responsiveness," *Legislative Studies Quarterly* 2 (1977): 233-54.
7. Richard F. Fenno, Jr., *Home Style: Representatives in Their Districts* (Boston: Little, Brown, 1978).
8. On congressional elections see David R. Mayhew, *Congress: The Electoral Connection* (New Haven, Conn.: Yale University Press, 1974); Barbara Hinckley, *Congressional Elections* (Washington, D.C.: CQ Press, 1981); Gary C. Jacobson and Samuel Kernell, *Strategy and Choice in Congressional Elections,* 2d ed. (New Haven, Conn.: Yale University Press, 1983); Edie N. Goldenberg and Michael W. Traugott, *Campaigning for Congress* (Washington, D.C.: CQ Press, 1984); and Marjorie R. Hershey, *Running for Office* (Chatham, N.J.:

Chatham House, 1985). For a broader perspective on elections and representation, consult Lyn Ragsdale, "Responsiveness and Legislative Elections: Toward a Comparative Analysis," *Legislative Studies Quarterly* 8 (1983): 339-78.

9. Gary Orfield, *Congressional Power: Congress and Social Change* (New York: Harcourt Brace Jovanovich, 1975).

10. For extended treatment of these philosophical visions of Congress, see Roger H. Davidson, David M. Kovenock, and Michael K. O'Leary, *Congress in Crisis: Politics and Congressional Reform* (Belmont, Calif.: Wadsworth, 1966), 15-36; and John S. Saloma III, *Congress and the New Politics* (Boston: Little, Brown, 1969), chaps. 1-2. Advocacy of these normative perspectives, admittedly, is largely limited to those outside Congress, mostly academics. For a partial exception, see Richard Bolling, *Power in the House* (New York: Capricorn Books, 1974). Bolling recognizes, however, that "the role of the political leader is vastly different from that of the philosopher, political theorist, or anyone who tries to analyze social problems. . . . All of these can and should be purists. . . . The political leader's role is to achieve as promptly as possible an *effective* solution" to these problems (20-21). Reform is likely to reflect a short-run perspective that promotes such practical solutions.

11. James M. Burns, *Congress on Trial* (New York: Harper, 1949); James M. Burns, *The Deadlock of Democracy* (Englewood Cliffs, N.J.: Prentice-Hall, 1963); and Joseph S. Clark, *Congress: The Sapless Branch* (New York: Harper and Row, 1964).

12. For a statement of this possible shift in Congress's role, see Samuel P. Huntington, "Congressional Responses to the Twentieth Century," in *The Congress and America's Future*, 2d ed., ed. David B. Truman (Englewood Cliffs, N.J.: Prentice-Hall, 1973), 6-38.

13. American Political Science Association, Committee on Political Parties, *Toward a More Responsible Two-Party System* (New York: Rinehart, 1950); Richard Bolling, *House Out of Order* (New York: Dutton, 1965).

14. James Burnham, *Congress and the American Tradition* (Chicago: Regnery, 1959).

15. Alfred de Grazia, *Republic in Crisis* (New York: Federal Legal Publications, 1964); and Alfred de Grazia, *Congress: The First Branch of Government* (Washington, D.C.: American Enterprise Institute, 1966).

16. In "Congressional Responses" Huntington captures the dilemma precisely: "If Congress legislates, it subordinates itself to the executive; if it refuses to legislate, it alienates itself from public opinion. Congress can assert its power or it can pass laws, but it cannot do both" (7). Reform, at least that guided by a broad view of Congress's place in national politics, makes this choice explicitly.

17. Observers inside and outside of Congress do not always, or even regularly, use even these narrower standards to organize their critiques of the legislature. To be sure, in *Power in the House* then-representative Bolling cites the need for a "responsible budgetary process" (259), and Warren Weaver, a Capitol Hill correspondent, describes the legislature as "clumsy" and "unresponsive" (see Weaver, *Both Your Houses: The Truth about Congress* [New York: Praeger, 1972], 3). But, on the whole, most critics voice specific complaints about committees, weak parties, archaic procedures, and difficult personalities. Nonetheless, these particular legislative shortcomings fall easily into categories that relate to Congress's alleged inefficiency, lack of sensitivity to public opinion, and inaccessibility to citizens' scrutiny. Thus,

responsibility, responsiveness, and accountability offer convenient rubrics under which to classify and assess the common criticisms of Congress.

18. These are not the only criteria available to evaluate the legislature's performance. For other perspectives see Roger H. Davidson and Walter J. Oleszek, "Adaptation and Consolidation: Structural Innovation in the House of Representatives," *Legislative Studies Quarterly* 1 (1976): 37-65; Charles O. Jones, "How Reform Changes Congress," in *Legislative Reform and Public Policy*, ed. Susan Welch and John G. Peters (New York: Praeger, 1977), 11-29; Walter J. Oleszek, "A Perspective on Congressional Reform," in *Legislative Reform and Public Policy*, 3-10; Samuel C. Patterson, "Conclusions: On the Study of Legislative Reform," in *Legislative Reform and Public Policy*, 214-22; and Leroy N. Rieselbach, "Congressional Reform: Some Policy Implications," *Policy Studies Journal* 4 (1975): 180-88.

19. Richard Nixon made a similar argument about his 1972 reelection. He believed his Vietnam policy was both successful (responsible) and approved by most citizens (responsive).

20. This last contingency is the most likely result of reform, to the extent that it is even possible to anticipate what reform will produce. Members will inevitably be reluctant to give up what they consider their legitimate prerogatives. The issue, in realistic rather than utopian terms, is how to combine legislative functions most effectively and organize Congress most efficiently to approximate any observer-critic's particular vision.

Congress in Action: A Critical Assessment   2

Congressional observers of the 1950s and 1960s—those who preferred a responsible legislature that could compete on even terms with the president for policy influence as well as those who preferred a responsive assembly attuned to constituent concerns—found Congress wanting. They leveled three charges, which can be expressed in bold terms: 1) *Congress was, at best, only imperfectly responsible;* it had yielded much of its decision-making authority to the executive branch, especially in foreign relations. 2) *Congress was only modestly responsive;* it often listened, but did not act and did little to call forth less frequently heard societal voices. 3) *Congress was held accountable far more in theory than in practice,* an unsatisfactory situation that was not entirely the fault of the legislature itself. The critics of Congress marshaled persuasive evidence in support of each of these propositions and they recommended an extensive reform agenda.[1] The legislature's performance, they asserted, could be improved on all fronts. What they may have failed to appreciate sufficiently, however, is that reforms designed to improve performance in one area may have unintended and unanticipated repercussions in other facets of legislative activity.

To the reformers of the 1950s and 1960s, Congress's troubles did not seem momentary aberrations. Its fundamental structure and organization had undergone only modest alterations over a half-century. The 1910-11 "palace revolution" in the House of Representatives that constrained the powers of Speaker Joseph Cannon marked the beginning of the modern legislative era. From then through the 1960s, with the single and notable exception of the Legislative Reorganization Act of 1946, the main outlines of congressional organization and procedure evolved slowly but surely. Change tended to be adaptive and incremental, not fundamental or wholesale. For example, in 1961 membership on the

House Rules Committee was increased to provide stronger leadership control over the flow of legislation to the floor, but the panel continued to thwart the Speaker and his lieutenants periodically. Similarly, the Senate adopted the "Johnson Rule" (named after Texas Democrat Lyndon B. Johnson, the Majority Leader) to guarantee junior members a better committee assignment. (The majority party member with the longest continuous service on a committee automatically assumed the committee chair.) But despite the rule, senior senators retained what many saw as excessive influence. (The rule did not affect seniority; it pertained to committee assignments, not to the chair.) Senators who served during the Harding or Coolidge years, returning to the Capitol 50 years later, would have recognized clearly the basic outlines of congressional politics in the Kennedy-Johnson era.[2]

A Decentralized Institution

In general, Congress by the mid-1960s had become "institutionalized."[3] Year after year many of the same legislators operated in the same settings, using the same procedures. The congressional modus operandi was one of fragmentation and decentralization, with authority and influence widely although not equally dispersed among the 535 senators and representatives. Many legislators had a direct and immediate impact on congressional decisions, mainly those within the jurisdictions of the committees on which they served. In such circumstances, congressional politics was coalition politics; that is, proponents of particular proposals—through bargaining, compromise, negotiating, "logrolling," or "mutual backscratching"—assembled fragments of political power into winning coalitions. By seeking support in committee, on the floor, and in conference, they tried to push bills through the multiple stages of the legislative process to the president's desk.

The dispersal of power in Congress by the mid-1960s, which resulted in decision by bargain and compromise, was a product of numerous conditions. The electoral process stimulated member independence of central authority—presidential or partisan. Electoral triumph, especially in the smaller House districts, is almost always the product of the candidates' own efforts in their own constituencies.[4] Given this fundamental fact, most legislators pay prime attention, particularly early in their careers, to their districts "where the votes are" and where the ultimate decisions about their continuation in office will be made. Incumbents, having learned the ropes, begin their reelection efforts with substantial advantages over their challengers.

Therefore, few incumbent representatives were turned out of office during this period, but a sufficient number lost every two years to reinforce the inclination of those who survived to court their constituents and to resist national, centralizing forces that might jeopardize their electoral security.

The internal organization, formal and informal, of Congress also sustained the individual legislator's independence. The specialized standing committees, the chief agents of congressional decision making, constituted the major decentralizing force in Congress. The committees operated relatively free of restraint; what they decided was often what the parent chamber enacted. To put it another way, committees, especially House committees, were the repositories of congressional expertise; members tended to be legislative specialists on the topics within the panel's substantive jurisdiction. Nonmembers were often prepared to defer to committee expertise, to accept committee recommendations. Of course, they expected and generally received reciprocal deference in their own areas of specialization.

The committee, then, was a highly independent body with substantial influence over legislative activity. Its chairperson, as the single most important member of the panel, wielded the greatest influence. Chairpersons varied considerably in the degree to which they exercised their powers, but, protected by the seniority rule, many possessed the independence to shape what their committees did. Their capacity to make their own views, or those close to them, prevail within their separate committees and the reciprocal deference among committees made the fragmented, divided character of legislative authority clearly visible. In short, committee decisions were very often synonymous with legislative action.[5]

At the same time, the political parties, which might have had centralized legislative authority, were weak. The party leadership—the Speaker of the House, floor leaders, and the whips—had few genuine sanctions with which to enforce discipline on the disparate party membership. As noted, legislators tended to vote their districts rather than the party line if tension between the two occurred. Committee considerations—the use of seniority to select committee leaders and the protection of committee expertise and power—often militated against supporting the party. Party leaders were not without some influence, but it was based on persuasion rather than compulsion. With these means, parties sometimes acted cohesively, but on balance they lacked the power to countervail, regularly and effectively, the centrifugal forces that electoral and committee realities generated.[6]

Congressional rules and procedures contributed directly to the fragmented, decentralized character of the legislature. They required a bill to move past many "veto points," at which the measure either succeeded or died. They defined and defended committee jurisdictions, thereby serving to insulate the panels, to minimize the possibilities that they would be circumvented, and to guarantee that the major decisions would be made there. The position of legislative minorities was buttressed in the House by the Rules Committee and the rule of unlimited debate, the well-known if not notorious filibuster in the Senate.[7] By the 1960s numerous congressional procedures sustained a system of multiple centers of influence and promoted bargaining as a way to resolve conflict in Congress.[8]

Finally, like any other organization, Congress operated within a context of mores and practices, nowhere codified but demonstrably observable. These informal traditions, or norms, fostered diffusion of power. Senators and representatives alike were enjoined to specialize in a few policy areas, to defer to one another's expertise, to treat each other courteously, and, in general, to behave in ways that minimized hostility and friction. This "legislative culture" permitted the lawmakers to try to carve out for themselves a niche where each could eventually exert some influence over congressional decision making. Many succeeded, content to possess a fragment of power even at the cost of eschewing authority beyond their narrow focus of concern.[9]

Thus, Congress during the 1960s appeared to its critics as a highly decentralized, fragmented institution. Electoral considerations, the committee structure, formal rules and procedures, and informal norms and expectations diffused authority widely among the lawmakers. Negotiation and compromise were the chief modes of decision making; bargaining provided the only viable means to assemble the fragments of power into workable coalitions. Political parties, the potential centralizing force, proved unable to overcome the divisive forces.

In consequence, the critics found Congress incapable or unwilling to act decisively. They pointed to its failure to provide comprehensive national health insurance for all citizens; partial coverage—Medicare for the elderly, Medicaid for the poor—they deemed inadequate. They faulted Congress for delay in redressing the civil rights grievances of black Americans. Only after extraordinary developments in the mid-1960s—the assassination of President John F. Kennedy, the unprecedented and graphically televised civil rights movement, and an enormous Democratic landslide electoral victory in 1964—was the legislature goaded into enacting major civil rights legislation. Critics cited similar failures with respect to aid to education and environmental protection.

Decentralization, they argued, made creative policy making difficult if not impossible. To win reelection, members often deferred to the president or delegated to the bureaucracy rather than confront politically controversial policy choices.

Responsibility: Policy Making in Congress

Policy making in a decentralized legislature is a complicated, painstaking process. To enact policy, those in favor must move their legislation through subcommittee, full committee, the Rules Committee (in the House), and out onto the floor where a majority must vote for passage. If the process can be repeated in the other house and a conference committee can resolve all differences in the two chambers' versions, then and only then will some new policy, or modification of an old policy, be *authorized*. For most programs, money must be *appropriated* to implement them. The entire process is then repeated, with appropriations bills sent through the subcommittees and full committees of the Appropriations panels in the House and Senate.[10] It is the need to move across, around, or over these imposing hurdles that gives congressional politics its distinctive coalitional character. To assemble a winning coalition at each of these stages requires bargaining skill and patience that must be sustained over many weeks and months.

Given this picture of congressional practice, it is not surprising that critics judged the national legislature as deficient on responsibility grounds. Extraordinary situations do occur, as they did in the early New Deal period and the Great Society era of 1964-65. On each occasion an exceptional coincidence of events gave the Democratic party both the presidency and an overwhelming majority in each house of Congress.[11] Top-heavy legislative majorities make the weakness of party discipline tolerable and provide the dominant party with incentives to advance a major legislative program.[12] But ordinarily conditions are far less favorable.

Where partisan control of government is divided, with one party controlling the presidency and the other holding a majority in at least one house of Congress (as was the case in 10 of the 22 years between 1950 and 1972), prospects for cooperative and inventive lawmaking are substantially reduced. The government's failure to reduce domestic petroleum consumption in the face of severe supply shortages created by the 1973 Arab oil embargo is typical of conflictual policy making under conditions of divided control.[13] Even when the president and the congressional majority share a common party label, responsible lawmaking seldom follows, for nominal majorities show a decided tendency to

23

evaporate when the roll is called. Thus, policy making in Congress flows from slow, arduous negotiations that often cross rather than follow party lines.

This policy making by negotiation is especially apparent in domestic affairs, where Congress retains much authority and is less likely to defer to executive initiatives; the end result regularly reflects the impact of legislative deliberation and decision. Congress seems to prefer to respond to presidential proposals, to demand that the chief executive set the national agenda. Congressional criticism, particularly when the Democrats command the majority, is commonplace when, in the lawmakers' judgment, the president is lax in proposing a legislative program. Once that program is forthcoming, however, the legislators are more than willing to alter the president's proposals dramatically or to reject them entirely. Throughout the prereform period numerous conflicts over executive proposals to cut farm price subsidies or reduce federal support for rivers and harbors projects (which Congress regularly rejected) or to change national health insurance or civil rights legislation (which Congress was frequently unwilling or unable to pass) amply testified to the legislature's ability to resist and defeat undesired presidential initiatives.[14]

When Congress is prepared to substitute its own priorities for the executive's, it provides ammunition to those who criticize it for irresponsibility. As suggested earlier, the congressional process is less than efficient. To assemble a winning majority takes time; many independent interests must be accommodated. Critics of Congress during the 1950s and 1960s pointed to extended hearings, lengthy "mark-up sessions,"[15] long periods of delay, and filibusters and other dilatory tactics as evidence of the legislature's inability to act decisively. These critics did not always recognize that time may be the essential ingredient in legislative decision making, that delay may permit action by allowing a specific compromise to be reached. Still, their basic argument was sound: Congress moved ponderously. Furthermore, the negotiated agreements that did command a majority were often modest in scope—proposals for major change having been sacrificed to secure the support of critical power holders.[16]

For example, in 1965 President Lyndon Johnson proposed a bold and expensive initiative to deal with poverty and crime in inner-city slums. As originally drafted, "Demonstration Cities" legislation would have given a dozen or so cities large sums, to be spent under the watchful eye of federal bureaucrats, to promote racial integration and renovation of blighted areas. Passage of the program, however, required compromise: proponents had to drop integration as a goal, relax the national government's administrative control over the program, and, more important, make many more cities (eventually 150) eligible to participate. Each compromise added congressional votes to the coalition supporting model cities legislation—from southern conservatives who objected to federal control of local political activities and from representatives of cities added to the list of recipients. What began the legislative process as a "demonstration project" to show that massive federal intervention could renew decaying urban centers finished as another "pork barrel project" that divided funds widely and ineffectively among the constituencies of many members of Congress.[17] Such policy transformations are common congressional practice.

In sum, Congress's output in domestic matters was neither radical nor rapid. Congress seemed in no hurry to respond to interest groups or executives, but preferred to develop its own domestic programs in its own way and at its own pace. Those who saw responsibility as demanding more efficient development of more imaginative and innovative programs found congressional performance unsatisfactory.

From the point of view of responsibility, congressional performance seemed even worse in foreign relations. Over a number of years, culminating in the 1960s and early 1970s, the president capitalized on several advantages to dominate foreign policy making. The commander-in-chief power, one of the Constitution's most explicit grants of authority, enabled the chief executive to commit military forces, as Harry Truman did in Korea, on his own initiative. A near monopoly of expertise—the State Department and Foreign Service, the Pentagon, and the intelligence community all report directly to the White House—permitted the president to cast foreign policy issues in terms favorable to his proposals. The Supreme Court, in *United States v. Curtiss-Wright Export Corp.* (299 U.S. 304 [1936]), suggested that the president is "the sole organ of the nation" in international relations, giving the executive a forceful claim to manage the country's diplomatic contacts with the rest of the world. Finally, and perhaps most important, the lessons of history taught Congress that its decentralized organization and often slow-paced decision-making style were frequently inappropriate, especially when speed or secrecy were involved, in foreign policy making.

For all these reasons, Congress came to defer to presidential expertise in military matters. The Armed Services committees were merely "real estate" panels, concerned with the management of military installations and content to leave the more critical issues of military strategy and procurement to Pentagon generals and White House executives.[18] Diplomatic initiatives, such as President Richard Nixon's rapprochements with China and the Soviet Union, were executive in origin and conduct. The executive branch negotiated tariff agreements under broad congressional delegations of power, which the legislature renewed and extended at regular intervals. Wars were under total presidential control; in the Korean and Vietnam wars Congress supported military efforts initiated by presidents without invoking its constitutional right to declare war.

This is not to argue that Congess could not have influenced American foreign policy at any time. Control over the purse strings, which the Constitution grants, enables the legislature to deny funds for executive policy initiatives. The increasing unpopularity of the Vietnam conflict prompted numerous proposals to cut off money for military involvement in Southeast Asia. But only during the last days of American involvement in the war, in early summer 1973, did Congress succeed in forcing the president's hand. In June the legislature tacked onto a $3.3 billion supplemental appropriations bill, enacted to keep the government operating in the new fiscal year beginning July 1, a provision cutting off funds for bombing in Cambodia. President Nixon vetoed the bill and the House sustained his action, but lest the government go out of business for lack of money, he accepted a compromise and signed a second supplemental bill prohibiting spending for military purposes in Indochina after August 15, some six weeks hence, without prior legislative approval. On the whole, however, the substance of the nation's Indochina policy—from its earliest inception in the Eisenhower and Kennedy administrations to the end of direct American involvement during Nixon's presidency—reflected the policy choices of the chief executive rather than Congress.

Likewise, Congress could have reclaimed for itself the power to set tariffs, which it had delegated legislatively to the president, or to designate some independent agency to negotiate trade agreements, but it did not do so. The legislature tried with only modest success to keep closer tabs on military matters by insisting that funds for weaponry be authorized on an annual, not a long-term, basis.[19] The lawmakers gave shape to the foreign aid program: they made major cuts in the president's fund requests, reallocated money from military to economic forms of aid, and denied money to various countries (Vietnam, Cambodia, Angola, and—temporarily—Turkey). Yet the president remained central and Congress peripheral in foreign policy making. As Sen. Adlai E. Stevenson III (D-Ill.) put it: "Congress is . . . unfit to formulate foreign policy or to effectively oversee its implementation in all parts of a fast moving world."[20] Responsibility for America's international relations rested, in the eyes of legislators and the public, in the White House, not on Capitol Hill.

This tendency to place responsibility for domestic and foreign policy on the president rather than on Congress seemed, then, to have some justice to it. The legislature was not preeminent in policy making much of the time, and when it was, it was only after an extended period of deliberation and debate. Congress was not the responsible initiator of public policy; rather it slowly molded, and gave legitimacy to, policies that usually originated outside its chambers.

Responsiveness: Representation in Congress

When the spotlight shifted from responsibility to responsiveness, Congress appeared in a considerably better light. Its defects from one perspective became advantages from another; its vices, which some critics felt inhibited responsible policy choice, to others became its virtues because they fostered responsiveness. Congress's openness, decentralization, and bargaining style of decision making appeared admirable. The slow pace of Congress allowed time for those with a stake in policy outcomes to communicate their sentiments to members. The multistage process of lawmaking provided points of access to nonlegislators by identifying the places where external pressures could be brought to bear on the legislature. Congress was customarily more than willing to listen to what outsiders had to say.

To put it another way, Congress during the 1950s and 1960s had ample opportunity, and regularly took it, to attend to messages from interested parties, including the president, pressure groups, and the public. As noted, Congress chose to react to executive initiatives rather than set its own agenda. Moreover, the president possessed a full arsenal of weapons that comprised what Richard Neustadt called his "power to persuade."[21] Specifically, the president used his public popularity and professional reputation (his standing with Washington decision makers) to try to influence lawmakers; it was difficult for them to resist a popular and determined leader. He could argue on the merits of an issue, using speeches, press conferences, special messages, and his personal ability to command attention. He could call on party loyalty by shaping his appeals to partisan interests. He could deal with congressional committees by sending his chief aides and experts to testify at hearings; by courting the important committee members, especially the chairperson and ranking minority member; or by accepting committee amendments to bills to win votes. He could win over crucial supporters—committee chairpersons, party leaders, influential senators and representatives—through personal contacts. If he secured the support of these leaders, they in turn could use their authority to persuade their followers to back him.[22]

In congressional politics the president's persuasive powers rested on his ability to do lawmakers favors and to provide goods and services—such as endorsing particular bills, offering patronage positions, and helping political campaigns financially or by making personal appearances. If the president is highly regarded, such electoral assistance may benefit the local legislative nominee. While it is never entirely clear precisely to what extent any president uses these forms of persuasion—bargains struck are not always explicit and seldom widely publicized—they enabled the president to work from a position of strength to influence congressional decision making.[23]

President Johnson, for instance, broke a decade-old logjam in 1964 by persuading Congress to declare a "war on poverty." The bold legislation that resulted, the Economic Opportunity Act, contained provisions to provide jobs, education, and student aid; an assistance package for the rural poor; and the Jobs Corps, a training program for urban youth. The president made the legislation the central focus of his 1964 reelection campaign and put the substantial expertise of the executive branch to work designing a broad package of elements with widespread political appeal. When the bill was before Congress, Johnson gave it his personal attention. Northern Democrats, mostly liberals, could be counted on to back the chief executive. Southern support was courted: Phil M. Landrum (D-Ga.), a conservative with impeccable credentials (he had co-sponsored a restrictive labor reform bill hated by liberals) was persuaded to sponsor the act.

Johnson took his case to the public; the war on poverty theme was a winner. How could the opposition, mostly Republicans, favor poverty or oppose equal opportunity? White House lobbyists swarmed over Capitol Hill, and they played rough: "Republicans protested the threats and pressures they claimed were being used upon individual congressmen." [24] When necessary, the president made substantive concessions. For example, he mollified conservative foes by accepting an amendment permitting governors, as protectors of states' rights, to veto most projects proposed for their states. In the end the president captured enough southern conservatives and Republicans to win comfortable majorities in each chamber of Congress.

To the extent that President Johnson's constituency differed from the lawmakers'—and the differences between the president's national orientations and the supposedly more parochial perspective of members were widely noted[25]—points of view were introduced into legislative deliberations that otherwise might not have been heard or at least might have been less forcefully expressed. Congress, in short, was responsive to the president.

The legislature was also responsive to the views of organized interests. Lawmakers often worked closely with group representatives ("lobbyists") to promote mutually desired legislation. This is not to argue, as some observers did, that pressure group activity was decisive in lawmaking outcomes. Indeed, the most persuasive evidence from the 1950s and 1960s suggests that the interests did not call the legislative tune (and did not really pay the piper either); rather they worked in collaboration with, and sometimes at the request of, sympathetic members of Congress.[26]

Lobbyists sought to establish and maintain free and open lines of communication with members of Congress in positions to help them promote their specific causes. Much of their activity was designed to sustain this access; they often ran service operations to supply information, assistance, and contacts to lawmakers working for the views they wished to promote. In return for such support, the lobbyists hoped to be able to "make a pitch" to legislators concerning their clients' interests. The pressure group belied its name; it was more often a coalition partner than an irresistible force in the legislative process.[27]

Even this reliance on low-key tactics, on friendship and trust rather than bribes or threats, provided groups with ample opportunity to present their opinions. They appeared regularly as witnesses at committee and subcommittee hearings. They directly supplied research findings and documentary evidence to relevant legislators and members of their staffs. Through such channels, group postures became visible to the lawmakers whose own positions often had not yet crystallized. In some cases, however, the group provided only data that supported the legislators' existing judgments; it introduced no new perspectives. In any event, if responsiveness is defined as maintaining open and operative channels of communication, Congress was responsive, at least to organized group interests.

And here was the rub. While the national legislature did hear and have the chance to respond to the views of well-organized, well-financed interests—such as business, labor, agriculture, veterans, and the professions—other less affluent interests went unheard and unheeded. Access to Congress, its critics were quick to charge, was unequal. Because of congressional decentralization some groups had ties to important leaders while others related only to the rank and file. Important interests—the poor, blacks, women, and consumers—were often inadequately organized. Lacking money, experience, and lobbying know-how, such interests were unable to present their positions persuasively. What legislators heard, in short, was far from the full story; their intake of information depended on what messages were being sent as well as which communications they chose to hear.[28]

One other audience, the unorganized public, provided a focus for legislative attention. Members of Congress were not prepared to accept the executive branch or interest associations as the legitimate and incontrovertible voice of the people. To get a general sense of popular sentiment, they examined opinion polls and attended, perhaps more closely, to their own constituents' views expressed in conversations, letters, and local newspaper columns and editorials. A few members, recognizing the imperfect character of these information sources,[29] commissioned their own surveys; others relied more on intuition, on their sense of what their constituents believed. Most lawmakers did not really know accurately what the folks back home felt on any but the most dramatic issues of the day.

On the whole, Congress at mid-century responded moderately well to a variety of interests. The legislature could not avoid getting messages, loud and clear ones in many instances, from the executive; indeed, Congress demanded such communications. Interest groups also abounded, using their access to transmit their views to legislators who found those views helpful and often solicited them. Lawmakers also felt the need to gauge local sentiment; they were careful to avert possible electoral sanctions by considering citizen opinion before they acted. Moreover, the decision making process in Congress contributed to responsiveness. The legislature's decentralization and fragmentation, as well as the slow pace that its bargaining style of conflict resolution imposed, guaranteed numerous points of access and time to transmit messages. Not only did Congress listen, but when conditions were right—when the messages were clear and decisive—it also acted. During the Great Society era of the mid-1960s, the legislature passed significant new legislation on employment, education, equal rights, health care, and environmental protection.[30] A long time in coming, these initiatives suggested that Congress would respond if the pressures were great enough. On all fronts—executive, group, individual—critics did find, however, room for improvement. These defects became the targets of reformers seeking to enhance the responsiveness of Congress.

The Accountability of Congress

These same defects, especially popular indifference to the legislature, help explain why the public did not hold Congress more accountable for its actions. Accountability, citizen control through the ballot box, requires three conditions to function properly. First, those making the judgment, the ,voters, must be aware of the behavior of the legislators whom they are to hold to account. Second, the citizens must have some views of their own, some desirable policy goals that they expect the legislators to attain. Third, if legislative behavior and citizen preferences do not match, the electorate must have some way to express its dissatisfaction: in other words, voters must have candidates, in the party primary and general election, whose views coincide with their own. Congressional observers in the 1950s and 1960s found that these three conditions were poorly met. In legislative politics, accountability operated inadequately.

Because the prerequisites for accountability were seldom found, members of Congress were free to act without popular control on all but the most dramatic and emotional issues.[31] In direct contrast to the first condition, the citizenry was generally unaware of the major details of legislative behavior. Polls regularly revealed that close to half of the population was unable to name their elected representatives. Few understood the complexity of the congressional process with its myriad decision points. Even the most visible act, the roll call vote, was unknown to many voters.

To add to the confusion, legislators exploited the possibilities of a decentralized organization. They acted in inconsistent ways, working against a bill in committee, but later voting in support when a roll call vote was taken. Or, in the House, they could take one position on teller votes, where they filed past tellers and were counted for or against a measure but were not listed individually, and another on recorded votes that put each individual's stand clearly on the public record. Congressional procedures enabled members to be all things—friend and foe—to all bills and immeasurably complicated the citizen's task of understanding congressional politics. Finally, the media of communication did not help much. Understandably, the single chief executive was more "newsworthy" than the multimember legislature. Dramatic events in Congress were the exception not the rule, and coverage of the legislature was modest, even in the most comprehensive media. Thus, citizens who were attentive to legislative politics had a hard time comprehending fully what their representatives were up to in Washington.

Citizens who tried to be attentive were relatively few. Those who formed their own views and goals—the requirement of the second condition of accountability—were scarcer still. Voting studies from the 1950s amply demonstrate that voters' ballots were cast more on the basis of the citizens' party identification—their standing loyalty to one or the other of the major political parties—than on their views about the issues

of the day.[32] While there is reason to believe that the 1950s were the na-
dir of issue orientation—the "bland leading the bland"—it is doubtful
that the upsurge in concern for issues and performance in the following
decade was sufficient to satisfy the second accountability criterion.[33] The
voters' rejection of presidential candidates who sought to offer choice—
Barry Goldwater in 1964 and George McGovern in 1972—seems to
reflect a general perception of the losers' "unsuitability" more than
an awareness of their specific substantive views (although the
former admittedly may have followed from the latter). If this was
true for presidential contests, it was certainly true for less well-
publicized legislative races. Voters' choices in congressional
elections seldom reflected detailed awareness of the candidates' issue
positions.

The third condition for accountability, the opportunity for meaningful choice, was not well satisfied either. In theory, electoral contests
provide voters with the chance to substitute candidates with whom they
agree for incumbents whom they oppose, but in practice, two major
factors limited the effects of elections: the relatively uninformed character of the voters and the slight chance that the voters' preferred
candidates often had to win. If citizens knew neither what the incumbent did in Washington nor what the major issues were in any
campaign, they were unlikely to render an unequivocal, issue-related
verdict at the polls, even when a clear substantive choice existed
between incumbent and challenger (and it did not in numerous
districts). Most constituencies were "safe" for the incumbent or for the
incumbent's political party. In fact, there was little turnover in Congress
throughout the prereform period; more than two-thirds of the House
seats remained Republican or Democratic without change. What shifts
occurred in Congress reflected what happened in about 100 highly
competitive House districts.[34]

Moreover, change was not uniform. Variations in the nature of
district electorates tended to cancel out the possibility that one set of
views would gain ascendancy in Congress. Voters in some districts chose
liberal challengers over conservative incumbents, but the reverse occurred in other constituencies. When the balance in the competitive
districts tipped in one direction, as it did toward the Democrats in 1964,
a strong legislative majority came into existence, and substantial policy
change in Congress ensued. Most commonly, however, the competitive
districts did not swing uniformly to one party, and the overall composition of Congress has varied little from year to year. These modest
changes in composition did not appreciably affect the ideological
outlook of the entire legislature.[35]

Accountability, then, worked in imperfect ways. Elections were held every second year, and the citizens on occasion did vote "no," at least in a few states and districts. But, in reality, these ballots seemed to be cast on the basis of little information about the incumbents' legislative performance, with scant concern for the issues that separated sitting lawmakers from their challengers, and in many districts with only a slight chance to send a new member of Congress to Washington. Stability was the chief characteristic of the national legislature during the 1950s and 1960s. The change that did take place stemmed from electoral reversals in a few states and districts and was rarely sufficient to alter Congress's substantive outlook more than marginally.

Summary

The Congress of the 1950s and 1960s was a stable, institutionalized assembly with fixed routines for conducting its business. Its dominant characteristic was decentralization, which dispersed power among 535 members and mandated a bargaining, coalition-building style of decision making. The formal rules and informal norms of the legislature sustained fragmentation, and the political parties—the potential force for centralizing congressional operations—were too weak to overcome the divisive tendencies built into the structure of Congress. These circumstances engendered substantial criticism of Congress, setting the stage for the reform drama that unfolded during the 1970s.

Critics of Congress, however, seldom invoked broad philosophic visions of the legislature—either executive force or legislative supremacy models—to guide their assessments; these remained the preserve of a few academics and interested observers. Rather, most critics, particularly the members of Congress themselves, focused on practical, day-to-day matters that revealed congressional defects. Their commentary came from both the political left and the right. Liberals wanted more policy action, conservatives preferred less; both felt frustrated in their inability to discover and control what Congress, as an institution, was doing. Each had its own reform agenda, and each came to the conclusion, as the 1960s wore on, that reform was imperative.

Generally speaking, the sum of the critics' arguments was that Congress was something less than ideal in terms of its responsibility, responsiveness, and accountability. It simply was not equipped to be responsible on a regular basis; its organization and procedures were not designed to allow efficient and speedy formulation of policy. Congress had delegated much of its policy-making power to the president, especially in international relations. Only the war in Indochina had, by the late 1960s, provided much incentive for Congress to flex its muscles and try to recapture its atrophied authority. The legislature's performance with respect to the responsiveness criterion was better. The same structural shortcomings that inhibited responsibility encouraged representativeness. Many groups—but not all, and particularly not those interests lacking money and skill—could find the time and the locus in the legislature to present their views prior to the enactment of policy. Congress was better suited to listen than to act, and more inclined to do so. Finally, Congress was held accountable, in the sense that dissatisfied citizens could, and occasionally did, retire its members; in practice, these citizens lacked the knowledge, the incentive, or the electoral opportunity to exercise meaningful popular control over public policy. In short, whatever the evaluative criterion employed—responsibility, responsiveness, or accountability—critics of various persuasions found Congress wanting and determined to reform it. As the 1960s came to an end, moreover, conditions were conducive to launching a major effort to change Congress, and the reformers quickly undertook to do so.

NOTES

1. See ch. 1, pp. 6-9 and notes 11-19.
2. On the evolution of congressional structure and process in the period after 1910, see George B. Galloway, *The History of the House of Representatives*, 2d ed. (New York: Crowell, 1976); Nelson W. Polsby, "The Institutionalization of the U.S. House of Representatives," *American Political Science Review* 62 (1968): 144-68; Nelson W. Polsby, Miriam Gallaher, and Barry S. Rundquist, "Growth of the Seniority System in the U.S. House of Representatives," *American Political Science Review* 63 (1969): 787-807; Charles S. Bullock III, "House Careerists: Changing Patterns of Longevity and Attrition," *American Political Science Review* 66 (1972): 1295-1300; Joseph Cooper and David W. Brady, "Institutional Context and Leadership Style: The House from Cannon to Rayburn," *American Political Science Review* 75 (1981): 411-25; and Randall B. Ripley, *Congress: Process and Policy*, 3d ed. (New York: Norton, 1985), chap. 1.
3. Polsby, "Institutionalization."
4. John W. Kingdon, *Candidates for Office* (New York: Random House, 1968); David A. Leuthold, *Electioneering in a Democracy: Campaigns for Congress* (New York: Wiley, 1968); Jeff Fishel, *Party and Opposition: Congressional Challengers in American Politics* (New York: McKay, 1973); Marjorie Randon Hershey, *The Making of Campaign Strategy* (Lexington, Mass.: Lexington Books, 1974); and David R. Mayhew, *Congress: The Electoral Connection* (New Haven, Conn.: Yale University Press, 1974).

5. On committees in the 1960s, see William L. Morrow, *Congressional Committees* (New York: Scribner's 1969); and George Goodwin, Jr., *The Little Legislatures: Committees of Congress* (Amherst: University of Massachusetts Press, 1970).

6. On parties and party leadership during the 1960s, see Randall B. Ripley, *Majority Party Leadership in Congress* (Boston: Little, Brown, 1969); Lewis A. Froman, Jr., and Randall B. Ripley, "Conditions for Party Leadership: The Case of the House Democrats," *American Political Science Review* 59 (1965): 52-63; Charles O. Jones, *The Minority Party in Congress* (Boston: Little, Brown, 1970); Louis P. Westefield, "Majority Party Leadership and the Committee System in the House of Representatives," *American Political Science Review* 68 (1974): 1593-1604; and Randall B. Ripley, *Power in the Senate* (New York: St. Martin's, 1969).

7. Subject to the approval of the full House, the Committee on Rules defines the terms—the length of time for debate, the permissibility of amendments—under which the chamber considers a bill. On some occasions in the 1950s and 1960s, the committee refused to permit legislation approved by other standing committees to reach the floor. See James A. Robinson, *The House Rules Committee* (Indianapolis, Ind.: Bobbs-Merrill, 1963); and Spark M. Matsunaga and Ping Chen, *Rulemakers of the House* (Urbana: University of Illinois Press, 1976). The filibuster rule in the Senate (technically, the cloture rule) specifies the conditions under which debate can be terminated and a vote forced. Minorities, especially those opposed to civil rights, used unlimited debate in the prereform era to force the majority, eager to pass other legislation, to make concessions or to abandon bills entirely. See Raymond E. Wolfinger, "Filibusters, Majority Rule, Presidential Leadership, and Senate Norms," in *Readings on Congress*, ed. Raymond E. Wolfinger (Englewood Cliffs, N.J.: Prentice-Hall, 1971), 296-305.

8. For a full description of the rules and their strategic implications in the 1960s, see Lewis A. Froman, Jr., *The Congressional Process: Strategies, Rules and Procedures* (Boston: Little, Brown, 1967).

9. On norms, see Donald R. Matthews, "The Folkways of the U.S. Senate: Conformity to Group Norms and Legislative Effectiveness," *American Political Science Review* 53 (1959): 1964-89; Ralph K. Huitt, "The Outsider in the Senate: An Alternate Role," *American Political Science Review* 55 (1961): 566-75; William S. White, *Citadel: The Story of the U.S. Senate* (New York: Harper, 1956); Herbert B. Asher, "The Learning of Legislative Norms," *American Political Science Review* 67 (1973): 499-513; and Richard F. Fenno, Jr., "The Internal Distribution of Influence: The House," in *The Congress and America's Future*, 2d ed., ed. David B. Truman (Englewood Cliffs, N.J.: Prentice-Hall, 1973), 63-90.

10. On appropriations politics in the 1960s, see Richard F. Fenno, Jr., *The Power of the Purse: Appropriations Politics in Congress* (Boston: Little, Brown, 1966) and Stephen Horn, *Unused Power: The Work of the Senate Committee on Appropriations* (Washington, D.C.: Brookings Institution, 1970).

11. The Great Depression and the Hoover administration's inability to cope with

it led voters to turn to Franklin Roosevelt and the Democrats in large numbers in the elections of 1932, 1934, and 1936. The singular combination of the assassination of John F. Kennedy and the 1964 Republican debacle, with Barry Goldwater at the top of the ticket, gave Democrats a genuine working majority for a brief period in the mid-1960s.

12. For an assessment of the possibilities for genuine policy change in Congress, see Gerald C. Wright, Jr., Leroy N. Rieselbach, and Lawrence C. Dodd, eds., *Policy Change in Congress* (New York: Agathon, 1986).

13. See Walter A. Rosenbaum, *Energy, Politics and Public Policy* (Washington, D.C.: CQ Press, 1981).

14. Most commonly, conflict revolved around Congress's efforts to impose its preferences—for public works, emergency housing, milk price support legislation—on an unwilling president. For capsule summaries of a host of policy struggles, see Randall B. Ripley and Grace A. Franklin, *Congress, the Bureaucracy, and Public Policy,* 3d ed. (Homewood, Ill.: Dorsey Press, 1984). The president's response was to veto objectionable bills: Richard Nixon vetoed 40 public bills; Congress overrode (by a two-thirds vote in each house) only 5. The legislature was more successful in imposing its preferences on Gerald Ford, overriding 12 of his 66 vetoes.

15. In these sessions the committee goes over the bill line by line, often substantially amending it, to produce the final version of the legislation on which the full committee or the entire chamber will be asked to act.

16. On some occasions a powerful individual can single-handedly block legislation. Chairman Wilbur D. Mills (D-Ark.) of the House Ways and Means Committee personally held off enactment of national health insurance for the elderly. Only when Mills became convinced of the need for such a program and steered an acceptable bill through his committee did Medicare become law. See Theodore R. Marmor, *The Politics of Medicare,* rev. ed. (Chicago: Aldine, 1973); and John R. Manley, *The Politics of Finance* (Boston: Little, Brown, 1970).

17. See Randall B. Ripley, *The Politics of Economic and Human Resource Development* (Indianapolis, Ind.: Bobbs-Merrill, 1972), chap. 5; and R. Douglas Arnold, *Congress and the Bureaucracy: A Theory of Influence* (New Haven, Conn.: Yale University Press, 1979).

18. Lewis A. Dexter, "Congressmen and the Making of Military Policy," in *New Perspectives on the House of Representatives,* ed. Robert L. Peabody and Nelson W. Polsby (Chicago: Rand McNally, 1963).

19. Raymond H. Dawson, "Congressional Innovation and Intervention in Defense Policy: Authorization of Weapons Systems," *American Political Science Review* 56 (1962): 42-57.

20. Quoted in Judy Gardner, "Congress More Cautious in Post-Vietnam Era," *Congressional Quarterly Weekly Report,* June 28, 1975, 1349.

21. Richard E. Neustadt, *Presidential Power* (New York: Wiley, 1960).

22. Of course, contemporary, postreform presidents continue to use many of these same techniques to persuade Congress.

23. The president did not, nor does he now, make all these contacts personally. He had a large liaison staff at his disposal to assist in persuading members of Congress to go along with his policy proposals. On liaison in the prereform period, see Abraham Holtzman, *Legislative Liaison: Executive Leadership in Congress* (Chicago: Rand McNally, 1970). Executive branch lobbying efforts were not always supportive of the chief executive's programs, although they often seemed to be. The agencies sometimes asked Congress to depart from official executive requests because they were not satisfied with the authority or funds requested for them. Some bureaus—the Army Corps of Engineers, for instance—developed cozy relationships—often referred to as *iron triangles* or *subgovernments*—with congressional committees and concerned interest groups and became virtually immune from executive control. The Corps, as chief construction agency for rivers and harbors projects, sought to enlarge its mission; congressional subcommittees (the House Appropriations Public Works Subcommittee, for example) were eager to expand their influence and their ability to serve their constituents; citizens and the interest associations that represented them were happy to have the benefits that public projects provided. Each component of the iron triangle had incentive to push for bigger construction programs, and presidents were regularly frustrated in their efforts to hold the fiscal line. See John A. Ferejohn, *Pork Barrel Politics: Rivers and Harbors Legislation, 1947-1968* (Stanford, Calif.: Stanford University Press, 1974); Arthur A. Maass, "Congress and Water Resources," *American Political Science Review* 44 (1950): 576-93; Douglass Cater, *Power in Washington* (New York: Random House, 1964); and J. Leiper Freeman, *The Political Process*, rev. ed. (New York: Random House, 1965).

24. James L. Sundquist, *Politics and Policy: The Eisenhower, Kennedy, and Johnson Years* (Washington, D.C.: Brookings Institution, 1968), 146. This paragraph leans heavily on Sundquist's account (chap. 4) of the war on poverty.

25. Samuel P. Huntington, "Congressional Responses to the Twentieth Century," in *The Congress and America's Future*, 2d ed., ed. David B. Truman (Englewood Cliffs, N.J.: Prentice-Hall, 1973), 6-38.

26. For instance, Raymond A. Bauer, Ithiel de Sola Pool, and Lewis A. Dexter, *American Business and Public Policy*, 2d ed. (Chicago: Aldine-Atherton, 1972), IV, suggest that lobbyists had less "clout" than generally believed, that they were often understaffed and inadequately financed, and that they sought to avoid "pressure tactics" and "hard sell." See also Lester W. Milbrath, *The Washington Lobbyists* (Chicago: Rand McNally, 1963); and Lewis A. Dexter, *How Organizations Are Represented in Washington* (Indianapolis, Ind.: Bobbs-Merrill, 1969). For the traditional, classic view of interest groups as more powerful policy-making participants, see David B. Truman, *The Governmental Process*, 2d ed. (New York: Knopf, 1971); and Grant McConnell, *Private Power and American Democracy* (New York: Knopf, 1966).

27. This stress on the supportive rather than an aggressive posture of interest associations does not mean that other, more traditional techniques of

influence were not used. Groups did hire intermediaries, influential constituents of the legislators, to express interest group sentiments. Public relations campaigns and even bribery were also used. Some did get involved in the electoral process, seeking to reward their friends and punish their enemies. Yet, on balance, such tactics were relatively costly and inefficient. Direct communication was more effective and the preferred method of group involvement.

28. For the classic exposition of the "mobilization of bias" in the interest group system, see E. E. Schattschneider, *The Semi-Sovereign People* (New York: Holt, Rinehart and Winston, 1960).

29. Well-to-do citizens, those with more education and higher incomes and with more leisure time, communicate more often than do low-income constituents and are quite atypical of the full electorate. Thus, members are unlikely to get a fair sampling of constituent opinion. See Angus Campbell et al., *The American Voter* (New York: Wiley, 1960); and *Elections and the Political Order* (New York: Wiley, 1966).

30. Sundquist, *Politics and Policy*.

31. This point should not be overemphasized. As noted, electoral uncertainties did compel members of Congress to worry about constituents' reactions and thus introduced some link between governor and governed. But this connection was probably stronger than empirically necessary, given the reality of voters' attention to Congress. In fact, legislators had few worries about most single acts or votes. See John W. Kingdon, *Congressmen's Voting Decisions* (New York: Harper and Row, 1973). Rather, members needed to cultivate the impression among their constituents that they were alive, well, and, most important, working hard for the state or district.

32. See Campbell et al., *American Voter* and *Elections and the Political Order;* and Donald E. Stokes and Warren E. Miller, "Party Government and the Saliency of Congress," *Public Opinion Quarterly* 26 (1962): 532-46. Stokes and Miller found that in the off-year congressional election of 1958, only 7 percent of those polled gave issue-related reasons for their votes. For confirmatory evidence from 1970, see Stanley R. Freedman, "The Salience of Party and Candidate in Congressional Elections: A Comparison of 1958 and 1970," in *Public Opinion and Public Policy*, 3d ed., ed. Norman R. Luttbeg (Itasca, Ill.: Peacock, 1981), 118-22.

33. See, for example, David RePass, "Issue Salience and Party Choice," *American Political Science Review* 65 (1971): 389-400; Richard W. Boyd, "Popular Control of Public Policy: A Normal Vote Analysis of the 1968 Elections," *American Political Science Review* 66 (1972): 429-49; and Gerald M. Pomper, "From Confusion to Clarity: Issues and American Voters, 1956-1968," *American Political Science Review* 66 (1972): 415-28.

34. Charles O. Jones, "Inter-party Competition for Congressional Seats," *Western Political Quarterly* 17 (1964): 461-76. In 1968, when Richard Nixon barely edged out Hubert Humphrey for the presidency, only 8 (of 404) House incumbents seeking reelection were defeated (3 in the primary, 5 in the

general election). At the other extreme in 1964, when Lyndon Johnson buried Barry Goldwater in a Democratic landslide, 50 incumbents (of 394 who entered the lists) lost their seats (5 in primaries, 45 in the fall contest). Thus, even "major" swings brought only a modest-sized new contingent to Congress; without "new blood," the ideological composition of Congress changed only slightly.

35. One study found that in the 1966 off-year House elections that selected the 90th Congress (1967-68), losing candidates, as a group, bore a striking ideological similarity to the winners. Had the defeated nominees actually won, the resulting House would have been slightly more liberal in foreign policy but slightly more conservative in the domestic sphere. To be sure, if the national electorate had followed party or liberal-conservative inclinations strongly in one direction, the resulting Congress would have been strikingly different from the 90th actually elected. But such unidimensional swings in partisan or ideological preferences, encompassing virtually all electoral districts, are unknown in the annals of American political history. See John L. Sullivan and Robert E. O'Connor, "Electoral Choice and Popular Control of Public Policy," *American Political Science Review* 6 (1972): 1256-58.

Reform Initiatives since 1970 | 3

Under the lash of numerous critics, Congress in 1970 began to enact a broad series of reforms designed to improve its performance. The reformers shared one ambition: making Congress "better." But what constitutes a "better" Congress? There was and is little agreement. A few reformers have proposed changes intended to move the legislature toward a sweeping philosophical vision of what Congress should be, but these proponents of executive force or congressional supremacy have found few interested in their theoretical insights. Others have focused on smaller but more manageable matters, directing their attention to specific steps designed to make Congress more responsible, more responsive, more accountable, or some combination of these desirable yet often incompatible attributes. This pragmatic perspective, nurtured by the events of the 1960s in particular, dominated the reform movement that flowered during the 1970s; Congress moved in several directions rather than consistently toward any one reform vision. Even though the reforms sought improvements in the responsibility, responsiveness, and accountability of Congress, their net impact ironically may have been to preserve, or even extend, the decentralized character of the legislature.

To chart the causes, course, and consequences of congressional change is no easy task. For one thing, *reform*—defined as intentional efforts to reshape institutional structures and processes—is only one, and perhaps not even the most important, facet of organizational alteration. *Change*—more broadly defined as any shift, intended or inadvertent, evolutionary or revolutionary, in basic institutional patterns or procedures—may occur more randomly and unobtrusively. In addition, the content of public policy, the values—money, power, symbolic preferment—that statutes or other legislative activities confer,

41

may reflect either reform or change, as defined, or both. Thus change appears basic; a variety of causes may stimulate new forms of organization and action and lead to new institutional outcomes. In this light, reform is best seen as a type of change, an *explicit* effort to bring about preferable results through specific structural or procedural alterations. The analyst's task is to sort out the causes and shape of change, including reform, and to assess its impact, if any, on Congress's performance. This formidable challenge is taken up in this and the subsequent chapter.

As David Rohde and Kenneth Shepsle make clear, change may flow from a multiplicity of forces.[1] First, events outside the assembly may impinge directly on it. Domestic recession or international crisis may pose problems that highlight congressional deficiencies; failure to cope with old or new issues is likely to encourage reformers to come forward with proposals to make Congress work better. Second, membership turnover may bring to the legislature new personnel with different backgrounds, experiences, and perspectives; newcomers may operate the existing congressional machinery in ways quite at variance with old routines, or they may seek to rebuild the legislative engine to make it perform more efficiently.[2] Alternatively, events may induce or compel incumbent members of Congress to reassess their views, leading to either policy change, reform, or both.[3] In short, events and new members, neither planned nor predictable, may contribute as much or more to legislative change than any self-conscious reform movement.

Members of Congress are the chief agents of reform; unless and until they choose to act, there will be no reform.[4] Lawmakers treat reform, as they do more "substantive" issues, in incremental style. They are seldom if ever moved by broad visions of the ideal Congress; rather they respond, in the short run, to circumstances of the moment. Reforms tend to be political, pragmatic, and more-or-less spontaneous reactions to seemingly irresistible forces. They have been piecemeal, not wholesale; individually modest, not radical; ad hoc, not the products of comprehensive planning.

In addition, the reformers' motives are mixed, not pure, making it difficult to determine precisely the purposes of the changes they propose. Some ostensible goals are far easier to defend than others; the rationale for institutional engineering may belie its true intent. For example, who can fault the desire of Congress to regain public prestige lost during the late 1960s?[5] Similarly, wanting to make the legislature more effective or efficient in producing public policy is hardly controversial. It is somewhat riskier, however, to propose reforms that increase legislative influence relative to the executive. There are those who prefer presidential to congressional power. Likewise, to suggest reforms to bring about desired policies, or to reverse unfavorable outcomes, is likely to elicit opposition from those satisfied with the legislature's current output (or lack thereof). Finally, personal considerations of members—the desire to improve their electoral fortunes or legislative power—may underlie their reform sentiments, although these concerns are seldom openly advertised.

Overall, then, it is hard to know with certainty what reformers have wanted to accomplish. The reforms they did adopt, implemented incrementally and sequentially over a half decade, were compromises not always consistent with one another. Moreover, the reforms are hard to distinguish from the consequences of other, unplanned changes that occurred over the same period. Any efforts to specify precisely what the reforms of the 1970s actually produced are treacherous. This disclaimer notwithstanding (valor being the lesser part of discretion), it is possible to identify three sets of reforms—those promoting responsibility, responsiveness, and accountability—that Congress adopted and that contribute to congressional performance today.[6]

Two broad aims seem to have motivated these efforts. The first was to "democratize" Congress, to diffuse influence more widely among members and citizens, to give more of them a greater opportunity to participate meaningfully in congressional deliberation and policy making. The second was to reassert congressional power, particularly vis-à-vis the president, to recapture influence unwisely lost to the executive branch, to make Congress a more effective policy maker. These efforts occupied the better part of a decade, and the reforms they spawned were implemented without reference to broad theories or even to one another.

Reform Background

A singular combination of events, new issues (or dramatically altered old ones), and personnel turnover in Congress set the stage for the reformers to win approval of much of their agenda. Vietnam was surely the catalyst. When President Lyndon Johnson asked Congress for a free hand to fight in Indochina, the legislators were more than happy to comply: no representatives and only two senators voted against the Gulf of Tonkin Resolution that gave the president carte blanche to conduct the conflict as he saw fit. But as the war dragged on toward an unsatisfactory conclusion and as the public became increasingly impatient with the nation's inability to "win" the fight, lawmakers' frustrations grew. They sought, without success until the very end, to influence the course of the war once it became obvious that presidential policy was not working. Their failure to move either Johnson or Richard Nixon to alter course made clear their impotence vis-à-vis the "imperial presidency" and led to calls for a reassertion of legislative authority.[7]

Controversy over the federal budget taught a similar lesson: Congress was at a serious disadvantage in any policy competition with the executive branch. The costs of the Vietnam conflict dislocated the federal budget; the effort to pay for both "guns and butter," the war and a multitude of "Great Society" social programs, led to soaring inflation and deficits. Spending seemed out of control, and Congress's budgetary mechanisms appeared incapable of checking a runaway budget. Nixon confronted Congress directly: he insisted that it adopt a cap on federal spending and he began to impound duly enacted appropriations that he thought entailed excessive costs.[8] Members of the legislature concluded, grudgingly although correctly, that they were poorly prepared to push their own fiscal priorities in the face of presidential power and persuasion.

During the mid-1960s, a set of difficult and emotional policy concerns also confronted the country. Civil rights issues aroused racial antagonisms. The Supreme Court's 1954 decision in *Brown v. Board of Education* declared segregated schools unconstitutional. The civil rights movement, featuring peaceful marches and protests that all too often turned violent, brought black Americans' claims forcefully to public attention. The Civil Rights Act of 1964 and the Voting Rights Act of 1965 increased the salience of their cause. The civil rights issue was no longer simply a residue of slavery, restricted to the southern states; housing, access to public accommodations, busing for school desegregation, equal employment opportunity, and voting rights affected all sections of the nation and the lawmakers who represented them.[9] Similarly, other items, such as environmental protection, energy, school prayer, abortion—previously ignored or treated gingerly—rose to the top of the policy agenda, and Congress found that it was ill-prepared to deal with them. Congress, suffering from a collective, institutional "inferiority complex," called for reform.[10]

Also during this time a new spirit of democracy, of expanded political participation, pervaded the country. Johnson's "war on poverty" stressed community action and sought to involve ordinary citizens, the beneficiaries of social programs, in the planning and implementation of federal welfare activities. Previously unrepresented or underrepresented interests—not only the poor and minorities but also consumers and women—began to organize and to press their claims on government: the public interest, or citizen lobby, movement flourished.[11] The Democratic party, fearing that rank-and-file partisans played too small a part in the presidential selection process, dramatically revised its nominating procedures. New party rules, adopted after 1968, drastically reduced the role of party professionals—the alleged "bosses"—and created a system in which the nominee was chosen, for all practical purposes, by citizens in state caucuses and primary elections.[12] In short, more involved citizens made louder and more numerous demands on their elected representatives, who, burdened by a growing workload, found themselves increasingly hard-pressed to respond.

The electoral process further transformed Congress. Membership turnover, low during the 1960s, rose sharply. In the 91st House (1969-71), there were 36 freshmen (23 members of the 90th retired; 13 lost their reelection bids); that is, 8 percent of the House were serving their first term while 18 percent were in the tenth term or more. A decade later, in the 96th House (1979-81), there were 77 freshmen (18 percent of the House) replacing 49 retirees, 24 defeated representatives, and 4 who either resigned or died; members with 10 or more terms of service constituted 13 percent of the House.

In the Senate the story was the same. Turnover increased dramatically. In the 91st Senate there were 14 freshmen (replacing 6 retirees and 8 losers); in the 96th there were 20 (succeeding 10 retirees and 10 election victims). From an alternative vantage point, 31 percent of the 91st Senate had less than a full term of service, while 10 years later the figure was 48 percent.[13] There was, in short, a great infusion of "new blood" in Congress during the 1970s.

The newcomers recognized Congress's failings, inheriting from their predecessors a long-standing dissatisfaction with Congress's performance. In the 1946 House elections, for instance, Republican challengers won 55 previously Democratic seats, mostly from northern liberals. The Democrats remained the majority in the House, but the surviving conservative southerners dominated the party and, under the seniority tradition, acceded to a disproportionate share of powerful committee chairmanships. They allied in a conservative coalition with the Republicans in Congress to block liberal policy initiatives. Consequently, throughout the 1950s there was constant but unavailing agitation by liberals to modify the seniority system, gain power in congressional policy making, and enact progressive legislation.

The newcomers of the 1960s and early 1970s were younger, more policy oriented, and more independent minded; and as a result less predisposed to adhere to the modus operandi than was the earlier generation of lawmakers. They balked at the traditions of the institution,

45

refusing to accept norms like apprenticeship that required them to refrain from active participation in congressional deliberations until they had supposedly "learned the ropes" or to defer to the wise counsel of committee leaders—chairpersons and ranking minority members—until they had acquired the requisite specialization. They were, in short, unwilling to obey the adage of Speaker Sam Rayburn (D-Texas): "To get along, go along." [14] Moreover, many of these new members found it electorally advantageous to run for Congress by running "against" Congress,[15] to criticize the legislative establishment and upon arriving in Washington to adopt a critical, reformist view of congressional structure and procedure. Finally, the new electoral circumstances that protected most incumbents from November surprises at the polls—effective personal campaign organizations and the ready availability of funds from the proliferating political action committees (PACs)[16]—gave new members the independence they needed to pursue their own political agendas, agendas that included reform.

Thus, the reform spirit grew. Congress's inability to influence American foreign policy in Vietnam spurred on the reformers. Watergate, that extraordinary congeries of scandals—more far-reaching than the bungled burglary at the apartment complex that gave it its name—provided the final impetus. President Nixon, preoccupied with defending himself and his subordinates, had little time to lead the legislature. As the Watergate revelations unfolded, his popularity plummeted, as did his persuasive power. Nixon's political weakness gave Congress the courage and the opportunity to act to redress its grievances against the executive. Nixon's resignation (and his successor's controversial pardon of the "disgraced" ex-president) handed the Democrats a major triumph in the 1974 midterm elections: 75 freshman Democrats, many of them liberals, were elected to the 94th Congress (1975-77) and sustained the reform spirit.[17]

This extraordinary concatenation of circumstances stirred up a wave of congressional self-evaluation and analysis; without these elements of basic change, it is doubtful that reform would have followed. In 1965 Congress established a Joint Committee on the Organization of Congress. The committee's wide-ranging examination of the legislature's organization and procedures led eventually to passage of the Legislative Reorganization Act of 1970. In 1972 Congress established a second committee, a Joint Study Committee on Budget Control, that laid the groundwork for the Congressional Budget and Impoundment Control Act of 1974.

Each chamber pursued its own course as congressional introspection grew. The House formed three separate reform panels: the (Bolling)

Select Committee on Committees in 1973-74; the (Obey) Commission on Administrative Review in 1977; and the Select (Patterson) Committee on Committees in 1980.[18] Not to be outdone, the Senate launched the (Hughes) Commission on the Operation of the Senate in 1975, the Temporary Select (Stevenson) Committee to Study the Senate Committee System in 1976, and the (Culver) Commission on the Operation of the Senate in 1975.[19] An impressive welter of ideas emerged from these committees; many were adopted (more were not!).

The liberal Democratic Study Group (DSG)[20] nurtured the seeds of reform, which first bore fruit when Congress enacted the Legislative Reorganization Act of 1970. Policy problems that appeared intractable extended the growing season, new members tilled the fields, and the reformers brought in a bumper crop of changes during the ensuing years. But they did not inevitably reap what they had intended to sow (in fact, they did not always know precisely what they had planted), and their harvest was often bitter.

A Democratizing Trend: Responsiveness and Accountability ___

Nevertheless, these conditions were conducive to significant reform; they created for members of Congress both incentives and opportunity to alter the ways in which the legislature conducted its business. The first major thrust of the reform movement was to make Congress more democratic by offering more senators and representatives a greater chance to influence congressional policy making, oversight, and representation. This effort, in turn, consisted of two streams of reform: one aimed at responsiveness, the other at accountability. The first sought to permit more voices from inside and outside the legislature to be heard, and perhaps heeded, in congressional deliberations and decisions. The second required those debates and choices to take place in the open, presumably subject to citizen scrutiny. Congress, in consequence, would be more democratic; more members, responding to more interests, would contribute to its activities, and they would do so in plain sight of the public.

Redistributing Committee Power

As a first step the House and later the Senate loosened the hold of committee leaders on their panels. Many members, especially liberal and junior legislators, chafed under the restrictions on their participation and policy influence that the old, committee-dominated regime imposed. The committee chair, often in collaboration with the ranking minority member, dominated the panel. Formal leaders were chosen by seniority; the majority party member with longest continuous service on a committee automatically became its chairperson. In the eyes of the critics, this meant that longevity, physical and political, rather than expertise or political skill, determined who would manage committee deliberations. Specifically, because so many "safe" Democratic seats were in the South, conservatives from below the Mason-Dixon line acceded too frequently to the top committee posts and used the power of those positions to block northern liberals' policy initiatives.[21]

In 1971 both parties in the House decided they could employ criteria other than seniority to choose chairpersons; each empowered its party caucus, the meeting of all party members, to vote on whether to accept the recommendations of the party committee on committees for chairperson or ranking minority member. The Republican procedure called for a conference vote on its committee on committees' nomination, a recommendation not necessarily based on seniority. The Democrats adopted a plan, sometimes described as a "Kamikaze system," whereby 10 committee members could force a vote in the Democratic Caucus on their chairperson. The requirement to stand up publicly to oppose powerful chairpersons served to deter challengers, but liberals on the District of Columbia Committee did seek to oust Chairman John L. McMillan (D-S.C.); they objected to his longstanding opposition to home rule for Washington, D.C. McMillan survived on a 196-96 caucus vote. This challenge may have contributed to his defeat in his district's 1972 primary.

In 1973 the House Democrats went one step further: they determined that the full caucus should vote on the nominee for each committee chair and, if one-fifth of the members so desired, by secret ballot. In practice, all decisions followed seniority; negative votes against the senior committee member ranged from 2 to 49 and in no instance reached one-third of those cast. The Republican Conference raised two challenges, but in both cases the seniors retained their chairs by three-to-one margins. A hint of change reached the Senate in 1973 when Republicans adopted a proposal under which committee members would elect the ranking minority member from among their own number without regard to seniority; no ranking minority members were unseated under the new process. Two years later the Senate Democrats accepted a plan (not used until the outset of the 95th Congress in 1977) to vote in full caucus by secret ballot for chairperson on request of the caucus; in such voting, members need not adhere to seniority.

It was the House Democrats, however, who first used new procedures to mount a successful challenge to a sitting chairperson. In 1975 they permitted rank-and-file members of the caucus to nominate candidates for committee chairperson if the caucus rejected the committee on committees' original choice. More important, they used the new process. The caucus—its ranks enlarged by the addition of 75 freshmen, mostly liberals—actually deposed three southern committee chairpersons: W. R. Poage (Texas), 75, of the Agriculture Committee; F. Edward Hébert (La.), 74, of the Armed Services Committee; and Wright Patman (Texas), 81, of the Banking, Currency, and Housing panel. These aged oligarchs were succeeded by younger northerners: Thomas Foley (Wash.), 45; Melvin Price (Ill.), 70; and Henry Reuss (Wis.), 62. Foley and Price had been the second-ranking Democrats on Agriculture and Armed Services, respectively, while Reuss stood fourth on the seniority ladder on the Banking Committee.[22] Wayne Hays (Ohio), rejected for renomination by the committee on committees for another term as chair of the House Administration Committee, averted defeat in the caucus; freshmen whose campaigns he had supported with funds at his disposal as chairperson of the House Democratic Congressional Campaign Committee helped reverse the initial decision.[23]

Later in 1975 the Democratic Caucus applied the same procedures for selecting committee chairpersons to selecting subcommittee chairpersons of the Appropriations Committee, positions that have important budgetary responsibilities. A decade later, at the start of the 99th Congress (1985-87), the caucus replaced octogenarian Melvin Price (Ill.) with Les Aspin (Wis.), a younger liberal, in the Armed Services Committee chair.[24] While seniority has been followed more often than not, it is now clear that the principle is not inviolate; chairpersons are on notice that they may be unseated if their peers deem their behavior unacceptable.

If committee leaders had been less powerful—more presiding officers than independent, autonomous actors—the conflict over seniority would have been less heated. But they were not. In the prereform period, committee chairpersons commanded substantial influence. In consequence, the democratizing trend produced a number of reforms that limit the ability of chairpersons to dominate their panels. The Legislative Reorganization Act of 1970, for example, allows the ranking majority member to preside over committee business if the committee leader is absent. If a chairperson in the House fails to move consideration of a bill within seven days after the Rules Committee grants a rule, a committee majority can so move. The 1970 act also guarantees all members the opportunity to participate fully in committee hearings (for instance, by empowering minority members to call their own witnesses), limits the ability of chairpersons to use proxy votes by mandating that they be given only in writing and for specific legislative business, and grants extra staff assistance to minority members.

In addition, the 1970 reorganization act allowed senators, effective in the 92d Congress (1971-73), to serve on only three committees (two major, one minor) and to chair only one committee and one subcommittee of a major panel.[25] During the 1970s the House also moved to reduce the concentration of power. The Democrats took numerous steps: no member could chair more than one legislative subcommittee, serve on more than two full committees, or be a member of more than one exclusive committee.[26] Each Democrat was entitled to serve on one exclusive or major committee. Chairpersons of exclusive or major committees could not chair any other committee or a subcommittee on a committee other than the one they led. No member could serve on more than a total of five subcommittees. Thus, both the Senate and House effectively guaranteed members "a piece of the action" earlier in their careers and ensured that committee chairs could no longer monopolize leadership positions on their panels.

Most important, perhaps, in the House, the reforms devolved much full committee power on the subcommittees. As noted, new rules made it easier for junior members of a full committee to attain positions of authority on that panel's subcommittees. In 1973 the Democratic Caucus designated all party members on each standing committee as the committee caucus and empowered them to choose subcommittee chairpersons, establish subcommittee party ratios, and set subcommittee budgets. The boldest step taken by the caucus in 1973, however, was to adopt a "subcommittee bill of rights." [27] This manifesto declared that full committees should respect the jurisdiction of each of their subcommittees. All legislation referred to a full committee was to be parceled out to the appropriate subcommittee within two weeks. Subcommittees were empowered to elect their own leaders; write their own rules; employ their own staffs; and meet, hold hearings, and act on legislation. Each subcommittee was entitled to its own budget. The "bill of rights" was a declaration of subcommittee independence from the full committee and its chairperson. Finally, in 1974 the Democratic Caucus required all full committees with more than 20 members to create a minimum of four subcommittees.

During the course of the decade, House Democrats also established procedures to facilitate members' accession to positions of subcommittee power. They instituted bidding procedures that permitted all members, even the most junior, to secure desirable subcommittee assignments and leadership posts. Bidding was in order of seniority. Each full committee Democrat was guaranteed a choice of one subcommittee membership before any could claim a second subcommittee slot; each member thus could seek an advantageous subcommittee assignment, and each could secure a reasonably senior slot on some subcommittee. A similar process governed the selection of subcommittee chairpersons: members requested (bid for) the top spot on their preferred subcommittees; the full committee caucus ratified their choices, by secret ballot when there was competition for a particular subcommittee chair. In sum, these reforms not only restricted the number of positions any member could hold but also virtually guaranteed that the available assignments would be shared widely among all the committee members. Broad participation in subcommittee activity became possible.

Control over staff was dispersed as well. Under the 1971 House reforms, the full committee chairperson could no longer hire all panel staff. Each subcommittee leader, chair and ranking minority member, was granted authority to employ a professional staff member for the committee. In 1975 the Senate went further, granting all senators some committee staff of their own. Previously, full and subcommittee chairpersons had controlled staff recruitment, but a new procedure permitted all senators not already authorized to hire staff personnel to recruit an aide to assist them with each of their three full committee assignments.[28] These changes effectively reallocated committee power from senior leaders to rank-and-file members.

The democratizing impulse also led to direct attacks on two powerful House committees: Rules, and Ways and Means. The Rules Committee determines the conditions under which legislation is considered on the House floor. A "closed" rule—to its critics, the "gag" rule—allows the committee to limit or eliminate the opportunity to propose amendments to pending bills; thus, the committee can, and sometimes did in the 1950s and 1960s, prevent a majority from voting its will. To reduce this possibility, the Democrats in 1973 adopted a complicated procedure requiring the party delegation on Rules to allow a floor vote on any amendment if 50 party members called for a vote and the full party caucus agreed.[29]

Ways and Means also felt the lash of the democratizers. Under the chairmanship of Wilbur Mills (D-Ark.), the committee did not use subcommittees; all business was conducted in full committee with Mills presiding. The 1974 resolution requiring all committees with more than 20 members to establish at least four subcommittees was directly aimed at Ways and Means; permanent, expert, independent subcommittees were intended to undercut Mills's power. Subsequently, the Democratic Caucus enlarged the committee by half, from 25 to 37 members, enabling more, and more liberal, representatives to secure seats on the panel. Like the changes on Rules, these reforms were designed to make Ways and Means more responsive to the will of rank-and-file Democrats.

Taken together, the committee reforms of the 1970s sought to decentralize Congress and to make it more democratic. Change was particularly marked in the more hierarchial House. Committee chairpersons would be less able to direct and dominate their panels the reformers believed; chairs would have to share their authority with subcommittee leaders and full committee majorities. In other words, more people, operating from power bases within committees and subcommittees, would have a share of congressional authority. Solutions to pressing problems would involve a larger set of participants; more members could influence the bargaining that eventually would produce new policies. More lawmakers, voicing differing sentiments and articulating a broader range of constituent opinions, would bring more points of view into play in legislative decision making. Democratizing reforms, in sum, were expected to extend congressional responsiveness.

These democratizing reforms could also serve additional purposes. For the individual member, ensconced in a subcommittee seat with budgetary, staff, and other resources attached, policy influence became a real possibility. This, in turn, would increase the participation in policy subsystems, the "iron triangles" that often permit congressional personnel, interest group representatives, and executive branch bureaucrats to shape basic policy choices.[30] Since the subcommittee has jurisdiction over certain policy topics, its members could contribute to the decisions on those matters that the subsystem manages. And of course policy influence would be readily convertible, through advertising activities and credit claiming, into reelection currency; informing the voters about what they had accomplished would not hurt electorally.[31] Using a newly won subcommittee slot, more members could "deliver the goods"—a rivers and harbors project or a defense contract—to their states and districts. Democratization, in short, was readily defensible (who could quarrel with the values of equality and participation?), but it also entailed more mundane and personal political considerations.

"Sunshine" Reforms: Less Secrecy, More Accountability

Democratization of Congress had a second aim, in addition to making the institution more responsive: improving Congress's public image. The reforms were a direct response to an increasingly hostile public. The prestige of Congress had been weakened not only by policy failure but also by a series of widely publicized scandals (from ordinary, old-fashioned corruption and conflicts of interest to Adam Clayton

Powell and Abscam, featuring nontyping typists and aquatic exhibition-ism in the Tidal Basin).[32] Paradoxically, constituents retained consider-able confidence in their own individual representatives, but concluded that Congress collectively was performing poorly.[33] To change this perception and restore popular approbation, the legislature adopted a series of reforms designed in large part to expose its operations to citizen scrutiny. To the extent that the voters could discover what their representatives were doing, and satisfy themselves that these activities were ethical, they would be able to hold Congress accountable and accept it as legitimate and untainted.

Members of Congress enacted several reforms to make legislative activities more accessible to interested citizens.[34] The Legislative Reorga-nization Act of 1970 opened up committee proceedings. It allowed televising, broadcasting, and photographing of committee hearings within limits left to the discretion of individual panels. In 1978 the House began televising its formal floor sessions, and with the advent of cable TV systems, the programs reached an increasing portion of the population over the C-SPAN network. The Senate, however, balked at televising its proceedings, fearing that it would encourage its members to "grandstand" rather than to focus on legislative business and would show the institution at its worst.[35]

In 1973 the House mandated that all committee sessions should be open to the public unless a majority of the panel voted in an open meeting to close them; this included the mark-up sessions in which committees prepared final drafts of bills (previously conducted behind closed doors in most committees) and conference committee meetings in which differences between House and Senate bills on the same subject were resolved. The Senate adopted similar "sunshine" rules in 1975. House committee members were required to vote by recorded roll call each day to close a committee meeting, and only the full chamber, also on a recorded roll call vote, could close a conference committee session. In both chambers executive sessions on secret or controversial matters remain possible, but the burden of proof falls on those who would exclude outside observers; they must persuade their committee col-leagues to keep the public out.

The 1970 act also required that legislators vote publicly in commit-tee and on the floor. Under the old rules only vote totals, not the positions of individual members, were recorded in committee. The revised procedures obligate committees to record and make available each lawmaker's committee votes.

A related reform shed light on congressional operations on the floor. Prior to the 1970 act, under certain circumstances no votes were recorded; there could be voice, standing, or unrecorded teller votes,[36] but in each instance the positions of individual legislators remained unknown. Only formal roll call votes were recorded. The act provided that, on demand of 20 House members, the names of those participating in teller votes be listed as they walked up the aisle. Eventually, the House switched to voting by machine—"electronic device"—to speed up the roll call process as well as to record individual positions more visibly. Those reforms were intended to enable attentive citizens to identify the supporters and opponents of particular legislative measures in committee and on the floor.

In the same vein, reforms were passed that disclosed members' campaign finances. In 1971 Congress enacted a modest bill, the Federal Election Campaign Act (FECA), and in 1974, following Watergate disclosures of manifold campaign finance abuses—satchels of cash, money laundering, funding of criminal activities—the legislature adopted sweeping amendments to the FECA. Contributions to primary, run-off, and general election campaigns were severely limited to $1,000 by individuals and to $5,000 by organizations. Spending ceilings were also imposed on candidates. Both donors and recipients were obligated to report, fully and promptly, even modest campaign contributions. The law created a Federal Election Commission (FEC) to oversee the statute; the FEC receives and makes available candidate spending reports. A variety of interest organizations, particularly Common Cause, a public interest lobby, analyze campaign finance information and publicize the sources of funds that flow to members of particular congressional committees and lawmakers promoting particular policies.

The constitutionality of the FECA was challenged, and in the case of *Buckley v. Valeo* (1976) the Supreme Court struck down the provision imposing spending ceilings on candidates on the grounds that it violated First Amendment guarantees of freedom of expression. The decision did sustain both the contribution limits and the reporting requirements of the act. Thus, while candidates were free to spend unlimited funds, they had to raise the money from relatively small contributions and to report in some detail the purposes for which they spent the funds. PACs soon became prominent sources of funds for congressional candidates. While each political action committee's contribution is limited by the act to $5,000 per candidate per election, groups of related committees—from single sectors of industry such as oil or defense—emerged as major suppliers of campaign money. Although each could give no more than $5,000, together they could provide candidates with large sums. Still, they must report what they give. The intent of these reporting requirements, enforced by the FEC, was to make known the sources and uses of campaign funds and thus lessen popular suspicions about legislators' finances.[37]

In 1977 and 1978 the Senate and House, respectively, adopted stricter codes of ethics to replace weak ethics legislation enacted in 1958 and 1968. The new regulations were designed to deter conflicts of interest by members by disclosing their general financial history to interested citizens and the media. In particular, senators and representatives were required to report their earned income, income from dividends and interest, honoraria received for lectures and other activities, the value and donor of gifts tendered, holdings in property and/or securities, and their outstanding financial obligations. Such disclosures should enable concerned citizens to discover to whom, if anyone, legislators are financially beholden and to assess whether members' personal interests impinge on matters about which they must vote or otherwise act.

In addition, the ethics codes imposed limits on lawmakers' acquisition and use of funds. Members could earn less as honoraria for giving speeches or offering advice to interest groups; income from such activities could not exceed 15 percent of their congressional salaries.[38] They were forbidden to collect "slush funds" (designated "office accounts") to supplement their official allowances and from spending campaign funds to defray their personal expenses. Candidates for reelection were prohibited from sending "franked mail"—sent at government expense to all "postal patrons" in the state or district—within 60 days of a primary or general election. Annual franked mailings for all members were restricted to not more than six times the number of addresses in the state or district. Representatives running for the Senate were prohibited from sending franked mail to residents outside the districts they currently represent.

Although members believed franked mail was essential to the representative function, to inform and educate constituents, reformers, including some in Congress, felt the perquisite conferred an unfair electoral advantage on incumbent legislators, and they moved successfully to restrict the practice. Finally, members of Congress were barred in any single year from taking gifts from interest groups or their lobbyists worth more than $100.[39] The intent here, as with the financial disclosure provisions, was to inhibit unethical behavior and to restore public confidence in Congress.

On their face, these sunshine reforms—open procedures, campaign finance regulations, and ethics codes—were designed to make it possible, although not necessarily easy, for the public to assess the degree to which members of Congress pursue their own interests at the expense of the public's. Yet other, less laudable motives may have prompted these reforms. Although little noted, there were clear implications for the political parties in mandating that Congress perform in public. The more visible any action, the more competing pressures—from the president, interest groups, and the public generally—come into play; the greater the number and power of such pressures, the less likely members will be to defer to party leaders and support the party line.[40] Financial disclosure could also be expected to influence, at least indirectly, the substance of policy. Forced to acknowledge the sources of their funds and obligations, members might be less likely to support their bankrollers' programs for fear of an appearance of conflict of interest. Similarly, controls on campaign spending have an obvious impact on election results. Limits on challengers' ability to fill their campaign coffers strengthen the well-documented advantage of incumbents (especially in the House).[41] In sum, even such praiseworthy reforms as increasing congressional visibility, and thus accountability, may conceal other less readily defensible intentions.

To increase member participation in legislative decision making, Congress also expanded the rights of the minority party.[42] The Legislative Reorganization Act of 1970 guaranteed the minority at least 10 minutes of debate on any amendment printed in the *Congressional Record* one day before debate on the legislation. It also gave the minority the opportunity to call its own witnesses, at least on one day of committee hearings, and three days in which to file its concurring or dissenting views on committee reports. In 1975 the minority won the right to hire a minimum of one-third of committee staff. Floor debate on conference committee reports was to be divided equally between majority and minority party members. These changes were intended to enlarge the minority's opportunities to make its voice heard in legislative deliberations.

House Democrats also moved to increase rank-and-file participation in the affairs of the party caucus. They required the Democratic Caucus to meet more frequently, at least once a month; they authorized all members, not merely the party leaders, to place items for discussion on the caucus's agenda. Furthermore, they permitted a majority of any state delegation to nominate a Democrat for a particular committee assignment; previously, the committee on committees had the exclusive power to nominate candidates for committee slots. The caucus also required the chairperson of the Democratic Congressional Campaign Committee, which provides assistance to party candidates for Congress, to be elected by the full caucus membership. In addition the party required the Speaker to name as House conferees members who were directly involved with a bill and preferably who supported its major provisions.

The requirement aimed to prevent the conferees from subverting the intent of the full House by yielding too easily to the Senate position on the bill. Finally, all members won the right to attend any full or subcommittee meeting (except of the Ethics panel), even if the session was closed to the public. Here, too, the goal was to expand member involvement in congressional affairs.

Overall, reforms redistributing committee power and increasing the visibility of congressional operations were designed to enlarge participation, by members and by citizens, in legislative decision making. Democratization, the reformers argued, should foster responsiveness and accountability.

A Trend toward Responsibility

The second basic thrust of the reform movement was a concerted effort to revive and revitalize Congress as an effective, that is, responsible, policy maker. The critics charged that Congress had abdicated its programmatic responsibilities, ceding much of its authority to the executive branch. Attempts during the 1970s to reclaim the legislature's proper policy primacy moved along several tracks. The reformers mounted a direct challenge to the president, enacting laws that strengthened Congress's ability to make its preferences prevail over his. They also sought to increase the ability of the majority party in Congress to move its legislative program ahead; a cohesive majority could act decisively, either to support a chief executive or to impose congressional priorities on a recalcitrant one. Finally, the legislature adopted new rules and procedures intended to reduce the opportunity for minority party members to impede the legislative process. All of these measures attempted to centralize legislative operations; more central authority, the reform proponents believed, would make Congress more efficient.

Taming the Executive: Reclaiming Power

During the prereform period, presidential assertiveness and congressional acquiescence had combined to create an imbalance between the two branches. The "imperial presidency," which Vietnam and Watergate symbolized, suggested that the legislature had lost or ceded its traditional powers to declare war, to control the federal budget, and to oversee the bureaucracy. Reform would enable Congress to renew its rightful role in the policy process, imposing its preferences on the president when it seemed sensible to do so.

To buttress its position relative to the executive, Congress reasserted its prerogatives in the foreign policy sphere, long a congressional concern. As far back as 1954, Senate reformers had tried to limit presidential discretion in foreign affairs by passing the Bricker amendment to the Constitution. This amendment, which was defeated by a single vote, would have curbed the practice of conducting diplomacy unilaterally through executive agreements rather than bilaterally through treaties, which require the advice and consent of the Senate.[43]

Other congressional efforts to restrict executive domination of foreign relations reached fruition in 1973 with passage, over President Nixon's veto, of the War Powers Resolution. Frustrated by its inability to influence the conduct of the war in Indochina in more than marginal ways and emboldened by the administration's Watergate embarrassments, Congress circumscribed the commander-in-chief's authority to commit military forces to combat without explicit congressional approval. The act enabled Congress to compel the executive to withdraw any troops sent into the field within 60 days (90 days if the logistics involved in removing the military units required it).[44] In theory, the president would cultivate congressional approval before sending troops into battle; without consultation there would be real risk of legislative reversal of the chief executive.

In a crisis the war powers procedures require the president to consult the legislature "in every possible instance" before committing the armed forces to hostile or potentially hostile situations. If he does deploy the troops, he must report in writing to Congress within 48 hours. This report triggers the 60-day congressional review period, and unless the lawmakers declare war or in some other way approve the use of force (by appropriating funds, for example), the president must bring the troops home. In addition, the legislature can end American involvement in the conflict by passing at any time a concurrent resolution to that effect. (A concurrent resolution, enacted in identical form by both House and Senate, does not require the president's signature.)[45] Interestingly, the resolution reflects congressional concern about its collective, institutional capacity to oppose the president; Congress framed the statute so that legislative *inaction* would trigger U.S. troop withdrawal. The chief executive can introduce the armed forces into hostilities on his own initiative, but he is obligated to withdraw them unless Congress acts positively to approve the commitment.

Budgetary reform is another area in which Congress reasserted its policy-making authority. Impartial observers as well as critics long agreed that Congress failed to exercise its power of the purse effectively. Indeed, President Nixon justified his impoundment of appropriated funds on the grounds that Congress had been fiscally irresponsible.

In the prereform budget process the chief executive submitted to Congress a single, unified budget, which Congress, through its appropriations committees, then split into a dozen or more bills that were given separate, unrelated treatment. At no point did the interested lawmaker have occasion to review the total budget and to compare proposed expenditures with available revenue.[46] Rather, the full picture was not visible until all appropriations measures had been passed; thus the last bills in the series became major targets for reduction as the sums committed in the earlier bills began to mount. Funds cut at one point could be restored later in supplemental appropriations bills, a fact that probably encouraged legislators to make cuts for partisan purposes in the full knowledge that such reductions need not be permanent. What seemed necessary to remedy these defects—to reduce Congress's competitive disadvantage in the face of executive expertise and give the legislature the opportunity to set its own spending priorities—was to coordinate and centralize the congressional consideration of the budget.

Congress made the effort in 1974. Building on the recommendations of a 1972 Joint Study Committee on Budget Control, the legislature passed the Congressional Budget and Impoundment Control Act. This comprehensive bill created special budget committees in the House and Senate that can draw on the resources of a Congressional Budget Office (CBO), a unified, joint staff of skilled experts. The CBO is the legislature's equivalent to the executive branch's Office of Management and Budget (OMB); it provides Congress with independent budgetary expertise, reducing its need to rely on data generated by the executive. Each year budget committees are required to produce (by April 15) and Congress is required to pass (by May 15) a *first budget resolution* that clearly specifies "targets" for federal spending,[47] recommended levels of revenue, the size of the deficit (or surplus), and the total level of the public debt. Spending targets, allocated among 19 separate categories, are not binding; they merely indicate the budget committees' recommendations.

After passage of the first resolution, the appropriations committees of the House and Senate and the revenue committees (House Ways and Means, Senate Finance) take over. They may accept the budget committees' figures or they may reject them. Even in the former case, they have substantial freedom to maneuver because the resolution provides only grand totals and does not set spending ceilings for particular programs or agencies (although the budget committee may suggest them). The tax and spending panels operate in their accustomed fashions. So do the other standing committees, which continue to authorize programs within their jurisdictions much as they did before passage of the budget act. These committees and the full chambers must complete action on the authorization and money bills not later than a week after Labor Day. The budget committees and Congress then must produce a *second budget resolution* that "reaffirms or revises" the first. The second resolution, to be adopted by September 15, is binding and sets forth the government's economic policies for the new fiscal year, which begins October 1.[48] Any legislation that breaches the spending ceilings or revenue requirements of the second resolution is subject to a point of order—an objection that may block passage—on the floor of either chamber.

The budget committees have an additional weapon to control the spending of the legislative panels: *reconciliation*. The act empowers them to propose, in a bill, that the legislative committees reduce or increase spending or revenue within their respective jurisdictions to conform to the overall budget resolution. Again, these directives are in aggregates, not line items; the reconciliation instructions, which the full chamber must pass, may order a committee to save certain sums, but the committee retains the right to determine which programs within its jurisdiction will be cut. Severe restrictions on available funds may force committees to change entitlement programs, such as Social Security and food stamps, that ordinarily escaped scrutiny under the prereform budget procedures. These committee decisions, made in response to reconciliation instructions, are merged in a reconciliation bill that Congress must enact by September 25, just prior to the onset of the new fiscal year.

The Congressional Budget and Impoundment Control Act of 1974 also includes curbs on the executive practice of impounding funds authorized and appropriated by Congress. If the president wishes to defer, or delay, spending, either house can compel expenditure of the funds by passing a resolution to that effect. If the chief executive seeks to terminate programs, he must persuade both houses to rescind, or cancel, the appropriation within 45 days; if the chambers do not act, he must spend the funds. Here, too, Congress wrote the law so that the legislature could have its own way with a minimum of effort. To rescind appropriations, the president must secure a resolution from both houses; inaction by either obligates him to spend the money. To defer expenditures, one house must act positively; if neither house votes a resolution of disapproval, the request to defer is automatically approved. These anti-impoundment procedures enable Congress to insist on its own spending priorities and to diminish the power of the chief executive to spend selectively.[49]

Overall, the budget act gives the legislature new budgeting resources through the budget committees and the CBO, a new means to look at the broad contours of the federal budget and determine its own spending and revenue priorities in a timely fashion, and a method to control impoundment and force presidential compliance with its spending decisions. To do so, however, required political compromise that merged innovative mechanisms with older, established procedures that serve the needs of individual lawmakers. In fact, the act became law because it satisfied the members' mixed motives.

Virtually all observers agreed that the old budgetary process was in shambles and that something had to be done. Congress as an institution was under fire for its failings, and the act was, symbolically at least, a counterattack. Reformers argued that the revised procedures would help Congress to recapture lost power, to improve its performance, and to enact new and better policies. Most important, it would achieve these goals without undue disruption of the existing budgetary process. Vested interests of appropriations and tax committee members would survive. The new methods did not replace old ways of doing business; instead they were grafted on to them. They defined and circumscribed the power and influence of the old centers of authority to some extent, but they were not expected to reallocate that power and influence dramatically. Reformers saw many potential benefits and few costs in the refined process.

To rectify further its disadvantages in information and analytic capacity vis-à-vis the executive, Congress created the Office of Technology Assessment (OTA), which would advise members on the implications of scientific developments. In addition, Congress expanded the budgets and enlarged the staff of two existing agencies: the Congressional Research Service (CRS) of the Library of Congress and the General Accounting Office (GAO). It also greatly increased members' personal and committee staffs and the use of computers to improve members' access to information.[50] In these ways Congress sought to compete more effectively with the executive; no longer would it readily defer to an administration presumed to possess superior information.

Finally, during the 1970s Congress began to assert, more forcefully than in the previous decades, already established powers. The Legislative Reorganization Act of 1946 had formalized the legislature's obligation to exert "continuous watchfulness" over the agencies and bureaus of the executive departments. Greater information resources and more vantage points, particularly from independent subcommittees, increased congressional surveillance of the executive branch. More specifically, use of the legislative veto increased. The legislative veto is a procedure permitting either the House or Senate, or both chambers, to review proposed executive branch regulations or actions and to block or modify those with which they disagree. As noted, both the War Powers Resolution and the impoundment title of the budget act contained congressional veto provisions, as did more than 150 other statutes enacted during the decade. The veto took numerous forms, depending on the particular piece of legislation. It could be exercised by an individual subcommittee or full committee (or even informally by a panel's chairperson), by either House or Senate, or by both enacting a concurrent resolution. Some forms required congressional approval, in advance, of executive activities; others allowed the legislature to reverse, after the fact, administrative rules and regulations. Whatever the form, however, Congress could, within a specified period, block bureaucratic behavior it found objectionable. Some scholars and lawyers asserted the veto was unconstitutional, that it encroached on the president's prerogatives;[51] Congress exercised the veto independently, without the chief executive's approval.

But the legislature found the veto device attractive. It enabled Congress to delegate authority to executives without permanently ceding control over what the bureaucrats actually did. Lawmakers could duck hot issues, but correct administrative "errors" if bureaucrats' proposals seemed unwise or politically damaging; they could defer to experts but later countermand them when they made poor choices. The legislative veto and other forms of oversight as well enabled Congress to exercise more thorough surveillance of the bureaucracy and greater influence over the executive branch.[52]

Here, too, the imbalance in institutional power between the two elected branches was used as a convenient justification for reform. To redress that imbalance, reformers argued, the legislature needed to reassert its authority over military, budget, and administrative matters. But other purposes may well have supplemented the avowed justification. Ideology figured prominently in both the war powers and budget bills. Those who opposed involvement in Southeast Asia, mainly liberals, led the fight to curb the commander-in-chief. Liberals and conservatives joined forces to support budgetary reform for quite different reasons: liberals expected the new process to provide more funds for social programs and less for defense; conservatives expected the reverse and were also eager for the budget committees to control spending—particularly of the "backdoor" variety—and balance the budget.

In addition to ideology, policy and personal power considerations prompted reform. The centralizing effects of the budget act would certainly expedite budgeting, but they also would exact a major price from the traditionally powerful revenue and appropriations committees.

Members of these panels were quite obviously reluctant to hand over policy responsibility to the budget committees.

Similarly, use of the legislative veto might help Congress centralize control over a sprawling bureaucracy and, if exercised by committee, enhance the authority of congressional participants in those now ubiquitous "cozy triangles," or policy subgovernments.

William Schaefer and James Thurber argue that the veto was more likely to facilitate members' reelection goals and personal power than to promote coordinated congressional control of administration.[53] Again a relatively acceptable motive—to redress legislative grievances against a too-powerful presidency—may have concealed almost as much as it revealed about the congressional reformers' real intent. But whatever the members' underlying motives during the reform decade of the 1970s, they did move forcefully to "tame" the executive.

Centralizing the Parties: Improving Efficiency

Perceived inefficiency in congressional performance motivated a second cluster of reforms to improve legislative responsibility. The House Democratic Study Group (DSG), comprising liberals long dissatisfied with Congress's failure to enact creative social programs, provided the impetus. A decentralized decision-making structure impeded coherent policy formulation, and the reformers professed a desire to make it easier for Congress to act. They hoped to convert the Democratic Caucus into a disciplined force for progressive legislation. And they rallied majority Democrats to impose some partisan discipline.

The liberals acted to strengthen the party apparatus in three ways. First, extending modest changes made in 1973, the Democratic Caucus in 1975 established a new procedure for making committee assignments. In 1973 the party leaders—the Speaker, the floor leader, and the whip— were permitted to sit with the Ways and Means Committee Democrats, who had traditionally served as the party's committee on committees, to make committee assignments. In 1973 the Democrats also had established a 24-member Steering and Policy Committee, composed of the party's elected leaders (the Speaker, floor leader, and caucus chairperson), 12 members elected by the Democratic Caucus to represent geographic regions, and 9 others appointed by the Speaker (including the party whips and representatives of the Congressional Black Caucus, women members, and freshman Democrats).[54] Then in 1975 the Democratic Caucus dramatically stripped the Ways and Means contingent of its committee on committees' powers, transferring them to the Steering and Policy Committee. The shift put the party's committee assignments into the hands of a more liberal body in which the party leaders had a strong voice.[55] The caucus retained the right to vote on each nominee for a committee chair and to approve Steering and Policy's slates for panel assignments.

Second, the caucus enhanced the personal power of the Speaker to move legislation forward. In addition to his powerful role in the Steering and Policy Committee, the Speaker won the right to nominate the Democratic members of the Rules Committee, subject to caucus approval. By so doing, the reformers hoped to yoke that panel firmly to the leadership. In addition, the caucus assumed the power to instruct the Rules Committee to act in specific ways, presumably to prevent favored programs from expiring in that sometimes defiant panel. The Speaker also gained new ability to regulate the flow of legislation to and from committee. He was authorized to refer bills to more than one committee, either simultaneously or sequentially, and to set time limits on committee consideration of measures. He could also create ad hoc committees to facilitate coherent treatment of complex policy issues. (Speaker of the House Thomas P. O'Neill, Jr. [D-Mass.], used this device effectively to coordinate President Jimmy Carter's 1977 energy programs.)

The leadership also supplemented existing techniques of vote gathering. The whip system was enlarged to improve communications between leaders and the rank-and-file. The Speaker frequently created informal task forces of members interested in particular bills to advise, plan strategy, and lobby for the legislation. Involving more members in enacting policy was intended to increase party cohesion. On the Senate side, the Temporary Select Committee to Study the Senate Committee System proposed a modest reform, passed in 1977, that gave the leadership new controls over bill referrals and scheduling.[56]

Third, the Democratic Caucus strengthened party discipline by insisting that Democrats maintain working majorities on the exclusive Appropriations, Rules, and Ways and Means committees.[57] They set the membership ratios at roughly two-to-one (two Democrats for each Republican), regardless of the overall balance between the parties in the full chamber. This step improved the prospects that party (liberal) legislation would receive favorable treatment in these panels. The caucus also retained the authority, if two-thirds of its members chose to exercise it, to instruct House committees to report legislation.[58]

In sum, reforms influencing committee assignments, the Speaker's authority, and party membership on committees centralized the power of the Democratic party in the House. A more responsible Congress was, ostensibly, the reformers' chief goal.

In addition, both chambers sought to realign and rationalize their committee jurisdictions. In the House the defenders of the status quo managed to remove all but the most routine features of the Bolling committee's 1974 reform proposals. The resulting reform was more cosmetic than anything else with respect to committee jurisdictions; the old order, preserving existing vested interests, remained largely intact. The reform legislation proposed to abolish Post Office and Civil Service; to divide Education and Labor into two separate committees; and to alter seriously the jurisdictions of Ways and Means, House Administration, and Merchant Marine and Fisheries. More sweeping recommendations (for example, to rotate committee members so that vested interests would not develop in particular assignments and to combine the authorization and appropriations phases of the budget process, heretofore distinct, in a single committee) were not even proposed; it was evident from the outset that such "radical" notions could not command majority support. In addition, the Bolling panel sought to bar committee chairpersons from casting absent members' votes by proxy; such a step would reduce the leader's capacity to shape committee decisions.

These proposals aroused howls of protest from those who saw them as threats to their own influence. Members of committees slated for abolition quickly took the lead in opposing the select committee's legislation. Representatives serving on panels whose jurisdictions would be similarly pared sought to retain control of policy areas of concern to them. Committee chairs, fearful of losing some bases of authority, expressed skepticism about the wisdom of the reforms. Committee staff, anxious about their jobs, joined the opposition. So, too, did interest groups, eager to preserve their familiar and well-established relations with committees. The Bolling proposals cut too close to the bone for too many members; they created more losers than winners. The result was predictable: the legislation was referred to the Democratic Caucus's (Hansen) Committee on Organization, Study, and Review, which in effect bowed to the opponents, gutted the select committee's proposals, and produced a set of reforms, more symbolic than meaningful, that the House eventually enacted.[59]

Senate reformers fared better; they won approval of modest but meaningful committee changes. The number of committees declined from 31 in the 94th Congress (1975-77) to 24 in the 95th (1977-79). Subcommittees fell from 174 to 117. In consequence, senators went from an average of 18 full or subcommittee assignments to 11. By the 98th Congress (1983-85), there were 16 full committees, with 103 subcommittees; senators averaged a little less than 11 assignments to these panels. More important, jurisdictions were rationalized, although considerably less than the Stevenson committee initially proposed.[60] Sharper demarkation of committee jurisdictions was intended to enhance congressional efficiency by reducing overlapping, redundant, and time-consuming treatment of legislation.

Curbing Minorities: Rules Changes

Reformers also attempted to improve congressional effectiveness by reducing the opportunities for minorities to thwart the majority and by speeding up consideration of legislation. As noted, the new budget process made possible the centralization of congressional fiscal policy making. Beyond this, the Senate significantly weakened the opportunity for minority use of unlimited debate, the *filibuster*. In March 1975, after weeks of acrimonious discussion and complex parliamentary maneuvering, the Senate voted to modify its infamous cloture rule (Rule 22), making it a little easier to cut off debate. Previously, two-thirds of those present and voting (67 senators if all were in attendance; 64 or 65 under ordinary circumstances) were required to invoke cloture; under the new rule three-fifths of the full membership (60 votes) could end debate.

The new procedure was, in fact, a compromise; liberals had wanted a simple majority of those present and voting to be able to force a conclusion to a filibuster.[61] Senate rules permitted 100 hours of debate after cloture was invoked, and filibuster proponents soon found that they could prolong the agony: if they introduced amendments prior to cloture, these would be in order after the vote, and they regularly prepared for such a contingency by introducing hundreds of amendments. The possibilities for a postcloture "filibuster by amendment" were restricted by a 1979 change that required the vote on final passage to come within the 100-hour period.[62]

The House also expedited consideration of legislation and reduced the opportunities for excessive delay. The reorganization act of 1970 allowed committees to meet while the House was in session, except under special circumstances. It permitted suspending quorum calls and dispensing with the reading of the *Journal* (a printed record of the proceedings of the previous session), unless a majority insisted. Quorum calls summon an appropriate number of members (100 in the Committee of the Whole, 218 when the House sits formally) to the floor for a vote. By the end of the decade, the use of repeated quorum calls as a dilatory tactic had been restricted. One vote, at the beginning of the legislative day, was often sufficient to establish a quorum.

The roll call process was also simplified. As noted earlier, an electronic voting system was instituted, and the rules allowed clustering of votes on rules, passage of bills, and conference reports at particular times so that members did not need to come to the floor so frequently. Subsequent votes in the series could be limited to five minutes. The number of members required to demand a recorded vote in the Committee of the Whole was increased from 20 to 25. These were modest steps, to be sure, but they made it easier for the 435-member institution to conduct its business.

Like courting popular approval or reviving the separation of powers, improving congressional responsibility (effectiveness or efficiency) was used as a convenient justification for reform. Strengthening the parties and the Speaker of the House, undercutting minority power, and reorganizing committee jurisdictions had implications beyond efficiency. Centralization would increase the influence of Congress against the executive, reformers argued; a strong legislature would be better able to impose its preferences on the administration. Moreover, a disciplined and productive legislature would look good to the citizens, leading to a rise in its popular standing. More significantly, of course, policy and personal goals could also be achieved. Those in command of an efficient policy process—the party leaders—would have a loud voice in the programs enacted—as well as considerable power to promote their own personal goals. Jurisdictional realignments, especially in the Senate, did move some programs from one committee to another, but many, more sweeping changes in committee jurisdiction were rejected. Clearly, whatever the intrinsic attractiveness of arguments about responsibility, they will readily yield in the face of practical pressures relating to influence and ideology.

The Road Not Taken: The Limits of Reform

Reform requires certain facilitating conditions. When critics and members of Congress concur that reform is needed, the latter, the actual reformers, will be inclined to act. They feel obliged to respond to the institution's needs, but the distance they are prepared to travel is limited. They will do what they must, but they are seldom eager, in any altruistic sense, to follow paths that may diminish their personal power and prerogative. The reforms of the 1970s failed to reach the goals that some observers, particularly those who stressed the desirability of making Congress a more responsible policy maker, felt were most critical. Many proposals were rejected largely because they would have disrupted important relationships within Congress and between members and outside interests.

One serious charge leveled at Congress was that its archaic committee arrangements, especially the confused jurisdictions of multiple panels, greatly inhibited responsible policy formulation. Too many committees, with divided and uncertain tasks to manage, slowed down the legislative process, imposed unmanageable burdens on individual members, and deterred decisive policy choices. To remedy this defect, reformers attempted to realign and clarify committee jurisdictions. But, as noted earlier, the Bolling committee's most sweeping proposals were never enacted. Reform failed in the face of members' fears that they would lose their "turf" if the committee system was significantly restructured. A half-dozen years later a far more modest proposal—to create a new Energy Committee with jurisdiction over matters previously in the hands of the Commerce, Interior, and Public Works panels—met a similar fate. Proposed by Representative Patterson's Select Committee on Committees (1979-80), the plan was sidetracked in favor of rechristening Interstate and Foreign Commerce the Committee on Energy and Commerce.

Indeed, by 1977 the reform movement had ground to a halt. Proposals for reform continued, but favorable action never followed. The House in 1977 established a Commission on Administrative Review, which produced an agenda of 42 suggestions, including the creation of a new Select Committee on Committees, to improve congressional performance. The House overwhelmingly declined to consider the proposals.[63] The 1980 report of the Patterson panel recommended several rules changes to improve efficiency: reforms to minimize scheduling conflicts between committees, to empower the Speaker to assign primary responsibility to one committee when a bill was referred to more than one panel, and to limit the number of subcommittees and subcommittee assignments available to any member. These proposals never reached the House floor.[64]

The Senate also continued to nod in the direction of reform, but to no avail. In 1983 it received a report from two former senators, Abraham Ribicoff (D-Conn.) and James B. Pearson (R-Kan.), proposing a series of "quite radical" reforms, including fundamental reshaping of the committee system, major reform of the budget process, limitations on debate to take up a bill, and elimination of an individual senator's ability to block action by placing a "hold" on legislation.[65] No action ensued. In 1985 the Senate failed to act on recommendations from Representative Quayle's Temporary Select Committee to Study the Senate Committee System. The committee proposed, most notably, to enforce rules limiting senators to service on three committees, to limit subcommittee assignments, and to abolish some 30 existing subcommittees.[66]

In short, experience shows that when Congress reaches the fork in the road that requires choice between reform, particularly to promote responsible policy making, and personal prerogative, the outcome is seldom in doubt. Unless there are compelling reasons to follow the reform path, and there have been few since the mid-1970s, reform will be the "road not taken."

Summary

Against a backdrop of pervasive disappointment with Congress's performance, a new generation of younger, more independent-minded legislators challenged executive policy-making dominance and tackled institutional reform. They were roused to action by recent history: congressional impotence during most of the Vietnam War and weakness of the executive branch after Watergate. They were not inspired by grand visions of the ideal Congress; they did not talk in terms of executive force or congressional supremacy philosophies. Rather, they reacted in typical legislative fashion, pragmatically and incrementally, with mixed motives, to reshape the structures and processes of the legislature. Over the decade of the 1970s, the reform movement produced numerous alterations intended, first, to democratize Congress: to give more people, inside and outside the institution, access to and influence over the legislature's deliberations and decisions. Second, the reformers sought to improve congressional efficiency: to revive Congress's capacity to enact sound public policy.

To foster congressional responsiveness and accountability, reformers reallocated committee power, particularly to independent subcommittees, and obligated Congress to act in public, in the "sunshine." Revamped committee procedures offer more members, operating from secure institutional positions, a chance to influence congressional decision making. Open committee meetings, campaign finance regulations, and financial disclosure requirements help interested citizens to discover their representatives' unethical behavior and to act accordingly at the polls. These reforms, in sum, aimed to make member and public participation in legislative affairs more meaningful; the reformers were eager—for personal, political, and policy reasons—to create a more democratic Congress.

The second trend, toward responsibility, enhanced Congress's policy-making potential by reasserting legislative power vis-à-vis the executive, strengthening the political parties as centralizing mechanisms, and revising the rules to promote efficiency. The War Powers Resolution and Congressional Budget and Impoundment Control Act asserted congressional authority to impose its own preferences on the president and his administration. More powerful political parties, with revived caucuses and a strengthened Speaker in the House, could more readily advance creative programs to remedy the nation's pressing problems. Revised rules would inhibit, if not prevent, minorities from imposing roadblocks to passage of such innovative policies. A responsible Congress, in sum, would be able to exert its authority and prevail when its members believed they had programs to advance.

These reforms—for responsiveness, accountability, and responsibility—were in one sense complementary. An efficient, responsible Congress, making sound decisions with reasonable dispatch, would restore public confidence in the institution; so would subjecting congressional operations to citizens' scrutiny. Ideally, an open, responsive legislature could, especially if the parties were powerful enough to organize action, meld the diversity of political viewpoints into effective programs without unconscionable delay or debilitating compromise.

In a second sense, however, the reforms were incompatible. The ideal of prompt action reflecting broad participation might well be illusory in a fragmented, decentralized institution. Too many voices, too large a body of policy-making participants, might make policy formulation impossible or require so many compromises that the programs actually adopted would be unworkable or ineffective. Extended accountability, subjecting members to many more pressures from groups and citizens external to Congress, could readily lead to the same result.

The reformers, by definition optimists, opted for the former scenario, to the extent that they looked at the broad picture at all. They hoped that each of the steps they proposed and enacted would produce the desirable outcomes they projected. Whether they realized their hopes—what the changes they imposed actually produced—is the subject of the next chapter.

NOTES

1. David W. Rohde and Kenneth A. Shepsle, "Thinking about Legislative Reform," in *Legislative Reform: The Policy Impact*, ed. Leroy N. Rieselbach (Lexington, Mass.: Lexington Books, 1978), 9-21.
2. On this "replacement" effect, which brings new members with different outlooks to Congress, see Herbert B. Asher and Herbert F. Weisberg, "Voting Change in Congress: Some Dynamic Perspectives on an Evolutionary Process," *American Journal of Political Science* 22 (1978): 391-425; Paul Burstein, "Party Balance, Replacement of Legislators, and Federal Government Expenditures," *Western Political Quarterly* 32 (1979): 203-208; David Brady and Barbara Sinclair, "Building Majorities for Policy Changes in the House of Representatives," *Journal of Politics* 46 (1984): 1033-70; and David W. Brady, "A Reevaluation of Realignments in American Politics: Evidence from the House of Representatives," *American Political Science Review* 79 (1985): 28-49.

3. On member "conversion," incumbents' change in voting stance, see Barbara Sinclair, *Congressional Realignment, 1925-1978* (Austin: University of Texas Press, 1982); and Brady and Sinclair, "Building Majorities."
4. Charles O. Jones, "Will Reform Change Congress?" in *Congress Reconsidered,* ed. Lawrence C. Dodd and Bruce I. Oppenheimer (New York: Praeger, 1977), 247-60.
5. Glenn R. Parker, "Some Themes in Congressional Unpopularity," *American Journal of Political Science* 21 (1977): 93-109.
6. For useful sources describing the developments of the 1970s, see Lawrence C. Dodd and Bruce I. Oppenheimer, "The House in Transition," in *Congress Reconsidered,* 3d ed., ed. Dodd and Oppenheimer (Washington, D.C.: CQ Press, 1985), 34-64; Norman J. Ornstein, ed., *Congress in Change: Evolution and Reform* (New York: Praeger, 1975); Norman J. Ornstein and David W. Rohde, "Political Parties and Congressional Reform," in *Parties and Elections in an Anti-Party Age,* ed. Jeff Fishel (Bloomington: Indiana University Press, 1978), 280-94; Samuel C. Patterson, "The Semi-Sovereign Congress," in *The New American Political System,* ed. Anthony King (Washington, D.C.: American Enterprise Institute, 1978), 125-77; Susan Welch and John G. Peters, eds., *Legislative Reform and Public Policy* (New York: Praeger, 1978); Rieselbach, *Legislative Reform;* and James L. Sundquist, *The Decline and Resurgence of Congress* (Washington, D.C.: Brookings Institution, 1981).
7. See Sundquist, *Decline and Resurgence;* Thomas M. Franck and Edward Weisband, *Foreign Policy by Congress* (New York: Oxford University Press, 1979); and Cecil V. Crabb, Jr., and Pat M. Holt, *Invitation to Struggle: Congress, the President, and Foreign Policy,* 2d ed. (Washington, D.C.: CQ Press, 1984).
8. For details on this controversy, see Allen Schick, *Congress and Money: Budgeting, Spending and Taxation* (Washington, D.C.: Urban Institute, 1980), chap. 3; and Howard E. Shuman, *Politics and the Budget: The Struggle between the President and the Congress* (Englewood Cliffs, N.J.: Prentice-Hall, 1984), chap. 7.
9. For a comprehensive treatment of the civil rights movement, see Robert Kluger, *Simple Justice* (New York: Knopf, 1976).
10. Steven S. Smith and Christopher J. Deering, *Committees in Congress* (Washington, D.C.: CQ Press, 1984), 36.
11. Jeffrey M. Berry, *Lobbying for the People* (Princeton, N.J.: Princeton University Press, 1977); and Andrew S. McFarland, *Public Interest Lobbies* (Washington, D.C.: American Enterprise Institute, 1975).
12. Austin Ranney, *Curing the Mischiefs of Faction: Party Reform in America* (Berkeley: University of California Press, 1975); and William J. Crotty, *Decisions for the Democrats: Reforming the Party Structure* (Baltimore: Johns Hopkins University Press, 1978).
13. Norman J. Ornstein, Thomas E. Mann, Michael J. Malbin, Allen Schick, and John F. Bibby, *Vital Statistics on Congress, 1984-1985 Edition* (Washington, D.C.: American Enterprise Institute, 1984), tables 2-7, 2-8, 1-6, and 1-7. Any two Congresses are, of course, not typical. Here, however, the evidence of high turnover is clear. The percentage of representatives with three or fewer terms of service (the relatively junior) was 37 in the 91st Congress, 34 in the 92d, and 37 in the 93d; for the three subsequent Congresses, the figures were 44, 49, and 50. The basis for this high turnover differed markedly in the two chambers, especially after 1976. Before that year incumbents had excellent

prospects for reelection; from 1966 to 1974, for example, never less than 88 percent of House incumbents or 71 percent of incumbent senators who sought another term succeeded. (The mean success rates for these five elections were 92 percent in the House and 79 percent for the Senate.) After that, however, the situation changed. House incumbents continued to succeed in retaining their seats; over 90 percent won (even in the face of the Reagan 1980 landslide, 90.3 percent of House incumbents held their positions). In the Senate, in sharp contrast, the incumbent advantage declined drastically. The 1976, 1978, and 1980 elections saw the incumbent victory rate fall to 64, 60, and 55.2 percent, respectively. (In the postreform period, 1980-84, Senate incumbents regained their advantage, and most won handily.) In the 1970s, House turnover reflected voluntary retirement from Congress, while Senate membership change reflected voter preferences more directly. See John R. Hibbing, *Choosing to Leave: Voluntary Retirement from the U.S. House of Representatives* (Washington, D.C.: University Press of America, 1982).

14. David W. Rohde, Norman J. Ornstein, and Robert L. Peabody, "Political Change and Legislative Norms in the U.S. Senate, 1957-1974," in *Studies of Congress*, ed. Glenn R. Parker (Washington, D.C.: CQ Press, 1985), 147-88.

15. Richard F. Fenno, Jr., *Home Style: Representatives in Their Districts* (Boston: Little, Brown, 1978).

16. Herbert F. Alexander, *Financing Politics*, 3d ed. (Washington, D.C.: CQ Press, 1984); and Michael J. Malbin, ed., *Parties, Interest Groups, and Campaign Finance Laws* (Washington, D.C.: American Enterprise Institute, 1980).

17. On this infusion of new blood into Congress, see Eric M. Uslaner, "Policy Entrepreneurs and Amateur Democrats in the House of Representatives: Toward a More Policy-Oriented Congress?" in *Legislative Reform*, ed. Rieselbach, 105-16; Thomas E. Cavanagh, "The Dispersion of Authority in the House of Representatives," *Political Science Quarterly* 97 (1982-83): 623-37; and Burdett A. Loomis, "Congressional Careers and Party Leadership in the Contemporary House of Representatives," *American Journal of Political Science* 28 (1984): 180-202.

18. These committees and the commission were named after their chairmen: Richard Bolling (D-Mo.), David Obey (D-Wis.), and Jerry Patterson (D-Calif.). In addition, the House Democratic Caucus from 1970 to 1974 had its own body, the 11-member Committee on Organization, Study, and Review, chaired by Julia Butler Hansen (D-Wash.), making reform suggestions and reviewing the proposals that the Bolling panel advanced.

19. The respective chairmen were Harold Hughes (D-Iowa), Adlai Stevenson III (D-Ill.), and John Culver (D-Iowa).

20. Arthur G. Stevens, Jr., Abraham H. Miller, and Thomas E. Mann, "Mobilization of Liberal Strength in the House, 1955-1970: The Democratic Study Group," *American Political Science Review* 68 (1974): 667-81.

21. Barbara Hinckley, *The Seniority System in Congress* (Bloomington: Indiana University Press, 1970), provides a balanced view of the pros and cons of the prereform operation of the seniority system.

22. Barbara Hinckley argues that the three chairmen were vulnerable to removal because they were old *and* southern conservatives *and* autocratic in their dealings with committee members, and because there was a viable

challenger waiting in the wings. "Seniority 1975: Old Theories Confront New Facts," *British Journal of Political Science* 6 (1976): 383-99.

23. One additional shift in House committee leaders occurred in 1975. After a series of widely publicized escapades with an exotic dancer, Wilbur Mills (D-Ark.), 63, long reputed to be one of the most powerful men in the House and a thorn in the flesh of liberals eager to revise the tax structure, declined to seek reelection as chairman of the Ways and Means Committee. Presumably, he felt he could not retain his position. Al Ullman (Ore.), 60, the second most senior Democrat on the committee, won the chair. Subsequently, Mills publicly acknowledged that he suffered from alcoholism and began a lengthy period of treatment and convalescence. Mills eventually returned to work, but retired from Congress at the conclusion of the 94th Congress. Incidentally, deposed chairpersons Patman and Hébert also retired effective in January 1977.

24. While Price was too promilitary for some, much of the opposition reflected the view that at his age, in failing health, he no longer had the strength to run the committee.

25. All standing Senate committees except Veterans' Affairs and Rules and Administration are considered major committees; thus the assignment limits apply to 13 of the chamber's 15 regular panels.

26. In 1973 the House designated its standing committees as *exclusive* ("power" committees like Appropriations, Rules, and Ways and Means), *major* (policy committees such as Education, Banking, and Commerce), and *non-major* (less desirable assignments such as Post Office and House Administration).

27. David W. Rohde, "Committee Reform in the House of Representatives and the Subcommittee Bill of Rights," *Annals* 411 (1974): 39-47; and Norman J. Ornstein, "Causes and Consequences of Congressional Change: Subcommittee Reforms in the House of Representatives, 1970-1973," in *Congress in Change*, ed. Ornstein, 88-114. See also Thomas R. Wolanin, "A View from the Trench: Reforming Congressional Procedures," in *The United States Congress*, ed. Dennis Hale (Chestnut Hill, Mass.: Boston College, 1982), 209-28; and Smith and Deering, *Committees in Congress*, chap. 2.

28. Susan Webb Hammond, "Congressional Change and Reform: Staffing the Congress," in *Legislative Reform*, ed. Rieselbach, 181-93; and Harrison W. Fox, Jr., and Susan Webb Hammond, *Congressional Staffs: The Invisible Force in American Lawmaking* (New York: Free Press, 1977).

29. In February 1975 this procedure was used to permit the first House vote on whether to retain the controversial oil depletion allowance. This tax benefit for oil producers, designed to stimulate exploration for new petroleum sources, was denounced as a tax loophole by its critics. The Democratic Caucus voted 153-98 to instruct the party's Rules Committee contingent to permit a vote on an amendment to a major tax reduction bill, which the Ways and Means Committee had rejected, to repeal the allowance. The members of Rules complied with the instruction, and the full House voted to eliminate the allowance.

30. The so-called military-industrial complex is perhaps the classic example of an iron triangle. Allegedly, Armed Services committee and subcommittee members, defense contractors (Boeing Aircraft or General Dynamics Corporation), and Pentagon generals and their subordinates combine to control weapons procurement policy. The congressional participants gain influence

(and their constituencies get defense contracts), the industry earns profits, and the military gets the hardware it desires for national protection. On subsystem politics, see J. Leiper Freeman, *The Political Process*, rev. ed. (New York: Random House, 1965); and Randall B. Ripley and Grace A. Franklin, *Congress, the Bureaucracy, and Public Policy*, 3d ed. (Homewood, Ill.: Dorsey Press, 1984), 9-12. See also Hugh Heclo, "Issue Networks and the Executive Establishment," in *The New American Political System*, ed. King, 87-124.

31. David R. Mayhew, *Congress: The Electoral Connection* (New Haven, Conn.: Yale University Press, 1974).

32. Adam Clayton Powell (D-N.Y.) was excluded in 1967 from the House, charged with a variety of offenses including "improperly spending public funds, falsely reporting his expenditures, contemptuous conduct, and reflecting discredit on the House." Robert S. Getz, *Congressional Ethics: The Conflict of Interest Issue* (New York: Van Nostrand, 1966), 188. Abscam—for Arab Scam—was an FBI sting operation in which federal agents, posing as Arab sheiks, offered bribes to members of Congress, who accepted them. Wayne Hays (D-Ohio) kept his mistress on his staff payroll as a typist although she could not type. Wilbur Mills (D-Ark.) was present when his female companion, an "exotic dancer" named Fanny Foxe, took a plunge in the Tidal Basin.

33. Richard F. Fenno, Jr., "If, as Ralph Nader Says, Congress Is 'The Broken Branch,' How Come We Love Our Congressmen So Much?" in *Congress in Change*, ed. Ornstein, 277-87; Glenn R. Parker and Roger H. Davidson, "Why Do Americans Love Their Congressmen So Much More Than Their Congress?" *Legislative Studies Quarterly* 4 (1979): 53-61; and Timothy E. Cook, "Legislature vs. Legislator: A Note on the Paradox of Congressional Support," *Legislative Studies Quarterly* 4 (1979): 43-52.

34. Charles S. Bullock III, "Congress in the Sunshine," in *Legislative Reform*, ed. Rieselbach, 209-21.

35. House leaders retained careful control of the mechanics of television coverage. House employees operate the cameras, which focus only on the rostrum and avoid panning the (often empty) House chamber. In this fashion the public receives a more favorable image of the House and its deliberations.

36. Under House rules a device known as the Committee of the Whole House on the State of the Union is used to facilitate preliminary consideration of legislation. The Speaker need not preside; a quorum for conducting business is 100, not the 218 required when the House sits formally. Voting in the Committee of the Whole is by voice vote, standing vote (the presiding officer counts the "yeas" and then the "nays" as each group in turn rises), or teller vote (each group, yeas and nays, comes forward in the chamber to be counted as they pass between tellers). The 1970 reform required recording individual positions on the teller votes. See Norman J. Ornstein and David W. Rohde, "The Strategy of Reform: Recorded Teller Voting in the House of Representatives" (Paper presented to the 1974 Annual Meeting of the Midwest Political Science Association). When the Committee of the Whole concludes preliminary consideration, it "rises," the Speaker resumes the chair, and a quorum reverts to 218. The House then acts to review—ratify or reject—decisions taken in the Committee of the Whole. On congressional

rules, see Walter J. Oleszek, *Congressional Procedures and the Policy Process*, 2d ed. (Washington, D.C.: CQ Press, 1984).

37. On the 1974 FECA amendments, see *Congressional Quarterly Weekly Report*, October 12, 1974, 2865-70; on the *Buckley* decision, consult *Congressional Quarterly Weekly Report*, February 7, 1976, 267-74. More generally, see Gary C. Jacobson, *Money in Congressional Elections* (New Haven, Conn.: Yale University Press, 1980); and Alexander, *Financing Politics*.

38. This limit was later relaxed considerably. In the 99th Congress (1985-87), members could supplement their $75,100 salaries with honoraria of 30 percent, or $22,530.

39. *Congressional Quarterly Weekly Report*, March 5, 1977, and April 2, 1977; and Bullock, "Congress in the Sunshine." Both the House and Senate have ethics committees to investigate and resolve charges of improper behavior by members.

40. Lewis A. Froman and Randall B. Ripley, "Conditions for Party Leadership: The Case of the House Democrats," *American Political Science Review* 59 (1965): 52-63. See also Lawrence C. Dodd, "Coalition-Building by Party Leaders: A Case Study of House Democrats," *Congress and the Presidency* 10 (1983): 147-68.

41. Gary C. Jacobson, "Practical Consequences of Campaign Finance Reform: An Incumbent Protection Act?" *Public Policy* 21 (1976): 1-32. The political alignments on extending campaign finance reform—to reduce PAC contribution levels or to establish a system of public finance for congressional elections—nicely illustrate the problem of incompatible intentions. Republicans, the legislative minority throughout the reform period, vigorously opposed many features -of the scheme enacted, as well as proposals to enlarge it. They feared that the restrictions on fundraising would entrench the majority Democrats permanently. The Republican position, now that the party has won the Senate and aspires to take the House, bears watching. On the one hand, as incumbents, limits on funding should benefit them; on the other, as the "in party" *and* the ideological favorite of the burgeoning number of corporate PACs, they stand to gain a decisive advantage in contributions under the present arrangements. In either case, the usual justifications in terms of visibility and accountability may have little to do with the ultimate choice.

42. See Wolanin, "Reforming Congressional Procedures," on reforms expanding minority party participation.

43. Reformers also had reservations about broad delegations of authority for executive control of foreign trade policy; they held that Congress should determine tariff levels on its own initiative.

44. There are those who argue that by giving the executive virtual carte blanche for the 60-day period, Congress actually *enlarged* presidential power, granting him authority that the Constitution does not afford him. On the War Powers Resolution, see the sources cited in note 7; and Pat Holt, *The War Powers Resolution* (Washington, D.C.: American Enterprise Institute, 1978).

45. This procedure is one form of the *legislative veto* by which Congress has sought to retain the ability to block specific administrative actions; it reserves to itself the opportunity, within a given time period, to stop bureaucrats from implementing specific regulations even though Congress has empowered them to do so. The Supreme Court in *Immigration and*

Naturalization Service v. Chadha (1983) declared certain forms of the legislative veto—ones that were not presented to the president for signature—unconstitutional, but it remains unclear how, if at all, the decision will affect the War Powers procedures.

46. Such calculations about the relationship between revenues and expenditures are extraordinarily difficult and complex. For one thing, agencies, especially of the Defense Department, can "reprogram" funds; that is, with the approval of the appropriate committee, subcommittee, or ranking member thereof, they can spend them on activities other than those for which they were originally appropriated. For another, money is often "in the pipeline"—appropriated but unspent—and a cut in subsequent appropriations will not affect programs until unspent funds are exhausted. Finally, agencies may spend using "backdoor" procedures—through borrowing, permanent appropriations, or mandatory spending—that are beyond the legislature's annual appropriations power. Such abstruse provisions made accurate calculations about deficits (or surpluses) and the costs of government extremely problematic. For a summary of conventional budgetary practice, see *Congressional Quarterly Weekly Report*, April 28, 1973, 1013-18. See also Schick, *Congress and Money.*

47. Actually, the spending figures the act requires include budget authority—funds that can be obligated over a period of years—and budget outlays—sums that can be spent in the ensuing fiscal year.

48. Passage of the first and second resolutions is by concurrent resolution, not by law. Both the House and Senate must adopt the concurrent resolution, but it does not require the president's signature. The terms of the resolutions are implemented, however, in regular legislation.

49. On the budget process and the politics surrounding its adoption, see Schick, *Congress and Money*; Shuman, *Politics and the Budget*; Dennis S. Ippolito, *Congressional Spending* (Ithaca, N.Y.: Cornell University Press, 1981); Joel Havemann, *Congress and the Budget* (Bloomington: Indiana University Press, 1978); Kenneth Shepsle, ed., *The Congressional Budget Process: Some Views from the Inside* (St. Louis: Washington University Center for the Study of American Business, 1980); and Aaron Wildavsky, *The Politics of the Budgetary Process*, 4th ed. (Boston: Little, Brown, 1984).

50. On committee staff changes and computer use in Congress see Joseph Cooper and G. Calvin Mackenzie, eds., *The House at Work* (Austin: University of Texas Press, 1981); Fox and Hammond, *Congressional Staffs*; Michael J. Malbin, *Unelected Representatives: Congressional Staff and the Future of Representative Government* (New York: Basic Books, 1980); and Stephen E. Frantzich, *Computers in Congress* (Beverly Hills, Calif.: Sage, 1982).

51. The Supreme Court's *Chadha* (see above, note 45) has called some of these legislative veto provisions into question.

52. See Morris S. Ogul, *Congress Oversees the Bureaucracy: Studies in Legislative Supervision* (Pittsburgh: University of Pittsburgh Press, 1976); Joel D. Aberbach, "Changes in Congressional Oversight," *American Behaviorial Scientist* 22 (1979): 493-515; Lawrence C. Dodd and Richard L. Schott, *Congress and the Administrative State* (New York: Wiley, 1979); John R. Bolton, *The Legislative Veto: Unseparating the Powers* (Washington, D.C.: American Enterprise Institute, 1977); and William West and Joseph Cooper, "The Congressional Veto and Administrative Rulemaking," *Political Science Quarterly* 98

(1983): 285-304. On the 1983 Supreme Court decision, see Joseph Cooper, "Postscript on the Congressional Veto: Is There Life after Chadha?" *Political Science Quarterly* 98 (1983): 427-29.

53. William P. Schaefer and James A. Thurber, "The Causes, Characteristics, and Political Consequences of the Legislative Veto" (Paper presented to the 1980 Annual Meeting of the Southern Political Science Association).

54. By 1985, in the 99th Congress, the Steering and Policy Committee had grown to 31 members: 11 official party leaders, 8 appointed by the Speaker, and 12 elected from geographical regions. The leadership, quite obviously, continued to have considerable influence in the committee. In addition, in 1985 Speaker Thomas P. O'Neill, Jr., formed an informal group, dubbed the "Speaker's Cabinet," to advise him on various matters; its members included "key committee leaders," party officials, and spokespersons for differing ideological viewpoints. See *Congressional Quarterly Weekly Report*, December 8, 1984, 3054-55.

55. The voting record makes this clear: In the 93d Congress the 15 Ways and Means Democrats averaged 34.1 percent in support of the southern Democratic-Republican conservative coalition; in that same Congress the 22 Democrats subsequently appointed to the Steering and Policy Committee in the 94th Congress (Speaker Carl Albert and freshman representative William Brodhead did not vote in the 93d) averaged only 24.9 percent in support of the conservative coalition, a difference of 9.2 percent, nearly 1 vote in every 10. Similarly, in the 93d Congress Ways and Means Democrats averaged 61.3 percent on party unity while the 22 voting members of the 1975 Steering Committee cast 74.9 percent of their votes in support of the Democratic majority position, a difference of 13.6 percent. In short, the reformers could reasonably expect the Steering Committee, now empowered to make committee assignments subject to caucus ratification, to be decidedly less conservative and more inclined to back partisan majorities than the Ways and Means Democrats.

56. See Bruce I. Oppenheimer, "The Changing Relationship between House Leadership and the Committee on Rules," in *Understanding Congressional Leadership*, ed. Frank A. Mackaman (Washington, D.C.: CQ Press, 1981), 207-25; Barbara Sinclair, *Majority Leadership in the U.S. House* (Baltimore: Johns Hopkins University Press, 1982); David J. Vogler, "Ad Hoc Committees in the House of Representatives and Purposive Models of Legislative Behavior," *Polity* 14 (1981): 89-109; Lawrence C. Dodd and Terry Sullivan, "Majority Party Leadership and Partisan Vote Gathering: The House Democratic Whip System," in *Understanding Congressional Leadership*, ed. Mackaman, 227-60; Lawrence Dodd, "The Expanded Role of the House Democratic Whips," *Congressional Studies* 7 (1979): 27-56; and Judith H. Parris, "The Senate Reorganizes Its Committees, 1977," *Political Science Quarterly* 94 (1979): 319-37.

57. Action against Ways and Means illustrates the diverse implications of reform. On one hand, the moves against the tax panel reduced that committee's independence; it could less easily go its own way, confident that the full membership of the House would defer to its expertise. The reforms increased the party's potential to bring the committee under its centralized control, to make it more responsible. On the other hand, dispersing committee authority—to more members, serving on independent sub-

committees, meeting in open sessions—also had the potential to undercut control, to increase responsiveness to multiple points of view, at the expense of effective action. The need to react to many participants could make it more difficult for Ways and Means to formulate and secure passage of workable financial programs.

58. In 1975, however, perhaps in the spirit of democratization, the caucus yielded its seldom-used authority to dictate the members' roll call votes.

59. Roger H. Davidson and Walter J. Oleszek, *Congress against Itself* (Bloomington: Indiana University Press, 1977).

60. See Parris, "Congress Reorganizes Its Committees."

61. At the center of the reform controversy was the arcane question of whether the Senate can adopt new rules by simple majority vote at the start of each Congress. Despite Vice-President Nelson Rockefeller's affirmative ruling on this issue, the defenders of the filibuster, led by James B. Allen (D-Ala.), outmaneuvered the reformers and salvaged the compromise, which not only imposed the 60-vote, rather than a simple majority, rule, but also reversed Rockefeller's ruling and established that a two-thirds vote is still required to end debate on changes in Senate rules.

62. *Congressional Quarterly Weekly Report,* December 13, 1975, 2721-22, and February 24, 1979, 319-20. Here, too, the reforms promoted several goals: democratization (by letting smaller majorities invoke cloture) and responsibility (by permitting those majorities to act more easily).

63. *Congressional Quarterly Weekly Report,* September 3, 1977, 1855; September 17, 1977, 1973-75; and October 15, 1977, 2183.

64. *Congressional Quarterly Weekly Report,* March 29, 1980, 886, and May 3, 1980, 1173-74.

65. *Congressional Quarterly Weekly Report,* April 9, 1983, 695-96.

66. *Congressional Quarterly Weekly Report,* December 1, 1984, 3035.

The Impact of Congressional Reform | 4

That substantial and significant congressional reform has occurred is incontrovertible. Congress in the 1980s is markedly different from Congress in the 1960s. The legislature adopted broad changes ostensibly to promote responsiveness, accountability, and responsibility. These commonly cited justifications, however, may have concealed other electoral, policy, and power motives. From one perspective, the reformers have achieved their purposes. Congress is more democratic: more members and concerned citizens can participate in congressional deliberations. Congress is more visible: more of its operations, particularly in committee, are open to public scrutiny; more of its members' campaign and financial dealings are matters of public record. And Congress is potentially more efficient: it is more capable of imposing its policy preferences on the executive in foreign and domestic affairs when it opts to do so.

Congress is to some degree more responsive, accountable, and responsible as a result of reform. But is it "better"? To answer this question, of course, requires a value judgment. Any analysis will reflect the observer's views about what sort of institution the legislature should be. Differing hopes and expectations will lead to varying assessments. The proponents of executive force or legislative supremacy may render different verdicts on congressional performance; alternatively, each school of thought may laud different facets of the new Congress. Second, an unequivocal answer to the query may be impossible because it is difficult to attribute postreform behavior to the reforms themselves. Reform is, after all, part and parcel of broader change. Crises outside Congress, new issues or the fundamental transformation of old ones, and new members of Congress may contribute as much or more than specific reforms to the altered character of legislative activity.[1]

This chapter attempts to chart the intended and unintended consequences of reform. Because reform was undertaken in response to many influences—political and personal—and because it was not guided by any sweeping, widely shared vision of desirable legislative structure and process, its effects seem inconsistent and uncertain. The accumulation of evidence since 1977, when the reform impulse began to flag, suggests that the results of reform have been many and varied. Reformers' intentions have sometimes been realized, and sometimes not. Often quite unintended and undesirable consequences have resulted from reforms designed to enhance Congress's responsiveness, accountability, and responsibility.

Responsiveness and Fragmentation

Central to the reformers' efforts was a desire to democratize Congress. The reformers' chief targets were the full committees, dominated by powerful, sometimes tyrannical, conservative chairpersons. By lessening the power of committee oligarchs, they hoped to make Congress a more responsive institution. Thus, the reformers modified the seniority rule for selecting committee chairs, limited the number of committee leadership positions any individual could hold, altered the committee assignment process, and devolved much committee power to subcommittees.

Viewed narrowly, these changes may have accomplished their purpose, but from a broader, long-run perspective, their proponents may have won the battle but lost the war. Increased responsiveness may have exacted a high price. By slowing up the legislative process and requiring more elaborate bargaining to reach agreements among more numerous participants, it may have made congressional decision making more arduous.

Modifying Seniority

With respect to seniority, in the House at least, the old order has been altered. Although most committee and Appropriations subcommitteee chairpersons continue to be chosen on the basis of seniority, there have been a sufficient number of departures from the rule to restrain the most arbitrary exercise of chairs' authority. On three occasions in 1975 and another in 1985, the Democratic Caucus has removed the sitting chairperson from his post. In two of those instances—the selection of Henry Reuss (D-Wis.) to head the Banking Committee (1975) and Les Aspin (D-Wis.) to chair Armed Services (1985)—the new committee chair was not second on the seniority ladder, but well down the list of senior Democrats. In addition, in a few cases junior members have challenged seniors for subcommittee chairs under the bidding procedures instituted in 1973 and won. For example, in 1974 John Moss (D-Calif.) successfully challenged full committee chairman Harley Staggers (D-W.Va.) for the top spot on the Commerce Subcommittee on Oversight and Investigations. Similarly, in 1981 Gus Yatron (D-Pa.) was deposed as chair of the House Foreign Affairs Subcommittee on Inter-American Affairs, presumably because he was too conservative; the seat went to Michael Barnes (D-Md.).[2] At the very least, senior committee leaders are on notice that the caucus and their committee colleagues can vote to unseat them. The threat of sanctions probably has a similar restraining impact in the Senate, although to date that chamber has faithfully adhered to seniority in selecting committee chairpersons.

Spreading Committee Assignments

The reformers' second goal, after modifying the seniority rule, was to democratize the committee assignment process, and to some extent they succeeded. Opportunities to compete for preferred assignments are clearly greater. The new rules in both parties in both chambers guarantee all members a major committee post. In the House the Steering and Policy Committee, to which the assignment responsibilities were transferred from the Democratic delegation of Ways and Means, is more representative of the full party membership. Steering and Policy seeks to accommodate as many members as it can, trying to match members' requests and committee vacancies wherever possible. In allocating assignments, the committee will consider members' electoral needs, regional and state considerations, support for the party leadership, policy views, and seniority.[3] Indeed, members often wage extensive and intense campaigns for particular seats, writing long memoranda and soliciting support from committee chairpersons, lobbyists, and state delegations to buttress their applications and improve their chances.

Yet members do not always succeed in winning the places they covet. For one thing, there are not always enough seats to go around, especially on the most desirable panels. Second, the party leaders may intervene when seats on particularly critical committees are at stake. The Speaker personally controls nominations to the Rules Committee, and as leader and chair of Steering and Policy he may influence who receives assignments to the Appropriations, Budget, and Ways and Means committees. The party apparatus even calculates *leadership support scores* for incumbents who apply to change assignments, and Steering and Policy seemingly uses them in making decisions on transfer requests.

The leaders seldom involve themselves in the assignment process, but when they do their influence may prove decisive. Thus members have greater opportunity to find congenial places in committee, but there is no certainty that they will succeed in doing so.[4]

Freeing the Subcommittees

The major thrust of committee reform was to create and sustain independent subcommittees, and here the reformers have succeeded admirably. The House moved a long way from full committee government to subcommittee government when it adopted the subcommittee bill of rights and passed new rules granting more members subcommittee positions. House subcommittee reform "loosened the full committee chairs' stranglehold on subcommittee decision making."[5] But power has not increased uniformly across all subcommittees; nor is it clear that subcommittee influence over policy choice exceeds that of the full committees. In sum, subcommittees have assumed greater significance, but they are still not automatically the prime movers in the public policy decisions of Congress.[6]

As retirements increased during the 1970s, junior members advanced rapidly to assume subcommittee chairs. In the House, the subcommittee reforms did enable more (and junior) members to accede to positions of potential power. Limiting individuals to a single subcommittee chair opened up at least 16 leadership posts to members previously denied them.[7] Moreover, the number of House subcommittees grew—from 120 in the 92d Congress to 151 in the 94th—providing additional positions for still more majority members.[8]

The new subcommittee chairpersons are more liberal, more "typical" Democrats, thus making committee leadership more representative of the entire party.[9] Yet, as John Stanga and David Farnsworth suggest, seniority, although wounded in principle, survives in practice, and much of the reform-induced change is concentrated in a few committees.[10] Exclusive House committees remain the province of senior members, and on other panels there has been only modest reduction in the seniority of subcommittee chairpersons. Within the limits, however, it seems safe to say that more members have some subcommittee seat from which to seek influence than was the case in the prereform period.

More important, perhaps, most subcommittees are independent and active. In the 96th Congress they held hearings on nearly 80 percent of all bills initially referred to their parent full committees; the comparable figure for the prereform 91st Congress (1969-71) was 35.7 percent. Similarly, subcommittees conduct more meetings and hearings than previously: in the 96th Congress they held 56.1 percent of standing committee meetings and 90.7 percent of standing committee hearings, up from 47.9 percent and 77.0 percent, respectively, in the 91st Congress. Finally, subcommittees control their own bills on the floor: subcommittee chairpersons managed 66.9 percent of the bills that reached the floor from their parent full committees in the 95th Congress, up from 49.0 in the 91st.[11] Subcommittees are much busier since adoption of their bill of rights.

In addition, subcommittees are often expert (with their own staffs), and they are protected from outside interference by guarantees of jurisdiction, control over their own rules, and adequate budgets. Indeed, party leaders do not often seek to impose discipline on the subcommittees; they most regularly confer with subcommittee chairs on procedural matters, like scheduling, and only rarely lobby them with respect to the content of policy. In fact, committee leaders are more likely to initiate communications with party leaders than vice versa. Party leaders' demands are usually limited to issues of major significance, and they often are made after the subcommittee has already completed action. In general, the leadership "neither desires to influence nor is capable of influencing the specific legislative outcomes of the vast majority of subcommittee deliberations."[12]

Such subcommittee independence suggests that the impulse to democratize the committees, to give House members operating room to participate more fully in policy making, has increased legislative fragmentation. There are today more individuals and power centers to deal with in coordinating congressional policy making. Concomitantly, the legislature's ability to act at all, much less more forcefully, may have declined as decentralization increased.

But independence is not autonomy; the extent that subcommittees control the conduct of legislative business is limited. For one thing, subcommittees remain subordinate to the full committees, which ultimately make policy recommendations. Indeed, Steven Smith and Christopher Deering find that the most independent and active subcommittees are often the least autonomous; adventurous subcommittees, in policy terms, may be challenged and reversed in full committee.[13]

While House subcommittees initiate consideration of more legislation, the number of bills originating there that the full committees actually report to the House floor has not risen appreciably. In the 91st Congress 75.4 percent of reported bills were treated first in subcommittee; the figure for the postreform 96th Congress was 80.0 percent.[14] Beyond this, subcommittees—particularly those that deal with pork barrel, constituency matters such as rivers and harbors projects or agricultural subsidies—are regularly open to external, group influences.

As part of subgovernments, they may have to defer to the wishes of their policy-making partners. The broader range of participation in congressional affairs generated by the general movement toward democratization has led nonmembers to take a greater interest in committee and subcommittee operations, enlarging the range of opinions that subcommittees need to consider. In short, subcommittees are constrained by the full committees, by ordinary members of Congress, and by outside interests. Subcommittee government "has not been fully institutionalized" in the House.[15]

Variations on the Reform Theme

Not surprisingly, reform does not have consistent effects throughout Congress. As Richard Fenno has made clear, committee decisions are shaped by various influences: members' personal goals (reelection, power, policy influence), the environmental context within which the committee works, the panel's "strategic premises" (decision rules or norms), and its decision-making processes (specialization, partisanship, participation).[16] In short, committees differ, and change has a different impact on them.

For instance, Norman Ornstein and David Rohde find that the reforms of the 1970s coincide with membership turnover in distinctive ways. The House Agriculture Committee "implemented the full array of subcommittee-strengthening reforms," experienced major personnel change, and got a new chairperson, in the process becoming ideologically more moderate and regionally balanced. Yet despite these major alterations, because the new members' goals varied little from the motivations of the members they replaced, "little overt change in behavior or policy outputs occurred."[17] They also find that reforms have increased the independence and activity of many subcommittees on the House Commerce and Government Operations committees without significantly altering policy making behavior. Indeed, on the former, the shifts, if anything, inhibited policy activities.[18] On the House Foreign Affairs Committee, new members and new rules put liberal legislators into prominent subcommittee positions and pressured the committee chair into joining the more active panel members in placing more restrictions on presidential foreign policy leadership.[19] Overall, change and reform produced behavioral shifts in some committees and none in others.[20]

In fact, it may take wholesale change to jar a committee out of its customary routines, and the resulting consequences are often unintended and, to some interests at least, undesirable. The case of House Ways and Means is illustrative. Although long a target of liberals' hostility during Wilbur Mills's lengthy and successful tenure as chairman, the committee was reformed only when circumstances were conducive—when Mills's personal problems made him and his panel vulnerable. Mills was forced from the chair, and Ways and Means was stripped of its committee assignment powers, required to create subcommittees, enlarged from 25 to 37 members, and deprived of some procedural protection (the "closed rule") for legislation it reported. In consequence, the new chairman, Al Ullman (D-Ore.), failed to sustain the bipartisan consensus that had characterized the committee. The panel began to divide along partisan lines, and it suffered a series of humiliating defeats on the House floor.[21] Catherine Rudder concludes that the ability of Ways and Means to carry its proposals on the House floor was, in consequence of reform, seriously impaired.[22]

Planned reform and more general, unpredictable changes mix in distinctive fashions to influence subcommittee performance as well. David Price attributes changes in the House Commerce Committee's Subcommittee on Oversight and Investigations to the accession of John Moss (D-Calif.) to the subcommittee chair. Although replacing the sitting chairperson was only one aspect of a thorough-going reform—the parent committee rewrote its rules and reallocated its resources to accommodate its subcommittees—Moss was largely responsible for these changes. Price concludes that Moss's "goals and methods as a leader . . . made for alterations in the subcommittee's product and performance." Michael Malbin reaches a similar conclusion: subcommittee activity reflected Moss's legislative interests; reform per se was less critical.[23]

Again, the moral seems clear: reform and more general change influence full committees and subcommittees in different ways. On balance, democratization has increased members' opportunity to participate in congressional activity at the expense of the full committees, but it has not done so uniformly or with consistent effects on legislative policy making.

Nowhere is the variation in the impact of reform clearer than with respect to bicameralism. Reform and change moved the House some distance, if not all the way, toward subcommittee government. The Senate, in sharp contrast, changed very little. New members with new interests and a new spirit of independence promoted individualism in the House. But in the Senate personal freedom had long been the order of the day. The so-called Johnson Rule, dating from Lyndon Johnson's tenure as Majority Leader (1955-61), guaranteed each senator a major committee assignment; the existence of 16 or more standing committees in a body of 100 members has made possible multiple assignments.

Senators have been free to pursue their own interests since well before the reform era. With numerous and desirable assignments, they have had less need to seek subcommittee posts as a forum for influencing policy; they can achieve their purposes within the confines of the full committees.

In consequence, there has been only incremental change in the number of Senate subcommittees: 123 in the 92d Congress (1971-73); 140 in the 94th (1975-77); and 103 in the 98th (1983-85), after members' committee assignments were limited. Similarly, change was minimal in the overall place of subcommittees in Senate deliberations during the 1970s and into the 1980s. Throughout the period roughly 40-45 percent of bills referred to full committee were handled initially in subcommittee; the same percentages applied to bills reported by the full committees that had been the subject of subcommittee hearings. Subcommittee meetings and hearings, in fact, as a proportion of all such sessions, actually declined from the 91st to the 96th Congress. The floor leaders in the Senate manage most routine bills when they reach the floor and, reflecting the members' individualism, bill sponsors handle more important legislation. Thus, the subcommittee chairpersons manage a small and decreasing number of bills.

In short, Senate subcommittees, unlike those in the House, play an involved but not decisive part, as they have for many years. That role varies from full committee to committee, but on balance subcommittees are "generally much less significant" in the Senate than they are in the House.[24] The full committees continue to make the major decisions. Hard-pressed senators, short of time but not of influence in full committee and on the Senate floor, simply have less need to strengthen and use subcommittees.

Increasing Staff Resources

A final feature of the move toward democratization in Congress was the effort to give members and committees more staff assistance and better access to it. On this front the reformers have also accomplished much of what they set out to do. Members' personal staffs have grown enormously. Representatives and senators can use staffers for legislative as well as constituency service (reelection) purposes. This is especially true in the Senate, where each member is entitled to recruit a staff aide for each committee assignment. These resources, coupled with research assistance from the congressional support agencies—the Congressional Budget Office, the Office of Technology Assessment, the General Accounting Office, and the Congressional Research Service—give individual members access to substantial amounts of data. They can, of course, readily use this information to support their own policy goals and preferences.[25]

Diffusion of staff resources has proceeded apace in the House, but has been restrained in the Senate. In both chambers the number of committee staff members has increased dramatically. House committees had 702 staffers on their payrolls in 1970 and nearly three times as many (1,970) in 1983. Senate committee staff totaled 635 in 1970, peaked at 1,277 in 1975, and then declined slightly to 1,075 in 1983.[26] The reformed rules in the House permitted the subcommittees to have their own staff. Not all took immediate or full advantage of these provisions, but most did. Of total House committee staff in the 91st Congress (1969-71), 23.2 percent were employed by subcommittees; a decade later, in the 97th Congress (1981-83), the figure had risen to 39.8 percent. Senate subcommittees, in sharp contrast, employed a substantial proportion of committee staff—42.1 percent in the 91st Congress, but only 32.5 percent in the 97th.[27] Full committee chairs retain considerable control over staff hiring in the Senate; individual members, given their committee-involved personal staff, have a viable alternative to complete reliance on committee or subcommittee employees. Finally, new rules in both the House and Senate granted the minority one-third of committee staff positions, and by the 1980s most but not all panels had separate majority and minority staffs. In short, reforms gave members of Congress greater access to staff assistance in their own offices (Senate), in their sub-committees, or in both (House). Presumably, the improved staff resources improved congressional responsiveness.

The Impact of Democratization

These steps toward democratizing Congress intersect with broad trends in the country at large. The new electoral realities of the reform era contribute to the increased potential for congressional responsiveness. Members, particularly in the House, are regularly reelected with sizable vote margins, and they work hard to maintain their electoral security. They travel home on weekends; they maintain district offices and extensive casework operations; they assign many of their staff to "work the district"; and in general they strive to earn the goodwill, and the votes, of the "folks back home."[28] This acute—some say excessive[29]—sensitivity to constituents' sentiments enhances responsiveness.

In sum, the move toward democratization has spread authority, especially in the House, more widely among members. The reforms of the 1970s made the House more like the Senate.[30] Both chambers are decentralized. Under the threat of ouster, committee chairpersons must share their authority with full committee majorities and more active and independent subcommittee leaders. On the whole, more individuals have influence, at least on a small square of the legislative turf. From these bastions they can shape policy and enhance their public image. Electorally secure, fully staffed, and more assertive vis-à-vis the executive, contemporary members of Congress are in a position to respond to a wide variety of viewpoints. In this sense, the reformers have attained their purposes.

The reformers' success in democratizing Congress, however, has not been costless. Diffusion of power has damaged Congress's ability to make public policy effectively and efficiently.[31] In the House, subcommittees emerge as the chief culprits. Paradoxically, subcommittee growth and independence may make it more difficult for members to achieve their individual goals of electoral security and policy influence. For one thing, the increased number of subcommittees has expanded the representatives' workload; members have more places to be, more subjects to master, and even with increased staff help they may be unable to cope with the new demands on their time and energy. Indeed, some believe that members depend too heavily on these "unelected representatives" on their personal and committee staffs.[32] In any case, specialization and expertise in the House may have declined; fewer members—only those on a given subcommittee—may be well enough informed to deal decisively as specialists with particular policy issues. Fewer individuals take the lead in narrower policy domains, and as they leave Congress, or move to other full or subcommittee positions, the institutional memory of Congress, the ability to relate current problems to past performance, may be damaged.[33] This is not to argue that, as a whole, Congress has less expertise; on the contrary, increased staff and access to more and better data have enlarged its capacity. Rather, it is to suggest that on *any single topic* fewer members, ensconced in their subcommittees, are involved, informed, and in a position to exert influence.

In addition, the existence of more subcommittees may have made members of Congress more vulnerable to representatives of interest groups. Lawmakers with responsibility for particular programs are fewer in number and thus more easily identifiable. Lobbyists know whom to approach with useful information and valuable electoral aid; for their part, members have both opportunity and incentive to enter into mutually beneficial, in a narrow sense, relationships with group representatives and executive branch personnel with concern for particular topics. The broader, national interest may get less attention than it deserves in these circumstances. Finally, independent subcommittees add a new layer to the decision-making process. To pass, programs must now clear subcommittee and full committee hurdles. Committee and party leaders must consult more members, particularly because subcommittee jurisdictions are not always clearly defined and several panels may insist on considering the same piece of pending legislation. Indeed, jurisdictional struggles among subcommittees as well as among their parent panels are increasingly common. As noted in Chapter 3, the Bolling committee failed in its efforts to redefine and systematize committee jurisdictions; the 1977 Senate reforms improved but did not totally resolve the problem of overlapping committee jurisdictions. To deal with this organizational complexity takes time, and legislation may be slowed if not sidetracked altogether by the need to consider compromises and construct coalitions among so many participants.

In the Senate the story is different, but the result is the same. Individualism has long been the hallmark of senatorial behavior, and reform has not undercut individual members' freedom of action. The major impact of the relatively modest reform in the Senate was to provide members with augmented staff resources, which contributes to their independence from committee and party discipline. Senators, like representatives, are able to pursue their policy predilections in relatively unencumbered fashion. For Congress as a whole, then, reform has greatly enlarged the potential for individual participation in policy making, that is, for responsiveness. But the cost has been decreased ability to push innovative public programs through the legislative process. More responsiveness may mean reduced responsibility. By multiplying the number of power centers, reform and change have increased the need for elaborate bargaining and compromise to reach agreement.

Accountability and Permeability

The second lane on the reformers' road to a more democratic Congress, after improving responsiveness, was opening legislative deliberations and legislators' finances to citizen and mass media consideration. The more the public knows about lawmakers' legislative activity and connections to pressure groups, economic interests, individual campaign contributors, and political action committees (PACs), the greater its opportunity to hold members to account. In principle, sunshine laws, Federal Election Campaign Act disclosure provisions, and congressional codes of ethics have put legislators' accounts and activity on public display.

In practice, until recently, the vast majority of congressional proceedings—in subcommittee, full committee, on the floor, and in conference were public sessions; more than 90 percent of all such committee meetings were open. Members file their financial disclosure information with the Federal Election Commission and the media publicize it; the number of millionaires in the Senate—usually at least one-third of the membership—makes good copy. Citizens are in a much stronger position to evaluate the content and motivation of legislators' behavior and to hold them to account for it. To the extent that citizens make such judgments and act on them, they will participate more fully in legislative politics and the assembly will be more democratic. To the degree that lawmakers listen to the public verdicts and respect them, Congress will be more responsive to public preferences.

Yet beneath the seeming success of these reforms lies a different reality. For one thing, there is little if any persuasive evidence that citizens pay greater attention to Congress than they did in the prereform era. Polls reveal that the electorate is not better informed about legislative action. Voters seem no better able to name their incumbent representative, although many can recognize his or her name when it is presented to them.[34] There has been no visible increase in issue-based voting in congressional elections; incumbency and partisanship, more than policy positions, still shape voter consideration of Congress and congressional candidates.[35] Nor is there any sign that the public's assessment of Congress relative to other political institutions has become more positive. In December 1984, 28 percent of the respondents in a Harris poll professed "a great deal of confidence" in Congress (the figure for the White House was 42 percent). That same year 32 percent expressed "positive" feelings about Congress (thought it was doing an "excellent" or "pretty good" job), while 46 percent harbored "negative" views of the legislature (rated its performance as "only fair" or "poor"). Public confidence in Congress has not been appreciably restored.[36]

Second, with committee proceedings and voting now matters of public record, lawmakers can no longer hide behind closed doors and unrecorded votes; they must act in the open. With the media, citizens, and campaign contributors watching, they must take care to protect their electoral flanks. Increasingly, committees have resorted to "executive" or "informal" sessions, held prior to official meetings, where the members can talk freely and develop compromises without the intrusive presence of outsiders. As Rep. Bill Frenzel (R-Minn.), who began his legislative service as a self-proclaimed "open meeting freak," put it: "Since our meetings have been closed, our work has been less flawed . . . and our consensuses much stronger. I think it's the only way to fly."[37] The presence of lobbyists and administrative officials at public sessions—where they can monitor members' behavior, offer the texts of amendments, and notify their employers when and where to apply pressure—may have made it more difficult for committees to act decisively, to be responsible.

With the rise of single-interest groups and PACs during the reform era, legislators may be less willing to risk offending any potentially decisive electoral force. Prudence dictates caution, and lawmakers may feel obliged to resist party or presidential calls for support. Previously, members could help out undetected, in the quiet of the committee room or on a standing or teller vote on the floor, but at present there are dangers in doing so. Members may be loath to act at all, preferring to entrench themselves as ombudsmen, claiming credit for serving the district, or by limiting their policy making to "position taking," choosing sides on substantive questions only when it is safe to do so. They may even obfuscate their stands to minimize the danger of being caught on the wrong side of a policy issue that turns out to be controversial.[38]

Financial disclosure, mandated by the House and Senate ethics codes, has not had much visible effect either. There has been little if any diminution in the frequency of ethical problems representatives and senators have encountered since the disclosure provisions were first enacted in 1977. The Senate "denounced" Herman Talmadge (D-Ga.) for campaign finance improprieties. The House Ethics Committee has been busy. The House censured Charles Diggs (D-Mich.) and Charles Wilson (D-Calif.) for improper financial dealings and expelled Michael Myers (D-Pa.), snared in the Abscam net. Others implicated in Abscam chose to resign, presumably to avoid expulsion.

But if there has been no reduction in malfeasance in the aftermath of reform, the future may be more promising. Voters, for their part, have not been particularly sympathetic to those legislators revealed as corrupt in some fashion or other. In 1980 Talmadge was denied reelection, and the voters delivered a resounding verdict (matched only by those in the criminal courts), retiring from office all save one of those accused in Abscam. In addition, the electorate in Idaho narrowly defeated Republican representative George Hansen, convicted in 1984 of filing false financial disclosure forms. These are dramatic cases—featuring videotapes of money changing hands, allegations of coat pockets stuffed with cash, and conduct clearly offensive to many Americans' sense of morality. The effect of the ethics codes and disclosure statutes on more mundane conflicts of interest (for example, self-serving but legal behavior) remains unclear.

Finally, campaign finance reform has led to paradoxical results. On the one hand, the new election system—with its full disclosure provisions and its limits on contributions but none on expenditures—has seemingly helped to entrench incumbents, especially in the House. With presidential campaigns now federally funded in full, private groups, particularly the newly legitimized PACs, have channeled their resources into congressional contests. Federal Election Commission data and Common Cause studies suggest that these donors have preferred the safe course of contributing to incumbents, who hold potentially powerful committee or party positions in Congress, to the riskier strategy of funding challengers, who might someday hold prominent posts.[39] Incumbents start with sizable advantages inherent in the perquisites of office, and unless their opponents can raise and spend significant sums—often more than a quarter of a million dollars—their prospects range from zero to nil. Gary Jacobson concludes that "any measure that limits the money available to candidates benefits incumbents." [40] Certainly, contribution controls appear to have hindered hard-pressed House challengers. Senate contests, by contrast, tend to be more competitive. Challengers are more visible and attractive, better able to solicit the funds they need, and in consequence to unseat the incumbent.[41]

To whatever degree incumbent electoral safety reduces personnel turnover in Congress, legislative accountability, however plausible in principle, will be inhibited. Old members espousing old points of view will continue to serve, even if they are out of touch, in policy terms, with their constituents, because they can fend off serious challenges.

This is not to say that the link between funding and votes is not well publicized. On the contrary, specialized media and the large city daily press frequently note which groups contribute to which members of Congress and speculate about the possible effects of these donations on legislative behavior. For example, an Associated Press story reported that the PACs of the 20 largest defense contractors contributed more than $3.5 million to congressional and presidential campaigns in 1983-84.[42] They channeled their donations to key committee members. John Warner (R-Va.), a senior member of the Armed Services Committee, which has jurisdiction over the controversial MX missile, received $80,050 from defense industry PACs. Ted Stevens (R-Alaska), chairman of the Appropriations subcommittee that funds the MX, got $60,800 from these same PACs. In the House, the defense PACs gave Joseph Addabbo (D-N.Y.), chair of the Appropriations subcommittee that considers the MX, $48,403; four other subcommittee Democrats got contributions in excess of $34,000 each. Overall, 13 of the 14 senators who received $30,000 or more from defense PACs, and 17 of 20 House members to whom these PACs contributed at least $15,000, voted in March 1985 to build 21 more MX missiles.[43] Citizens can find out who bankrolls their elected representatives and how they vote, but the evidence, on balance, suggests that few seize the opportunity to hold their lawmakers to account.

On the other hand, campaign finance and personal disclosure requirements have made life difficult for members of Congress. During the latter half of the 1970s, record numbers of legislators chose to retire rather than risk the relentless exposure of their daily routines, and those of their families, to public scrutiny. Many left Congress at relatively young ages (in their fifties), having acquired substantial seniority and positions of some prominence and power. The rise of aggressive investigative reporting in the wake of Watergate no doubt accounts, at least in part, for this increased attention to the personal lives of legislators; events formerly left unreported—alcoholism, family problems, financial transactions, even brushes with the law—are now fair game for the media. Many lawmakers have found the rewards of legislative service not worth the long hours and loss of privacy and have chosen to pursue their careers elsewhere.[44] In the four elections from 1966 through 1972, an average of 18.5 representatives and 4.75 senators declined to seek reelection; in the reform era elections from 1974 to 1980, the figures were 43.3 and 7.5, respectively. The exodus slowed appreciably, however, in 1982 and 1984, when an average of 32 representatives and 3.5 senators retired. Members increasingly seemed prepared to endure the attention that their positions in Congress attracted.

The potential for citizen-enforced accountability is real, but unrealized. The public can, if it chooses, hold members accountable, but in reality it does not seem more aware of, or more sympathetic to, Congress or its members, their activities, or their performance. In sum, while congressional activity is certainly more accessible to citizens, as the reformers hoped, the weight of the accumulated evidence suggests that the sunshine reforms have had limited effects. In fact, visibility may contribute to legislative inertia. Ever aware that they are, in a real sense, on display, members may conclude that care and caution, inaction, is the wisest course. Rather than risk alienating constituents and groups whose reelection support they feel is vital, they may avoid controversy and decline to act. Thus, by increasing the possibility for external actors to participate in congressional politics, the accountability reforms may have made Congress not only more democratic but also more permeable —more open to outside pressures from voters and organized interests that reduce the institution's capacity to make effective public policy. Steps to increase accountability, like those to promote decentralization (responsiveness), may have inadvertently undercut congressional responsibility.

Responsibility and Centralization _____

Although reformers were eager to democratize Congress, to make it more responsive and accountable, they were not unmindful of the institution's shortcomings as an efficient policy maker. They moved to reduce congressional immobilism and inertia. Flowing directly from the legislative reaction to Vietnam and Watergate and aided by the Democratic sweep in the 1974 midterm elections was the effort to improve Congress's responsibility, the third fundamental thrust of the reform movement. Specifically, the reformers aimed at expanding the assembly's ability to assert and sustain legislative priorities even in the face of determined executive opposition. They also sought to strengthen the political parties in the hopes of providing at least a modicum of centralized, efficient direction to congressional policy making. To that same end they enacted a number of rules changes designed to ease the flow of legislation through a complicated legislative process. Once again, the reformers won some victories, suffered some setbacks, and occasionally produced results that they had not foreseen.

Battling the Executive

Nowhere is the difficulty in disentangling the effects of reform from those of more general political change more obvious than in evaluating the impact of the congressional assault on executive branch prerogatives. The War Powers Resolution and the Congressional Budget and Impoundment Control Act, the two most vigorous manifestations of congressional revival, were passed in 1973 and 1974, respectively—a time of popular discontent, rapid turnover in Congress, and a scandal-ridden and politically vulnerable presidency. Events, new issues, and new members converged to create the conditions in which Congress launched a major challenge to the executive. External change, then, may have contributed as much as internal reform to the state of executive-legislative relations during the late 1970s and the 1980s.

The War Powers Resolution. Overall, the available evidence on a decade of experience suggests a mixed set of outcomes. Congress has not used its newly claimed authority systematically to impose its will on the executive, especially in the military realm. But it has, from time to time, asserted its preferences with respect to particular programs, using its constitutional authorization and appropriations powers. With regard to the War Powers Resolution, the president has felt obliged to report to Congress in compliance with the act on five occasions. Only two were controversial: Gerald Ford's recapture of the ship *Mayaguez*, seized by

Cambodia in 1975, and Jimmy Carter's abortive effort in 1979 to free the American hostages held in Iran. Each episode lasted only a few hours; neither really offered Congress a chance to act in any meaningful fashion. Each president complied with the letter if not the spirit of the statute. The law obligates the chief executive to consult with Congress, where possible, in advance of committing troops to combat. Crisis situations make widespread discussion of military action difficult if not impossible, and presidents have limited their contacts with Congress to informing a select few (usually those expected to be sympathetic), rather than soliciting congressional opinion in advance of policy choices. The Iranian rescue mission does not provide a promising precedent for the consultation provisions of the War Powers Resolution. Given the long planning period that preceded the action, the Carter administration could easily have involved congressional leaders in its deliberations; it chose not to do so, and the members of Congress, while voicing a few complaints, largely acquiesced in the executive's behavior.

The resolution also required the president to report to Congress, within 48 hours, when he has ordered combat troops to face "hostilities" in the field. In all five cases the president has sent appropriate messages, but he has often asserted that he has done so as a courtesy, not in compliance with the act itself.[45] A sixth case—Ronald Reagan's use of U.S. Marines as part of a multinational peacekeeping force in Lebanon in 1983 and 1984—illustrates the difficulties. The president claimed that since there were no real or imminent hostilities in the area the act did not apply. But as violence escalated and the American forces incurred casualities, some in Congress protested Reagan's rejection of the resolution. Eventually a compromise emerged: Congress authorized the Marines to remain in Lebanon for 18 months; the president acknowledged his obligations under the War Powers Resolution. While Congress could claim a victory in winning acceptance of the resolution, the executive retained firm control over U.S. policy in the Middle East.

In reality, Congress has the opportunity to participate in military policy making only when troops remain in the field for substantial periods. Under these circumstances, Congress can act decisively, ordering the troops home if it wishes, or by default, doing nothing and thus requiring the president to cease military operations. The issue, of course, is whether the legislature will act, imposing its preferences on the commander-in-chief, who will most certainly invoke the "national interest," the nation's prestige and honor, and the gravity of the situation. There is no cause to believe with certainty that members of Congress would be prepared in such circumstances, to run the risk or assume the responsibility of overruling the chief executive.[46]

The War Powers Resolution may be more significant as a prior deterrent to precipitous or dubious armed intervention. Never entirely certain that Congress will approve their actions, presidents may think twice before committing troops abroad. For example, there was widespread speculation that the Ford administration in 1974 was considering direct intervention in the Angolan civil war. The foreign policy committees of Congress, especially Senate Foreign Relations, became increasingly concerned, given what happened in Vietnam, that American commitment of money and weapons might escalate into military support of our favored faction. Such forthright expression of concern may well have contributed to executive caution. No use of American troops was ever officially proposed.[47]

Congress's success in imposing its military and foreign policy judgments on the executive has been uneven. On the one hand, Congress has flexed its institutional muscle frequently. The Senate refused to ratify the second Strategic Arms Limitation Treaty (SALT II); repeatedly the legislature has blocked or delayed (using the legislative veto) arms sales, the export of nuclear materials, and numerous treaties with neighboring nations (for example, maritime treaties with Mexico and Canada failed in 1980). During the Reagan administration Congress regularly cut the defense budget below the president's request (but allowed it to rise dramatically above previous levels), imposed limits on production and deployment of the MX missile (but refused to eliminate the system entirely), delayed production of new forms of chemical weapons until 1985, and reallocated military and economic assistance to foreign nations. Thomas Franck and Edward Weisband see such actions as a beneficial reassertion of congressional foreign policy powers.[48]

On the other hand, some signs point to a revival of legislative deference to the executive. Heightened conflict with the Soviet Union over Afghanistan, Poland, and Central America as well as over arms control undermined liberals' pleas for defense cuts; military spending rose precipitously from 1981 until the soaring federal budget deficit and revelations of Pentagon mismanagement prompted Congress to hold the line on 1986 defense expenditures. Despite this cap on military spending, lawmakers still appear receptive to the views of the defense community. For instance, Congress backed away from a comprehensive charter to regulate the activities of the Central Intelligence Agency, and while it did assert its right to prior notice of covert operations overseas, it reduced from eight to two the number of committees entitled to be informed about CIA covert activities.[49] Fewer overseers, especially if carefully briefed, may mean less intense legislative scrutiny of CIA operations.

Similarly, the fiscal 1981 foreign aid authorization bill relaxed a number of constraints on presidential discretion, enacted in response to the Indochina conflict, to employ aid funds flexibly. In the same vein, after initially restricting intelligence operations in Nicaragua and barring all military involvement there, Congress in 1985 reversed itself. It removed the restrictions and voted nonmilitary "humanitarian" aid to the rebel "contras" seeking to overthrow the Sandinista government. One widely touted explanation for this abrupt policy change was that members of Congress, especially Democrats, feared that constituents would fault them for being "soft on defense." A heavy lobbying campaign by the White House and a visit to Moscow by Nicaraguan president Daniel Ortega seem to have fortified this perception. Furthermore, domestic problems with equally obvious electoral implications—the economy, taxation, social issues like prayer and abortion, or another "energy crisis"—may lead members to redirect their attention to the home front, leaving international matters to the executive.

In sum, while presidents can no longer count on customary congressional acquiescence to their foreign policy initiatives, the legislature's assertiveness may reflect less structural reform than more basic, evolutionary change. Even without reform, new members with new ideas on new issues, eager to secure the support of their constituents, may be willing to use basic legislative prerogatives to challenge the administration. As membership and situations alter, the old pattern of congressional subordination might readily recur. Members' policy preferences and political purposes more than institutional reforms may be the decisive determinants of congressional challenges to the executive.

The Congressional Budget and Impoundment Control Act. Assessment of the new budget process yields a similar picture: reform intersects with other forms of change to produce unpredictable results. Here the situation is complicated by different budgetary arrangements in the House and Senate. Moreover, the multiple motives of the reformers—recapturing fiscal power from the executive and pursuing liberal or conservative policy goals—inevitably led to differing budgetary perspectives. From any particular vantage point, however, the revised procedures have generated a variable record marked by both successes and failures.[50]

On the plus side, the 1974 act has clearly restored Congress's *potential* to assert legislative supremacy in fiscal affairs. The Congressional Budget Office—which Aaron Wildavsky describes as "the best source of budget numbers in Washington"— provides Congress with reliable information to formulate independent budget proposals.[51] There is little doubt that if and when Congress wants to act decisively, it can use the provisions and procedures of the act to do so. On numerous occasions congressional budget resolutions substantially reordered the executive's budget priorities. The new reconciliation process under the act presents the opportunity to impose discipline, to limit spending and deficits significantly. But promise is not performance; to date, Congress's willingness and ability to use the law to meet its proponents' aims has been limited.

Early experience with the new process, however, provided auspicious signs. Between 1975 and 1979 Congress observed the form of the new scheme; for the most part, it formulated a coherent budget, specifying revenues, outlays, and the size of the deficit, although it did deviate somewhat from the prescribed timetable. The process thus looked as if it could provide the desired coherence and efficiency. This was particularly true in the Senate. The Senate Budget Committee prospered under the bipartisan leadership of Edmund Muskie (D-Maine), the chair, and Henry Bellmon (R-Okla.), the ranking minority member. The committee was careful to conform to the chamber's norms, individualism and reciprocity, and to avoid direct challenges to the other standing committees.[52]

The situation in the House was quite different. Motives beyond a more rational budget process seem to have induced the chamber to limit the potential of its budget committee. House rules restrict service on the committee to three terms. Rotation of members reduces long-term possibilities for internal House influence and constrains development of committee norms and expertise. House rules also mandate membership for representatives of the other revenue-related committees and the party leadership—Appropriations, and Ways and Means have five seats each on Budget; each party designates one member. In consequence, assignments went to liberal Democrats and conservative Republicans who, in pursuing their policy preferences, stressed partisanship and ideology, leaving the panel polarized and volatile.[53] Partisanship, in fact, threatened the process, and the House was hard pressed to comply with the act, often passing the budget resolutions late and by slender margins.

While the House did act more-or-less responsibly in passing a budget, those who saw budget reform as a way to alter the substance of policy found the record of the 1970s less promising, uneven at best, and disappointing in general. Conservatives hoped the process would enable them to spend less for domestic social programs and more on defense; liberals desired to reverse these priorities. Congress did depart substantially from the president's fiscal proposals for 1976 and 1977, favoring social over military spending. This result, however, may have reflected the natural enmity between the Republican White House and the Democratic Congress as much as the operation of the budget process itself. In contrast, some analysts find the congressional impact on budgetary priorities during the 1975-79 period as moderate to low.[54]

In short, between 1974 and 1979 the new process, as process, worked reasonably well; as a device to alter spending priorities, however, the process proved unsatisfactory to many observers. In particular, reformers eager to slow the growth of federal expenditures and the national debt were distressed. The revised process deterred neither, and the budget and the debt continued on their seemingly inexorable upward path.[55] In fact, the new budget committees created by the act added another layer of participants in the budgetary routine on top of the appropriations and tax panels. More interests must be accommodated before a budget resolution can be adopted. In any case, in its early years the budget process did shift some influence to Congress and establish the basis for more efficient and informed congressional decision making; it did *not* always produce the substantive results its proponents preferred.

By decade's end, however, political economic circumstances had changed dramatically; so, too, had the operation of the new budget process. Economic conditions deteriorated rapidly during the Carter administration. Inflation and unemployment soared, government revenues declined, and the deficit swelled. There was simply too little money available to fund the multitude of federal programs on the books. Congressional budgeting rested on the assumption that the legislature would have ample resources to distribute—an untenable premise by the late 1970s; an age of scarcity, of limited resources, had replaced the old age of affluence. Conventional budgetary politics of distribution— dispersing funds to please the constituents and placate the special interests—could no longer suffice in a period of economic hardship.

Moreover, Congress itself changed during the 1970s. Its membership turned over rapidly, at least by conventional standards. Seventy-five freshmen Democrats won House seats in 1974; retirement rates rose rapidly in the latter half of the decade. New members took places in a legislative system that reform had altered fundamentally. The democratizing trend of 1970-77 gave them positions of influence, particularly in subcommittees, from which to shape policy. To strengthen their support back home, new members had great incentive to continue distributive budget practices at a time when the economy was unable to provide the money to sustain the programs they desired. Budgetary processes and economic realities collided.

The 1980 elections provided the catalyst for change. Not only was Ronald Reagan elected by a landslide, but the electorate also gave him working majorities in Congress—clear control of the Senate and in the House a revived conservative coalition of Republicans and Southern Democrats. Building on its political momentum, the new administration led the nation from an age of distribution into a period of redistribution. Reconciliation, used innovatively and in an unforeseen fashion, provided the means to reorient the budget process.[56]

Post-1980 budgeting was consistent with the responsible parties version of the executive force model presented in Chapter 1. Disciplined majorities in each chamber enacted a budget that largely reflected the president's preferences: $100 billion in spending cuts and program reductions over a three-year period (1981-83). Democratic alternatives, aimed at preserving the status quo, were turned aside.

The 1974 act envisioned reconciliation as a device to instruct committees to conform to the second binding budget resolution due in September. But the Reagan administration, building on a precedent of the 1979 budget cycle, employed reconciliation in conjunction with the first resolution due in May, thus setting the terms of the budget debate entirely to its liking. With the passage of reconciliation instructions early in the budget season, the issue was not whether to cut federal spending, but where and how much. Reconciliation imposes a ceiling on total permissible expenditures; defining the fiscal "pie" in advance requires congressional budgeters to allocate available funds among numerous claimants without exceeding the mandated spending limits. Since there is not sufficient money to go around, there inevitably will be winners and losers; that is, there will be redistribution as a result of stringent reconciliation resolutions.

In 1981 the Reagan administration had the votes to impose severe— opponents said Draconian—reconciliation instructions on House and Senate Committees. It achieved its purpose: "to limit the growth of . . . government by limiting the revenues available to be spent." [57] In practice, the reconciliation procedure culminates in a single bill, subject only to one take-it-or-leave-it, up-or-down vote.[58] It precludes individual votes on individual programs, proposed by numerous interests. In other words, reconciliation shifts discussion of the budget process from cuts in individual programs and their effects to a broader concern for the benefits that the total package of reductions will provide for the national interest.[59] The president proposed a budget and Congress in the early days of Reagan's rule disposed of it consistently with his preferences.

During Reagan's first term the budget process did little to restore Congress's influence in financial matters; to the contrary, it subordinated the legislature to the administration, as the executive force theorists would have it. In one sense the process was efficient; a centralized procedure produced a budget with dispatch early in the legislative session. But in another sense efficiency declined. Beset by fiscal constraints and partisan conflict between the Democratic House and the Republican Senate and White House, Congress became increasingly unable to pass appropriations bills. It became necessary to fund government programs by a *continuing resolution* that permits spending to continue at the previous year's level until an appropriations measure clears Congress; in 1983, 7 of the 13 regular appropriations bills were funded under a continuing resolution for the entire fiscal year. In addition, it became difficult to pass the second budget resolution; in response, Congress in 1981 decided that the first resolution would automatically become binding unless a second was passed. In sum, efficiency in terms of meeting the budget act's deadlines declined after 1980. Conservatives were relatively pleased with fiscal outcomes in the post-1980 phase of budgetary practice: social programs received a decreasing share of federal funds, defense an enlarged portion. But total spending did not decline, and the deficits soared to record heights. Liberals, conversely, took little solace in budget allocations under Ronald Reagan.

After 1983, however, Congress collectively used reconciliation to challenge at least some of the president's priorities. The House, where the 1982 and 1984 elections restored a working Democratic majority, forced the administration and the Republican-controlled Senate to back away from a proposal, passed in that chamber, to freeze the level of Social Security benefits for fiscal 1986. Similarly, the defense budget was cut substantially. Although the president requested an after-inflation rise of roughly 6 percent, the final budget figure reflected only a 3 percent increase to compensate for inflation. In addition, the president, with Senate support, sought to terminate more than a dozen federal programs, but the Democratic House successfully defended ongoing social policies; while many were cut, only one program (revenue sharing) was ended. The complicated politics involved in reaching these settlements, which reduced the growth rate but not the size of either government spending or the deficit, delayed the passage of the first resolution until August 1, 1985. Overall, many congressional priorities prevailed, indicating again that the legislature can, when it has the will to act, use the budget process to substitute its views for those of the chief executive.

In 1985, Congress acted forcefully to revise the budget process, at least temporarily, to deal with the deficit issue. With a reluctant endorsement from President Reagan, a coalition of House Democrats and Senate Republicans secured passage of a new scheme to balance the budget by 1991. The Gramm-Rudman-Hollings bill (after its sponsors, Senators Phil Gramm [R-Texas], Warren B. Rudman [R-N.H.], and Ernest F. Hollings [D-S.C.]) adds another dimension to the regular congressional budget routine. If the usual process fails to reduce the deficit by a specified amount—$36 billion a year, reaching zero in fiscal 1991—the president is obligated automatically to "sequester" funds, that is cut the budget to reduce the deficit to the required level. Some programs, Social Security for example, are exempt from cuts, but little discretion is left to the executive: the cuts are to come equally from the domestic and defense portions of the budget, at a fixed percentage sufficient to lower the deficit to the mandatory target for each year. Substantively, then, Congress has forced itself, and the president, to adopt policies that should eliminate the deficit over a six-year period.

Procedurally, the Gramm-Rudman-Hollings plan alters the budget process. The Congressional Budget Office and the Office of Management and Budget jointly determine the size of the projected deficit and specify the percentage of the cuts necessary to reduce it to the targeted level; the Comptroller General verifies their report. The ordinary budget process proceeds, but under an expedited, and mandatory, timetable. A reconciliation bill is obligatory, not optional, and must be enacted by June 15 rather than September 25. If Congress and the president cannot agree on a budget that meets the deficit reduction goal, the latter must issue on September 1 the sequester order imposing the necessary cuts. The order takes effect on October 1, the start of the fiscal year, and presumably guarantees that the deficit will not exceed the prescribed level for that year.[60] How the process will work in practice, of course, remains uncertain, but whatever the result, it is clear that the changed political and economic circumstances of the mid-1980s were conducive to a marked transformation of the budget process so adroitly crafted by the reformers in 1974.

With respect to impoundment, the budget act has had a clear and pronounced effect. The president is now considerably less able to regulate the flow of federal funds. Impoundment for policy purposes, as Richard Nixon practiced it, is now virtually impossible without legislative acquiescence, and the burden has been transferred to the executive to win that approval.[61] When Congress appropriates, it is far more probable that the funds will be spent.

Yet the anti-impoundment provisions have had unintended consequences as well. Traditionally, impoundment was a useful and non-controversial device that promoted efficient administration. Now all matters, even the most routine deferrals, must be reported to Congress. Members have complained that many hours are wasted on relatively trivial items, a concern that bureaucrats share.[62] More seriously, the 1974 act appears to give the president authority never previously acknowledged, namely, an opportunity to delay expenditures temporarily at least for policy purposes. The chief executive can rescind funds (previously appropriated but not spent) for 45 days until congressional inaction compels their release.[63] On the whole, the impoundment provisions of the budget act improve the legislature's chances to impose its priorities if it is determined to do so. Whether its resolve will hold and what such decisiveness will accomplish will depend, of course, on future conditions inside and outside Congress.

Information and Oversight. Similar uncertainties appear about the results of the "information revolution." From one perspective it is incontrovertible that members of Congress have greater access to more data than ever before. Increased staff resources, new agencies (Congressional Budget Office and Office of Technology Assessment), more effective old support facilities (General Accounting Office and Congressional Research Service), and improved computer technology enormously expand Congress's capacity to engage in serious analysis that can sustain legislative alternatives to executive initiatives.

These developments, however, are not necessarily entirely positive. For one thing, members of Congress may not have adequate incentive to seize these new opportunities. Fundamentally, senators and representatives are politicians, not objective analysts. They may well be searching less for optimal policies than for programs that will serve their political purposes. They want ideas that will satisfy their constituents, and they need solutions that will survive the bargaining and compromising of a decentralized legislature. For example, in the late 1970s and early 1980s, congressional committees tended to use Office of Technology Assessment studies of railroad safety, nutrition, energy conservation, and other issues to sustain members' views rather than to enlighten them in any substantive way. In other words, members used analysis "strategically" more than "analytically"—to rationalize their presumably politically acceptable positions more often than to "seek the truth" about complex policy questions.[64] Policy analysts who do not recognize the political needs of their principals will find their advice ignored. Where politics and analysis merge, the latter may be of considerable use to legislators; where they diverge, analysis is likely to receive low priority.

Moreover, information that these reforms make available may actually distract lawmakers from programmatic activities. Overwhelmed by "information overload," members may be increasingly inclined to look to staff for substantive guidance.[65] Conversely, staff personnel who are prepared to be "entrepreneurs" rather than impartial "professionals" may come to play powerful roles.[66] Dependence on the experts may undercut the members' ability to make genuinely independent judgments. Finally, there is an information management problem; members may spend more time and energy administering their large staffs than they do using the data that staff supply. While some offices now employ professional managers,[67] the risk remains that organizational confusion and chaos will impede legislators' ability to delve into the substance of policy questions.

For all the increased attention Congress has paid to gaining control of a "runaway" bureaucracy, it is not certain that much has been accomplished. More oversight activity—more hearings, more reports required, more legislative-bureaucratic contacts—has not necessarily meant more influence or at least not coordinated management of the executive agencies.[68] This probably suits most members of Congress, who for policy or reelection reasons prefer power over some small segment of the bureaucracy to broader forms of institutional control.[69] It is not that members lack the capacity to exercise close oversight of the executive branch; rather, they lack incentive to impair the cozy subgovernment relationships with executive agencies and interest groups, relationships that foster their electoral goals.[70]

Similar considerations undercut forceful use of the legislative veto. Beginning in the late 1970s, Congress increasingly reserved for itself the right to block bureaucratic actions, but it vetoed few executive proposals. Its ability to do so, of course, may induce administrative caution, but direct confrontations, particularly in domestic affairs, have been relatively few. In this recent period Congress did veto four Education Department regulations and blocked a Transportation Department rule that would have required used car dealers to reveal known defects in the autos thay offer for sale. But, on balance, members seem content to protect or enhance their own agency contacts rather than to engage in severe interbranch conflicts.[71]

In 1983 the Supreme Court greatly restricted the form and use of the legislative veto as an unconstitutional violation of the law-making procedure. Because veto decisions were, in effect, policy decisions, the Court concluded that their passage by concurrent resolution, which does not require the president's signature, was improper. Parts of Congress could not impose a veto; rather, the legislature as a whole must present veto resolutions to the chief executive for his acquiescence or disapproval. This requirement makes the veto much more difficult to use: not only must majorities in both chambers be mustered to exercise the veto, but when the president rejects a veto the legislature also must assemble two-thirds majorities to override. Congress has countered to some extent by enacting veto requirements in negative terms; that is, statutes provide that executive actions on particular topics *cannot* take effect until Congress legislates, by joint resolution, its approval and the president signs. Legislative inaction, then, imposes a veto on administrative decisions. These new tactics mean that Congress must treat veto-related issues as it would normal legislation—in committees and on the floor—and it must expend considerable time and energy on them.[72] The legislative veto survives, but in a form that reduces its overall effectiveness as a check on unbridled policy-making discretion by the executive.

In sum, the Congress of the 1980s is surely better equipped to wage war with the executive for policy leadership. New authority (the War Powers Resolution and budget act) and strengthened analytic capacity (expanded staff and information resources)—have strengthened the legislature's position to define and fight for its own priorities. But capability and its use are not necessarily synonymous. Whether Congress will, in fact, challenge the executive depends on less tangible elements of political change—events summoning members to take up arms and their willingness and determination to mount the attack. Reform has helped Congress to contest the president's proposals, but it cannot guarantee that the legislature will fight. In short, Congress can, but only sometimes will, marshal its enhanced institutional might to do battle with the administration. Congress can be a more responsible institution in the postreform period: its willingness is all.

Strengthening the Political Parties

Congressional reformers sought not only to rearm the legislature against the executive but also to reallocate authority internally. The standing committess and their allegedly autocratic chairpersons were the chief targets of reform. One thrust of the attack on the committee oligarchs was to strengthen the political parties. More cohesive, centralized parties would be better able to move a program through Congress efficiently and effectively, to overcome the opportunities for delay and defeat built into a fragmented, pluralistic institution. In reality, the legislators were unwilling to surrender more than a modicum of their individual freedoms to the party leaders, and the movement toward centralization has proved halting at best. The parties, on balance, remain weak.

There have been some specific party successes, however. Using its newly won right to approve committee chairpersons, the House Democratic Caucus did remove three elderly and supposedly arbitrary committee chairpersons, but little or no change in committee factional alignments, leadership patterns, or policy outcomes has followed. With more loyal, mainstream Democrats in place as leaders, these committees —Agriculture, Armed Services, and Banking—continued to act in customary fashion.[73] What can be said is that committee chairs are now on notice that they have no guarantee of retaining their positions, a fact that may shape the ways they use the powers available to them. The same seems true of subcommittee chairs. In fact, the message has not been lost on those who aspire to committee and subcommittee leadership positions. Sara Crook and John Hibbing find that the party loyalty of those near the top of the seniority ladder, in position to chair committees, has increased markedly since the adoption of these reforms. Potential leaders recognize the need to vote with their party's majority, to establish their credentials as reliable partisans worthy of responsibility.[74]

The Democratic Caucus has also won an occasional policy victory. In 1975 it voted to instruct the Rules Committee to permit an amendment repealing the oil depletion allowance, previously defeated in the Ways and Means Committee, to be offered on the floor, The amendment passed and eventually became law. But in general, the caucus has been unwilling or unable to impose discipline on its majority, leaving individualism to flourish.

In the Senate, where little effort was made to increase party power, members' freedom of action continues unencumbered. Even so forceful a Majority Leader as Robert Dole (R-Kan.) has struggled to keep his Republican colleagues in line. Especially since 1984, when 22 GOP senators began to prepare 1986 reelection campaigns, Dole has had a hard time finding common ground on budget, farm, international trade, and military issues. His troops march to their own drummers on these matters. Like other leaders, he has tried to curb members' independence without sanctions, using only modest means of persuasion, and he has not always succeeded in holding his party majority together.

The House Speaker, like the caucus, has made successful but infrequent use of postreform powers. While the Rules Committee, whose majority membership he appoints, usually supports the party leadership, even it balks from time to time.[75] For example, in 1980 the panel refused to comply with a request by Speaker Thomas P. O'Neill, Jr. (D-Mass.), for restriction on amendments to the fiscal 1981 budget reconciliation bill. And in 1985 Rules Chairman Claude Pepper (D-Fla.) "vowed to kill" a banking bill promoting interstate, nationwide bank operations that the Commerce Committee had approved.[76] Similarly, the Speaker used his newly granted power to establish ad hoc committees to win passage of outer continental shelf legislation in 1975 and 1976 and President Carter's energy package in 1977. Committee conflict—five committees shared jurisdiction over major aspects of the energy program—had threatened to make concerted and comprehensive action impossible.[77] More commonly, such intrusion by the Speaker into standing committee preserves and authority has seemed too risky, too unlikely to overcome the divisive and divergent preferences of individual party members.

The Speaker's enlarged bill referral powers may even have counterproductive consequences. While he can refer a bill to several committees at once and impose time limits on their consideration (which he did 4,148 times in the 95th Congress), multiple referrals greatly exacerbated the problem of coordinating congressional activity. Eric Uslaner reports that multireferred legislation lingers longer in committee, is more likely to be amended, and is less likely to pass if it reaches the floor, than single referrals.[78] Far from providing centralization, the Speaker's referral power may encourage House committees to assert their authority; indeed, full committee chairs often press jurisdictional claims to compensate for their otherwise declining influence.[79] House leaders' new powers have proven inadequate to overcome the decentralizing forces that the reform movement unleashed. And in the already individualistic Senate, party leaders' ability to manage the chambers has also declined.[80] In neither house has reform produced significantly stronger parties, better able to move their programs forward.

In fact, leadership rests on the talents and skills of those who rise to the top party positions. The Speaker and the floor leaders have few sanctions with which to compel their nominal followers to vote the party line. Party power remains more psychological—members want to back their party when and if they can—than tangible. Party leaders, in the last analysis, cannot force the rank-and-file to support their initiatives; they must entreat them to vote for party programs. Barbara Sinclair identifies two broad and often irreconcilable obligations of the party hierarchy: it must assemble coalitions to pass party bills and, at the same time, it must maintain "peace in the family."[81] Maintaining party harmony is an onerous chore, given the diversity of members' ideological positions, constituency commitments (including pursuit of electoral security), and vested interests. Leaders cannot readily induce their ostensible followers to "rally 'round" party positions when the rank-and-file confront so many pressures to go their own ways. Centralization—through reform or on some voluntary basis—is hard to achieve in these circumstances, and without it policy-making efficiency (responsibility) remains a will-o'-the-wisp.

Revising the Rules

Finally, procedural reforms have produced only minimal and often unanticipated effects. Dilatory tactics are somewhat more difficult to use and legislation is less likely to get enmeshed in parliamentary thickets in the House, although this is hard to prove conclusively. Easing quorum call requirements, voting by machine, clustering votes, and permitting committees to meet more readily all contributed to expediting the flow of business, but the impact of these reforms has certainly been marginal, with little effect on the substance of congressional policy making.

The major rules change spawned by reform was the revision of the Senate cloture rule (Rule 22). Sixty votes (not the simple majority that the reformers preferred), rather than two-thirds of those present and voting, became sufficient to terminate a filibuster. But the new procedures, including those reducing the postcloture filibuster by amendment, do not seem to have facilitated more rapid processing of bills. This is not because the cloture has not been invoked; in fact, it has been used more successfully in recent years. There were 103 cloture votes between 1917 (when the Senate enacted its first cloture rule) and 1975 (when the 60-vote rule was passed). Of these, 24 were successful, including 2 that concluded debate on altering the filibuster rule; 16 of these occurred between 1971 and 1975, indicating a marked decline in minority power. The filibuster claimed only one bill that would have passed under the three-fifths rule (a 1974 proposal to establish a consumer protection agency). In 4 other cases, 60 votes were cast for cloture, but subsequently the two-thirds needed to shut off debate was attained and the measures passed. Under a simple majority principle, 24 additional cloture votes would have succeeded.

Coincidentally, during the much shorter period from 1975 to 1984, 103 cloture votes again were taken. Of these, 46 succeeded, almost twice the rate in the prereform era. On 26 occasions, more than 67 members voted to end debate, suggesting that cloture would have been invoked even under the more stringent two-thirds rule. In 20 other instances, however, a filibuster was ended with fewer than the requisite 67 votes under the old rule (if all members were present); these may be cases where the easier procedure permitted the majority to prevail more readily.[82] In sum, the revised Rule 22 seems to have encouraged more filibusters, but enabled the majority to terminate debate somewhat more effectively. Still, more than half of the post-1975 cloture votes failed.

Apparently the norms concerning unlimited debate have shifted in the wake of broader congressional change. Historically, the filibuster was reserved for major matters about which an intense minority felt passionately (particularly civil rights issues). Now, by contrast, any topic seems fair game for extended discussion, led by a handful of senators (liberals as well as conservatives) or on occasion even a single member. This acceptance of seemingly frivolous filibusters has undercut the intended effect of reform.[83] It may be that in the 1980s, now that the Senate has curbed the postcloture filibuster, the reforms will reduce minority power. At present, however, the filibuster—conducted or merely threatened—continues to shape Senate floor action on much legislation.[84]

Summary

During the first half of the 1970s, critics of Congress enacted sweeping legislative reforms. Motivated by numerous factors—policy inertia, personal powerlessness, public disapproval, electoral protection—they sought to democratize Congress (to make it more responsive and accountable) and to centralize its operations (to make it more responsible and to reclaim lost policy-making power, particularly from the president). Congress changes its institutional procedures as it makes policy in other areas—slowly and in piecemeal fashion. Therefore, it is scarcely surprising that the impact of reform has been uncertain. Reforms have often been incompatible; reformers have won some victories and suffered some setbacks, often discovering that their alterations have led to quite unexpected or even undesirable results.

Certainly Congress is better positioned to oppose the president, but given the rapid change in membership and the shifting push of events it is not clear that there will be steady pressure on members to use their potentially powerful weapons. The ultimate consequences of the War Powers Resolution and the 1974 budget act, coupled with the increase in Congress's analytic capacity, remain impossible to predict. The legislature has been, on occasion, a more efficient, responsible decision maker, but it has also, in other instances, lacked the will to assert itself. Centralizing reforms are in place—new party and leadership authority in the House and a reduction in the ability of minorities to use dilatory tactics in both chambers—but they have seldom been employed decisively. In the absense of centralization Congress has been hard pressed to act responsibly.

On the other hand, reforms have made Congress more responsive. The attack on the full committees has dispersed political influence more widely; subcommittees have clearly become significant forces in congressional deliberations. More members, with ties to more interests, possess the potential to affect public policy (and to oversee and represent more effectively). Junior members have secured advantageous legislative terrain, but have cultivated it differently in different committees and subcommittees and on different policy questions.

In addition, since the passage of campaign spending, financial disclosure, and sunshine reforms, it is easier to hold Congress accountable. More can be known about congressional activity, but there is little reason to believe that more *is* actually known, at least by ordinary citizens. The legislature is certainly more accessible to the public, but that very permeability has increased legislators' vulnerability to external influences and weakened an already fragile basis for centralized leadership. Members of Congress seem to prefer decentralization, and they have attained it. Congress is unquestionably more democratic in the 1980s than in the 1960s, but at a price: it is less able to exert institutional power and to enact innovative programs. In short, reform prompted by mixed motives has produced mixed results.

One overriding lesson is unmistakable: reform is no panacea. Part and parcel of broad currents of change, congressional reform reflects a welter of societal and institutional forces. Altered circumstances undercut expectations and produce unforeseen outcomes; short-run success evolves into long-term disappointment. Given the myriad of influences shaping legislative performance—new personnel with different values and aims; new economic, social, or political conditions and issues; and the organizational character of Congress itself—reformers find that their best-laid plans often go astray.[85]

Legislative history makes clear the incremental nature and ephemeral quality of reform. After 1977 members seemed to feel that enough had been done. To be sure, some conditions demanded response. The loophole in the Senate filibuster rule was quickly closed; ethical transgressions were punished; the use of riders on appropriations bills was restricted. But on the whole the reform spirit flagged. After perfunctory consideration, proposals to clarify committee jurisdictions, to create an Energy Committee, to refine the budget process, and in general to improve legislative efficiency were brushed aside.[86] In the absence of strong facilitating conditions—supportive members, favorable public opinion, the stimulus of particular national and international events—reform foundered.

On balance, Congress has become more decentralized, more responsive to a multitude of forces inside and outside its halls, and, as a result, more hard pressed to formulate and enact coherent, responsible public policies. Structural reform has enlarged the number of power centers involved in making policy, and party power cannot mobilize them in support of programs that either challenge or sustain the president. "Sunshine" laws have exposed members to attentive publics, most often organized interests. More independent members, faced with more difficult policy choices (the "politics of scarcity" requires allocation of sacrifice rather than dispensation of largesse) find it politically expedient to duck controversy: to defer to others, to delay, or to obfuscate. In consequence, Congress in the 1980s seems less willing or able to frame and fight for its preferences. Paradoxically, greater individual influence adds up to reduced institutional authority.

What observers make of these manifold alterations in Congress and its mode of conducting legislative business depends, of course, on their values; what they see reflects what they want to see. For some, perhaps many, Congress is a "better" institution than it was a decade ago. It is, after all, hard to quarrel with openness, accessibility, egalitarianism, and independence, and Congress as a result of reform has more of these admirable attributes. For others, however, Congress still comes up short. It seems less able to process legislation, to counterbalance a strong president, or to overcome the obstacles to efficiency raised by a decentralized institution. The essential and enduring questions persist: Can a fragmented Congress do its job? If not, what reforms remain in order?

NOTES

1. For an imaginative but largely ignored plea to treat reforms as hypotheses to be tested scientifically and abandoned if disconfirmed, see Donald T. Campbell, "Reforms as Experiments," *American Psychologist* 24 (1969): 409-29.
2. On the Moss-Staggers contest, see David E. Price, "The Impact of Reform: The House Subcommittee on Oversight and Investigations," in *Legislative Reform: The Policy Impact*, ed. Leroy N. Rieselbach (Lexington, Mass.: Lexington Books, 1978), 133-47. On the ouster of Yatron, see *Congressional Quarterly Weekly Report*, February 7, 1981, 263. For three 1979 cases (two on Commerce, one on Government Operations) see *Congressional Quarterly Weekly Report*, February 3, 1979, 183-87.
3. Senate Republicans seem to be an exception here, giving more weight to seniority in resolving conflict over particular committee posts. See Steven S. Smith and Christopher J. Deering, *Committees in Congress* (Washington, D.C.: CQ Press, 1984), 242.
4. On committee assignments, see Smith and Deering, *Committees in Congress*, 237-46; Charles S. Bullock III, "House Committee Assignments," in *The Congressional System: Notes and Readings*, 2d ed., ed. Leroy N. Rieselbach (Belmont, Calif.: Wadsworth, 1979), 58-86; Steven S. Smith and Bruce A. Ray, "The Impact of Congressional Reform: House Democratic Committee As-

signments," *Congress and the Presidency* 10 (1983), 219-40; and Heinz Eulau, "Legislative Committee Assignments," *Legislative Studies Quarterly* 9 (1984): 587-633.

5. Christopher J. Deering and Steven S. Smith, "Subcommittees in Congress," in *Congress Reconsidered*, 3d ed., ed. Lawrence C. Dodd and Bruce I. Oppenheimer (Washington, D.C.: CQ Press, 1985), 190.

6. The work of Smith and Deering is the most intensive and current research on subcommittees, and the paragraphs that follow draw heavily on their efforts. See Smith and Deering, *Committees in Congress*, chap. 5; and Deering and Smith, "Subcommittees in Congress." See also Roger H. Davidson, "Subcommittee Government: New Channels for Policy Making," in *The New Congress*, ed. Thomas E. Mann and Norman J. Ornstein (Washington, D.C.: American Enterprise Institute, 1981), 99-133.

7. Norman J. Ornstein, "Causes and Consequences of Congressional Change: Subcommittee Reforms in the House of Representatives, 1970-1973," in *Congress in Change: Evolution and Reform*, ed. Norman J. Ornstein (New York: Praeger, 1975), 88-114; John E. Stanga, Jr., and David N. Farnsworth, "Seniority and Democratic Reforms in the House of Representatives: Committees and Subcommittees," in *Legislative Reform*, ed. Rieselbach, 35-47.

8. Norman J. Ornstein et al., *Vital Statistics on Congress, 1984-1985 Edition* (Washington, D.C.: American Enterprise Institute, 1984), Table 4-2, 109. The House in 1981 adopted rules limiting committees to eight subcommittees; those with fewer than six subcommittees at that time could create no more than six. In consequence, there were 130 subcommittees in the 98th Congress (1983-85).

9. Smith and Deering, *Committees in Congress*, 193-94.

10. Stanga and Fransworth, "Seniority and Democratic Reforms." It remains the case, however, that on average the length of time required for House Democrats to reach the top spot on subcommittees has declined with the adoption of the new rules; it takes longer to gain a subcommittee chair on the most prestigious panels. See Smith and Deering, *Committees in Congress*, Table 6.1, 191.

11. These data are from Smith and Deering, *Committees in Congress*, Tables 5.1, 132; 5.2, 133; and 6.3, 195.

12. Christopher J. Deering and Steven S. Smith, "Majority Party Leadership and the Effects of Decentralization" (Paper presented to the Everett McKinley Dirksen Congressional Leadership Research Center-Sam Rayburn Library Conference, Understanding Congressional Leadership: The State of the Art, 1980), 36.

13. In *Committees in Congress*, 161-62, Smith and Deering stress the distinction between independence and autonomy: the former refers to the ability to operate freely, without restraint; the latter pertains to the ability to make decisions stick at subsequent stages of the legislative process. Subcommittees may be independent but not autonomous.

14. Smith and Deering, *Committees in Congress*, Table 5.2, 133.

15. Ibid., 161.

16. Richard F. Fenno, Jr., *Congressmen in Committees* (Boston: Little, Brown, 1973).

17. Norman J. Ornstein and David W. Rohde, "Shifting Forces, Changing Rules, and Political Outcomes: The Impact of Congressional Change on Four House Committees," in *New Perspectives on the House of Representatives*, 3d ed., ed.

Robert L. Peabody and Nelson W. Polsby (Chicago: Rand McNally, 1977), 186-269. For confirmatory evidence, see Joseph K. Unekis and Leroy N. Rieselbach, *Congressional Committee Politics: Continuity and Change* (New York: Praeger, 1984), chap. 4.

18. Ornstein and Rohde, "Shifting Forces," 237-52.

19. Ibid., 252-61. See also Fred M. Kaiser, "Congressional Change and Foreign Policy: The House Committee on International Relations," in *Legislative Reform*, ed. Rieselbach, 61-71.

20. See also John Berg, "The Effects of Seniority Reform on Three House Committees," in *Legislative Reform*, ed. Rieselbach, 49-59; and Christopher J. Deering, "Adaptation and Consolidation in Congress's Foreign Policy Committees: Evolution in the Seventies" (Paper presented to the 1980 Annual Meeting of the Midwest Political Science Association).

21. Glenn R. Parker and Suzanne L. Parker, "Factions in Committees: The U.S. House of Representatives," *American Political Science Review* 73 (1979): 85-103; and Unekis and Rieselbach, *Congressional Committee Politics*. In *Congressmen in Committees*, Fenno describes Ways and Means in the 1960s, at the height of Mills's influence. See also John F. Manley, *The Politics of Finance* (Boston: Little, Brown, 1970).

22. Catherine E. Rudder, "Fiscal Responsibility and the Revenue Committees," in *Congress Reconsidered*, 3d ed., ed. Dodd and Oppenheimer, 211-22; Catherine E. Rudder, "The Policy Impact of Reform of the Committee on Ways and Means," in *Legislative Reform*, ed. Rieselbach, 73-89; and Bruce I. Oppenheimer, "Policy Effects of U.S. House Reform: Decentralization and the Capacity to Resolve Energy Issues," *Legislative Studies Quarterly* 5 (1980): 5-30.

23. Price, "The Impact of Reform," 154; and Michael J. Malbin, "The Bolling Committee Revisited: Energy Oversight on an Investigative Subcommittee" (Paper presented to the 1978 Annual Meeting of the American Political Science Association).

24. Ornstein et al., *Vital Statistics,* Table 4-3, 110; Smith and Deering, *Committees in Congress,* Table 5-1, 132; Table 5-2, 133; Table 6-3, 195; and 151. See also Deering and Smith, "Subcommittees in Congress."

25. Susan Webb Hammond, "Congressional Change and Reform: Staffing the Congress," in *Legislative Reform*, ed. Rieselbach, 181-93; and *Congressional Quarterly Weekly Report*, November 24, 1979, 2631-38.

26. Ornstein et al., *Vital Statistics,* Table 5-5, 124.

27. Smith and Deering, *Committees in Congress,* chap. 7 and Table 2-3, 52.

28. David R. Mayhew, *Congress: The Electoral Connection* (New Haven, Conn.: Yale University Press, 1974); and Richard F. Fenno, Jr., *Home Style: Representatives in Their Districts* (Boston: Little, Brown, 1978).

29. Morris P. Fiorina, *Congress: Keystone of the Washington Establishment* (New Haven, Conn.: Yale University Press, 1977).

30. Randall B. Ripley, *Power in the Senate* (New York: St. Martin's, 1969); and Norman J. Ornstein, "The House and Senate in a New Congress," in *The New Congress*, ed. Mann and Ornstein, 363-83; and Smith and Deering, *Committees in Congress,* chap. 5.

31. Lawrence C. Dodd and Bruce I. Oppenheimer "The House in Transition," in *Congress Reconsidered*, 3d ed., ed. Dodd and Oppenheimer, 34-64; James L. Sundquist, *The Decline and Resurgence of Congress* (Washington, D.C.: Brookings Institution, 1981); Walter J. Oleszek, "Integration and Fragmenta-

tion: Key Themes in Congressional Change," *Annals* 466 (1983): 272-90; and Smith and Deering, *Committees in Congress*.

32. Michael J. Malbin, *Unelected Representatives: Congressional Staff and the Future of Representative Government* (New York: Basic Books, 1980).

33. Smith and Deering, *Committees in Congress*, 148-49.

34. See John A. Ferejohn, "On the Decline of Competition in Congressional Elections," *American Political Science Review* 71 (1977): 166-76; Thomas E. Mann, *Unsafe at Any Margin: Interpreting Congressional Elections* (Washington, D.C.: American Enterprise Institute, 1978); and Kent L. Tedin and Richard W. Murray, "Public Awareness of Congressional Representatives: Recall versus Recognition," *American Politics Quarterly* 7 (1979): 509-17.

35. See Thomas E. Mann and Raymond E. Wolfinger, "Candidates and Parties in Congressional Elections," *American Political Science Review* 74 (1980): 617-32; Barbara Hinckley, *Congressional Elections* (Washington, D.C.: CQ Press, 1981); and Gary C. Jacobson, *The Politics of Congressional Elections* (Boston: Little, Brown, 1983).

36. *The Harris Survey*, release 1984, no. 112, December 17, 1984; release 1985, no. 47, June 13, 1985. In absolute terms public confidence in Congress has been restored somewhat. In 1985 public sentiment shifted sharply. For the first time in 20 years a popular majority (53 percent) gave Congress a positive rating; 46 percent were negative about the legislature. *The Harris Survey*, release 1985, no. 46, June 10, 1985.

37. *Congressional Quarterly Weekly Report*, July 6, 1985, 1316.

38. On problems of acting in public, see Lewis A. Froman, Jr., and Randall B. Ripley, "Conditions for Party Leadership: The Case of the House Democrats," *American Political Science Review* 59 (1965): 52-63; Fiorina, *Congress: Keystone of the Washington Establishment*; and Mayhew, *Congress: The Electoral Connection*. Party leaders recognize that members give priority to local interests. As House Speaker O'Neill noted, "Members are more home-oriented. They no longer have to follow the national philosophy of the party. They can get reelected on their newsletter, or on how they serve their constituents." *Congressional Quarterly Weekly Report*, September 13, 1980, 2696.

39. In the 1983-84 electoral cycle, for example, 71 percent of the more than $112 million PACs contributed to congressional candidates went to incumbents. *National Journal*, June 15, 1985, 1429. But the rise of ideological groups that support challengers, or at least oppose incumbents—such as the National Conservative Political Action Committee (NCPAC), which spent $19.3 million in 1983-84, and the evangelical Christian Movement's Moral Majority (see the four-part series, *New York Times*, August 17-20, 1980)—may augur reduced group support for incumbents. See Gary C. Jacobson, *Money in Congressional Elections* (New Haven, Conn.: Yale University Press, 1980); Herbert E. Alexander, *Financing Politics: Money, Elections, and Political Reform*, 3d ed. (Washington, D.C.: CQ Press, 1984); and Michael J. Malbin, ed., *Money and Politics in the United States* (Chatham, N.J.: Chatham House, 1984).

40. Jacobson, *Money in Congressional Elections*, 194. See also Mayhew, *Congress: The Electoral Connection*; and Fiorina, *Congress: Keystone of the Washington Establishment*.

41. Barbara Hinckley, "House Reelections and Senate Defeats: The Role of the Challenger," *British Journal of Political Science* 10 (1980): 441-60. In *Strategy and Choice in Congressional Elections*, 2d ed. (New Haven, Conn.: Yale University

Press, 1983), Gary C. Jacobson and Samuel Kernell argue that attractive challengers emerge and win when conditions favoring their party, usually the one that does not control the White House, enable them to secure substantial funding sufficiently far in advance of election day to wage a strong campaign against the incumbent. Such conditions occur only rarely, and most often the incumbents triumph.

42. Robert Parry, "Defense Firms Increase Political Donations," *Louisville Courier-Journal,* April 1, 1985, A4.

43. It is very difficult to prove that contributions buy votes. Members regularly deny that they do. A few members, professing candor, acknowledge the impact of donations: "You can't buy a congressman for $5,000 [the maximum PAC contribution to a single candidate in a single campaign]. But you can buy his vote. It's done on a regular basis" (Rep. Thomas Downey [D-N.Y.], quoted in *Time,* October 25, 1982, 20). For one study that finds only marginal effects of PAC contributions of legislators' roll call votes, see John R. Wright, "PACs, Contributions, and Roll Calls: An Organizational Perspective," *American Political Science Review* 79 (1985): 400-14.

44. For example, 35-year-old Rep. John J. Cavanaugh (D-Neb.), well-regarded in his district and in the House, retired in 1980 after two terms, in part because "the continuous campaigning is debilitating and campaign financing is corrupting" (Quoted in *New York Times,* August 31, 1980, 20). See also the "retirement" speech of Rep. Otis Pike (D-N.Y.) in *Congressional Quarterly Weekly Report,* February 25, 1978, 528-29. On the retirement phenomenon in general, see Joseph Cooper and William West, "The Congressional Career in the 1970s," in *Congress Reconsidered,* 2d ed., ed. Dodd and Oppenheimer, 83-106; and John R. Hibbing, *Choosing to Leave: Voluntary Retirement from the U.S. House of Representatives* (Washington, D.C.: University Press of America, 1982).

45. Indeed, all presidents have argued that the resolution is an unconstitutional encroachment on the executive's constitutional powers as commander-in-chief. See Louis Fisher, *Constitutional Conflicts between Congress and the President* (Princeton, N.J.: Princeton University Press, 1984); Cecil V. Crabb, Jr., and Pat M. Holt, *Invitation to Struggle: Congress, the President, and Foreign Policy,* 2d ed. (Washington, D.C.: CQ Press, 1984); and Thomas Franck and Edward Weisband, *Foreign Policy by Congress* (New York: Oxford University Press, 1979).

46. Randall B. Ripley and Grace A. Franklin conclude pessimistically that "the War Powers Act is not likely to be operational in the real world." *Congress, the Bureaucracy, and Public Policy,* 3d ed. (Homewood, Ill.: Dorsey Press, 1984), 235.

47. Just to be certain, Congress added an amendment to the Department of Defense (DOD) appropriations bill forbidding the expenditure of any funds for "any activities involving Angola directly or indirectly." Since CIA funds were hidden in the DOD appropriation, this action removed the legal basis for either overt or covert intervention in Angola. The amendment, however, was repealed in 1985.

48. Franck and Weisband, *Foreign Policy by Congress.*

49. Loch K. Johnson, "Legislative Reform of Intelligence Policy," *Polity* 17 (1985): 549-73.

50. See John W. Ellwood, "Budget Control in a Redistributive Environment," in

Making Economic Policy in Congress, ed. Allen Schick (Washington, D.C.: American Enterprise Institute, 1983), 69-99; John W. Ellwood, "The Great Exception: The Congressional Budget Process in an Age of Decentralization," in *Congress Reconsidered,* 3d ed., ed. Dodd and Oppenheimer, 246-71; Howard E. Shuman, *Politics and the Budget: The Struggle between the President and the Congress* (Englewood Cliffs, N.J.: Prentice-Hall, 1984); and W. Thomas Wander, F. Ted Herbert, and Gary W. Copeland, eds., *Congressional Budgeting: Politics, Process, and Power* (Baltimore: Johns Hopkins University Press, 1984).

51. Aaron Wildavsky, *The Politics of the Budgetary Process,* 4th ed. (Boston: Little, Brown, 1984), 238.

52. Lance T. LeLoup, "Budgeting in the U.S. Senate: Old Ways of Doing New Things" (Paper presented to the 1979 Annual Meeting of the Midwest Political Science Association); and Shuman, *Politics and the Budget.* This is not to suggest that there was no conflict between the Senate Budget Committee and other committees. See Louis Fisher, "Congressional Budget Reform: Committee Conflicts" (Paper presented to the 1975 Annual Meeting of the Midwest Political Science Association); Catherine Rudder, "The Impact of the Budget and Impoundment Control Act of 1974 on the Revenue Committees of the U.S. Congress" (Paper presented to the 1977 Annual Meeting of the American Political Science Association); and Joel Havemann, *Congress and the Budget* (Bloomington: Indiana University Press, 1978). Rather, it is to suggest that the Senate panel sought accommodation not confrontation during the early phases of the new process. See also Wildavsky, *The Politics of the Budgetary Process;* and James A. Thurber, "New Powers of the Purse: An Assessment of Congressional Budget Reform," in *Legislative Reform,* ed. Rieselbach, 159-72.

53. Lance T. LeLoup, "Process vs. Policy: The U.S. House Budget Committee," *Legislative Studies Quarterly* 4 (1979): 227-54; and Unekis and Rieselbach, *Congressional Committee Politics,* chap. 2.

54. James P. Pfiffner, "Executive Control and the Congressional Budget" (Paper presented to the 1977 Annual Meeting of the Midwest Political Science Association); Allen Schick, "Whose Budget? It All Depends on Whether the President or Congress Is Doing the Counting," in *The Presidency and the Congress: A Shifting Balance of Power?* ed. William S. Livingston, Lawrence C. Dodd, and Richard L. Schott (Austin, Texas: Lyndon B. Johnson Library, 1979), 124-42; LeLoup, "Budgeting in the U.S. Senate," and "Process versus Policy"; and Mark W. Huddleston, "Assessing Congressional Budget Reform: The Impact on Appropriations," *Policy Studies Journal* 9 (1980): 81-86.

55. Ellwood, "Budget Control."

56. Ibid.; and Allen Schick, "The Distributive Congress," in *Making Economic Policy in Congress,* ed. Schick, 257-73.

57. Shuman, *Politics and the Budget,* 270.

58. Ironically, so powerful was the force behind the Reagan administration's 1981 reconciliation bill that it was "brought to the House floor in emasculated form. . . . The details were not available until the morning of the vote. . . . Figures were crossed out and substitute amounts penciled in. Some pages were misnumbered. Provisions were written by hand in the margins. To add insult to injury, one substitute amendment included the name and telephone number of . . . a staff member of the CBO." Shuman, *Politics and the Budget,* 236. The bill passed anyway.

59. Ellwood, "Budget Control," 94.
60. For a full discussion of the Gramm-Rudman-Hollings bill, see Elizabeth Wehr, "Congress Enacts Far-Reaching Budget Measure," *Congressional Quarterly Weekly Report*, December 14, 1985, 2604-11. The plan remains controversial. It was adopted outside the ordinary legislative process: no committees in either house considered it; the Senate added it on the floor to a high-priority bill to raise the federal debt ceiling; the House agreed to move immediately to a conference. Some proponents believed the plan was the only way to reduce the deficit; others hoped that, because it would cut heavily into defense expenditures, it would force President Reagan to accept a tax increase. Still others challenged the bill's constitutionality, arguing that automatic, across-the-board cuts violate the constitutional requirement that Congress legislate appropriations and the president sign such legislation. In any case, the need to deal with the deficit seemed politically irresistible, and the plan passed readily and rapidly despite the many doubts about its legality and workability.
61. William G. Munselle, "Presidential Impoundment and Congressional Reform," in *Legislative Reform*, ed. Rieselbach, 173-81; and Shuman, *Politics and the Budget*.
62. Pfiffner, "Executive Control of the Congressional Budget"; and Wildavsky, *The Politics of the Budgetary Process*.
63. Schick, "Whose Budget?" 112-13.
64. See David Whiteman, "The Fate of Policy Analysis in Congressional Decision Making: Three Types of Use in Committees," *Western Political Quarterly* 38 (1985): 294-311. See also Charles O. Jones, "Why Congress Can't Do Policy Analysis (Or Words to That Effect)," *Policy Analysis* 2 (1976): 251-64; and Allen Schick, "The Supply and Demand for Analysis on Capitol Hill," *Policy Analysis* 2 (1976): 215-34.
65. Malbin, *Unelected Representatives*.
66. David E. Price, "Professionals and 'Entrepreneurs': Staff Orientations and Policy Making on Three Senate Committees," *Journal of Politics* 33 (1971): 316-36.
67. Hammond, "Congressional Change and Reform."
68. Lawrence C. Dodd and Richard L. Schott, *Congress and the Administrative State* (New York: Wiley, 1979); and Joel D. Aberbach, "Changes in Congressional Oversight," *American Behavioral Scientist* 22 (1979): 493-515.
69. Where some form of institutional control does seem warranted, Congress increasingly resorts to "riders" on authorization or appropriations bills to prohibit spending for particular purposes (for example, to bar the Justice Department from committing money to institute any legal proceeding to require busing for desegregation). In 1983 the House Democrats adopted new rules that tightened party control over the use of riders, presumably to restrict their use by conservatives who oppose party positions. See *Congressional Quarterly Weekly Report*, January 8, 1983, 8.
70. Dodd and Schott, *Congress and the Administrative State*; Morris P. Fiorina, "Control of the Bureaucracy: A Mismatch of Incentives and Capabilities," in *The Presidency and the Congress*, ed. Livingston, Dodd, and Schott, 124-42; and Mathew D. McCubbins and Thomas Schwartz, "Congressional Oversight Overlooked: Police Patrols versus Fire Alarms," *American Journal of Political Science* 28 (1984): 169-79.

71. Richard E. Cohen, "Congress Steps Up Use of the Legislative Veto," *National Journal,* September 6, 1980, 1473-77.

72. Joseph Cooper, "Postscript on the Congressional Veto: Is There Life after Chadha?" *Political Science Quarterly* 98 (1983): 427-29.

73. Unekis and Rieselbach, *Congressional Committee Politics,* chap. 4. See also Berg, "The Effects of Seniority Reform."

74. Sara B. Crook and John R. Hibbing, "Congressional Reform and Party Discipline: The Effects of Changes in the Seniority System on Party Loyalty in the U.S. House of Representatives," *British Journal of Political Science* 15 (1985): 207-26.

75. Stanley Bach, "The Structure of Choice in the House of Representatives: Recent Use of Special Rules" (Paper presented to the 1980 Annual Meeting of the American Political Science Association); and Bruce I. Oppenheimer, "The Changing Relationship between House Leadership and the Committee on Rules," in *Understanding Congressional Leadership,* ed. Frank H. Mackaman (Washington, D.C.: CQ Press, 1980), 207-25.

76. *Congressional Quarterly Weekly Report,* June 15, 1985, 1159.

77. Eric M. Uslaner, "The Congressional War on Energy: The Moral Equivalent of Leadership?" (Paper presented to the Everett McKinley Dirksen Congressional Leadership Research Center-Sam Rayburn Library Conference, Understanding Congressional Leadership, 1980); and Oppenheimer, "Policy Effects of U.S. House Reform."

78. Uslaner, "The Congresssional War on Energy," 12-13.

79. Oppenheimer, "Policy Effects."

80. Robert L. Peabody, "Senate Party Leadership: From the 1950s to the 1980s" (Paper presented to the Everett McKinley Dirksen Congressional Leadership Research Center-Sam Rayburn Library Conference, Understanding Congressional Leadership, 1980). See also Roger H. Davidson, "Senate Leaders: Janitors for an Untidy Congress," in *Congress Reconsidered,* 3d ed., ed. Dodd and Oppenheimer, 225-52.

81. Barbara Sinclair, *Majority Party Leadership in the U.S. House* (Baltimore: Johns Hopkins University Press, 1983).

82. These data are from the 1977-84 volumes of the *Congressional Quarterly Almanac.*

83. See Raymond E. Wolfinger, "Filibusters, Majority Rule, Presidential Leadership, and Senate Norms," in *Readings on Congress,* ed. Raymond E. Wolfinger (Englewood Cliffs, N.J.: Prentice-Hall, 1971), 296-305; and Patty D. Renfrow, "The Senate Filibuster System, 1917-1979: Changes and Consequences" (Paper presented to the 1980 Annual Meeting of the Southern Political Science Association).

84. For instance, in 1985 Senate conservatives led by Jesse Helms (R-S.C.) filibustered a bill to impose economic sanctions against South Africa in response to that nation's apartheid policy. The Senate invoked cloture, on an 88-8 vote, but the minority continued to use dilatory tactics and agreed to permit the chamber to vote on the bill only after liberal Democrats promised to drop amendments that would have made the bill even stronger. See *Congressional Quarterly Weekly Report,* July 13, 1985, 1364-66. A subsequent threat to filibuster the conference report on the bill forced the Senate to postpone a final vote on the measure for a month, until after its summer recess.

85. One careful study found that reform "had no direct impact on ... committee inputs and outputs once the effects of underlying trends attributable to complexity in the external environment" are considered. See Susan Webb Hammond and Laura I. Langbein, "The Impact of Complexity and Reform on Congressional Committee Output," *Political Behavior* 4 (1982): 237-63.

86. For more on the rejected proposals of the House (Obey) Commission on Administrative Review (1977), the House Select (Patterson) Committee on Committees (1979-80), and the Senate Temporary Select (Quayle) Committee to Study the Senate Committee System, see Chapter 3, pp. 67-69.

The Future Congress | 5

Congress has changed! The Congress of the 1980s has identifiable features that distinguish it from its earlier incarnations. Most significantly, it is more responsive. A larger number of interests inside and outside the legislature are in position to express their points of view. Devolution of full committee power to independent subcommittees has permitted more legislators, with secure power positions, to influence at least some portion of the congressional agenda. The new activists, intelligent, well-informed, and independent-minded, speak forcefully for their own views as well as for those of constituents important to them. In addition, the contemporary Congress is increasingly—potentially if not in practice—accountable. Concerned citizens can discover, if they so choose, much of what Congress does and, through sunshine statutes, much about the financial stakes lawmakers have in what they do. In these ways Congress is surely more democratic than it was in the recent past.

Responsiveness implies permeability; more openness and participation allow more interests access to Congress. This, in turn, suggests a diminution in responsibility, a decline in efficient production of policy. Despite more firepower in their arsenals—new powers for the Speaker and House Democratic Caucus, new rules to speed action—the political parties, as chief mechanisms for centralizing legislative operations, seem less capable of fostering coherent and workable programs. It is harder in the 1980s for Congress to face up to, much less resolve, the plethora of foreign and domestic "crises" that confront the country. Responsiveness and accountability expose the assembly to multiple pressures and make it accessible to many points of view. Permeability undercuts decisiveness, however; decentralization and fragmentation induce caution (some say cowardice). It often appears more profitable for members to avoid controversy, to minimize the political risks inherent in addressing complicated and emotional issues, than to confront and make hard policy choices. Constituency service, oversight, and other forms of nonpolicy representation afford electoral protection; policy analysis and innovation remain dangerous.

Needless to say, observers view this more democratic (more responsive and accountable), less efficient (less responsible) Congress differently. While the reform spirit has ebbed since the late 1970s, many remain dissatisfied with the Congress they see, and they continue to propose reforms. The recommendations they offer depend on their political perspectives and on which values—responsibility, responsiveness, accountability, or some combination of these criteria—motivate them.

The important lesson is that reforms designed to promote one value may have costs in terms of another. Reform evolves incrementally in response to political pressures and reformers' pragmatic motives. Piecemeal changes adopted over a number of years without benefit of a master plan do not always mesh well with one another. The record of reform is a record of anticipated and unanticipated results. Desirable outcomes may give way to detrimental ones as political circumstances evolve.

A recalcitrant Congress that can thwart a liberal president's social or foreign policy initiatives may look considerably more attractive when it blocks a conservative chief executive's efforts to decimate programs already on the books. A centralized budget process that allows the legislature to spend tax revenues for liberal purposes—over a conservative administration's opposition—may seem a good deal less defensible if it permits a conservative president to cut the budget drastically. In short, political perspectives color assessments of reform.

This chapter assesses the future Congress from the executive force and congressional supremacy perspectives presented in Chapter 1 and introduces a new vision, *majoritarian democracy*. It also attempts to evaluate the effects of recent proposals—such as the item veto and changes in the terms of service and timing of House and Senate elections—on legislative performance.

A Responsible Congress

Both the executive force and congressional supremacy models of Congress propose to increase legislative responsibility. The two variants of the former—the propresident and the responsible parties visions— seek to subordinate Congress to executive leadership. They advocate a centralized assembly that will promptly process the president's policy proposals. One version of the congressional supremacy view also prefers a hierarchical Congress able to act with dispatch. Reformers of this school, particularly the "Whigs," envision using a centralized legislative process to promote legislative priorities rather than to push through executive programs. (By contrast, the literary school favors a responsive rather than a responsible Congress.) Each proexecutive model attributes the legislature's inefficiency in formulating public policy to the fragmentation of power in Congress. Each proposes reforms intended to permit Congress to act promptly and effectively. These reforms, however, would reduce the assembly's political responsiveness.

The propresident point of view, which (in the pre-Reagan period) liberals most often espoused, suggests that the emergence of the president as chief policy maker and administrator is both inevitable and desirable. The separation of powers serves to restrict the executive; Congress can and often does block valuable presidential initiatives, particularly when government is divided, with one party controlling the White House while the other has a majority in one or both houses of Congress.[1] Congressional reform since the 1970s has exacerbated the president's leadership problems. To form winning coalitions in support of the administration's policies, the president must court numerous power holders in Congress, rather than, as in the prereform period, only a few senior solons. In general, the propresident reformers would reduce the separation between the branches by increasing the executive's capacity to move its ideas through the legislature expeditiously.[2]

Congress in the propresident model would devote its energies to nonpolicy activities: conducting oversight of the executive branch to ensure that agencies conducted their affairs honestly and in keeping with policy goals, and providing services to provide citizens with better contact with government. Thus, legislative attention would be confined to supervising the bureaucracy and serving the citizenry. Congress, in effect, would concede lawmaking to the president, occasionally modifying executive proposals but usually only legitimizing them—stamping them with the congressional imprimatur. In principle, Congress would be subordinate at all times to the president, regardless of whether a conservative or a liberal sat in the Oval Office. Efficient policy making, not particular programs, constitutes the goal of the proexecutive reformers. In its "pure" form, this perspective stresses efficient production of legislation; in reality, those who favor executive power probably prefer particular programs—those that sympathetic presidents propose. In both cases responsibility is central for the executive force proponents.

Frequently, this executive-dominance notion goes hand in hand with the idea of the responsible two-party system. This scheme would centralize the policy-making process through the agency of the disciplined political party.[3] The British Parliament provides a model of the sort of institutional arrangements that these reformers envision; they would incorporate into the legislative process some elements of the English system.[4] As leader, the president, like the prime minister, would have the unchallenged ability to win legislative approval for favored programs. Support from Congress would be virtually assured because the legislators, given their dependence on powerful political parties, could oppose the executive only at the risk of terminating their political careers. Popular accountability, not an independent legislature, is the control mechanism; the electorate would punish poor performance by voting the party in power out of office. According to the responsible party view, Congress would relinquish its lawmaking authority, concentrating instead on nonpolicy activites and becoming a part of the party "team."

Strengthening the presidency, whether or not within an invigorated party system, would entail altering both the internal operations of Congress and the system of electing legislators. With regard to congressional procedures, the propresident position advocates a number of reforms, all intended to reduce the ability of various minorities to block the president's program. Many of these changes would seek to use the legislative party caucus to centralize congressional activity. Most important, perhaps, these reforms would attempt to curb the independence and autonomy of congressional committees. In theory, propresident reformers approve of the 1971-77 steps to reduce the powers of the panel chairpersons, enabling a majority of committee members to control the chairs' behavior.[5] If the president under these circumstances can command a committee majority, he can move his proposals through committee. A more basic way to gain control of the committees would be to ensure that the chairpersons were party loyalists. The demise of the seniority rule makes it possible for party majorities to select as committee leaders cooperative colleagues, using party loyalty as a central criterion. The record to date, however, suggests that personal power and policy, not party standards, have come into play on the few occasions when seniority has not proven decisive in selecting committee and subcommittee leaders.[6]

Both modes of curtailing committee autonomy—replacing the seniority rule with an elective process and reducing the powers and independence of committee leaders—correspondingly elevate the legislative parties to more prominent positions. Executive-dominance reformers applaud such changes. Party leaders, they insist, should assume the role of presidential representatives on Capitol Hill rather than act as legislative emissaries to the White House, the current practice. The leaders of the president's party should commit themselves and their resources to advancing his program.

Party agencies, say these reformers, should pursue the same end. The caucus should be able to exercise power on behalf of the majority of its partisans. For example, it should control committee assignments, rewarding the faithful and punishing the disloyal. Reform has made this possibility a reality. House Democracts deprived Phil Gramm (Texas) of his seat on the Budget Committee after he cooperated with the Reagan administration's 1981 budget blitz by sponsoring the Republican alternative adopted in lieu of the Democratic plan. After his ouster, Gramm resigned from the party, ran for reelection as a Republican, and won easily. In general, however, using committee assignments as a lever to enforce party discipline remains the exception, not the rule.

Policy committees, from the propresident perspective, should set forth party positions, subject to review and ratification by the full party membership, and at the operating level, they should be empowered to schedule party-sponsored bills for prompt floor consideration. Some propose, in addition, to permit the party caucus to bind members to vote for party legislation, at least on a few major bills each year. In the House, as noted, the Speaker's new powers do afford some control over scheduling, authority Senate floor leaders have long enjoyed. But in reality the parties remain unable to compel their members' votes when party legislation is considered on the floor. In principle, such changes— if linked to responsible parties able to punish dissenters through control of the nominating process—would create powerful parties able to steer executive programs through the legislature.

The reformers seeking to smooth the congressional path of executive policies would change the rules of procedure as well. Here, too, the goal would be to reduce the ability of minorities, entrenched at particular veto points within a decentralized system, to block administration programs.[7] In the House the chief focus of reform has been the Rules Committee. The Speaker's ability to nominate members to that panel, noted previously, has converted Rules into a more reliable ally of the party leadership, lowering substantially one obstacle to moving party programs forward.[8] Another proposal, applicable to all committees, would alter the discharge rule. The number of legislators' signatures required to extract a bill from an unwilling committee would be reduced from the present 218, a majority of the full chamber, to some more readily attainable number, such as 150. Members' desire for committee independence, however, makes adoption of the reform remote. If enacted, such procedures would limit the ability of committees or subcommittees to block passage favored by a majority, including a presidential majority, in the full chamber.

Senate reformers' main target has been unlimited debate, and they have made some gains. Sixty senators can terminate a filibuster, and time limits preclude an extended postcloture filibuster by amendment. But it remains difficult to cut off debate; in 1985, to cite one instance, proponents of an experiment giving the president an item veto mustered 57 or 58 votes for cloture on three occasions, but failed to force a vote on the issue. Reformers continue to favor rules that permit a simple majority of those present and voting to end filibusters as well as to enact legislation. Other suggestions to control debate include eliminating various delaying tactics and distracting procedures;[9] limiting the amount of time any senator can hold the floor; requiring that debate be germane to the issue at hand; and reducing the number of opportunities to mount a filibuster on any bill.[10] Each of these proposed changes could curtail a minority's ability to tie up the Senate as a strategy to defeat specific bills.

A potential presidential weapon is often discussed in this context: the *item veto*. At present, the chief executive must accept or reject a bill in toto; an item veto would enable him to block enactment, subject to a congressional override, of single provisions without having to reject the entire bill. The item veto would eliminate one popular legislative strategy for asserting congressional policy-making initiatives: the inclusion of a few items opposed by the chief executive in legislation containing major programs he favors. Lawmakers assume the president will accept a few undesirable provisions rather than risk losing a matter of central concern.[11] Executive impoundment was used, especially by the Nixon administration, as a partial and probably unconstitutional substitute for the item veto. The Congressional Budget and Impoundment Control Act of 1974 enables Congress to limit drastically the executive's ability to impound funds without congressional concurrence. Other presidents have signed bills containing objectionable provisions and announced their intention to ignore such clauses; the validity of this practice, a sort of "informal" item veto, has yet to be tested in the courts. Enactment of the veto by statute or constitutional amendment would surely strengthen the president's hand vis-à-vis the Congress.[12]

In addition, propresident advocates favor electoral reforms to restrain the voting independence of members of Congress. They favor reforms requiring members to back party-endorsed (most often, presidential) policy proposals. The election process, they argue, should provide the president with political support sufficient to pass his agenda, at least if he has a legislative majority. To this end these reformers continue to suggest lengthening lawmakers' terms of office to four years in the House and eight in the Senate. Thus, all members of Congress would be selected simultaneously with the president. Presumably, they would sense their obligation to him, attributing their victories at the polls more to his efforts than to their own. Another possibility is to schedule presidential elections shortly before congressional contests so that voters would know who would be in the White House before casting their congressional ballots; this might encourage some to give the executive a legislative majority. Still another suggestion is to require all states to provide the electorate with an option to vote a straight party ticket; this might reduce the ticket-splitting that seems to contribute to divided government.

These electoral reforms might encourage loyalty to the White House, but they would not compel it; there is no certainty that such changes would reduce the propensity for elections to produce a president of one party and a Congress wholly or in part controlled by the opposition. Thus, the responsible party reformers desire to guarantee party government and, in consequence, presidential government. They would have new, centralized national party committees control the fate of the party's congressional candidates. Public funding of campaigns—tax dollars channeled to nominees through the parties—would reduce dependence on individual or political action committee (PAC) contributors and eliminate one pressure to reject presidential leadership. The parties would manage a national campaign on national issues. If the ultimate power to control congressional nominations—to exact loyalty pledges in advance and to deprive recalcitrant legislators of their seats—rested with the president and his national committee, then he, like the British prime minister, could count on the support of a reliable legislative majority.

Finally, the executive-dominance view advances some ideas that might break down the "we versus them" mentality so characteristic of divided government. One recommendation entails amending the Constitution to allow members of Congress to take cabinet jobs without giving up their seats in the legislature. More fundamental would be an amendment permitting the government to "fall," as in European parliamentary arrangements, if deadlock developed or if Congress found the president to be weak, ineffective, or incompetent (but not necessarily impeachable). New elections would follow the fall of the government. Finally, some propose altered party rules that would permit all congressional candidates, incumbents and challengers, and holdover senators to sit as delegates at their party's presidential nominating convention.[13] Each of these steps would encourage cooperation rather than conflict between the executive and legislative branches. Programmatic action, in consequence, might be more likely.

All these suggestions, whether adopted wholly or in part, singly or in combination, would alter the position of Congress in the national political process. Fragmentation of power would be diminished, centralization increased, committee independence restricted, the parties strengthened, and the rules altered to permit executive leadership to carry the day. In the responsible party vision, the executive would dominate the national party and, through it, the legislature. By controlling campaign finance, the parties would control congressional nominations and the legislative careers of the winners. The presidential candidate of each party would run on a clearly defined party platform, and the voters would select the program that best suited them. The victor would have a dependable legislative majority; the centralized, party-managed Congress would do the president's bidding.

This can be described as a responsibility-accountability scenario: responsible because effective solutions to pressing problems could be efficiently and promptly produced, accountable because voters could replace the governing party with an opposition that had persuaded the electorate that it could do more and do it better.[14] Responsiveness would be the price. Subordinate to executive-dominated, disciplined political parties, Congress would be unable to respond to citizen and group sentiments or translate them into policy. Their appeals would have to focus on the president. While he would have to calculate what public reaction to his initiatives might do to his party's fortunes, he would have broad authority to chart the country's course for four years (or six, if the occasionally discussed proposal for a single, six-year presidential term finds a receptive audience).

A second, less widely discussed vision that focuses, to some extent at least, on responsibility reflects the congressional supremacy perspective. This "Whig" view is, in a sense, the mirror image of the executive-dominance orientation. Congress would be the dominant force in national politics. The president, by contrast, would have considerably less initiative and would commit himself more to execution of congressionally determined policies than to advancing his own agenda.[15]

Realization of this congressional-dominance vision would require many reforms. One would be to centralize legislative operation in ways not unlike those that the proexecutive proponents propose. The power relations with the White House, however, would be reversed so that Congress would call the shots rather than respond to presidential leadership. James Burnham even proposes to dismantle the federal apparatus and turn most of its present duties over to the state and local governments.[16] Most observers, however, discount the congressional-dominance vision as unrealistic. The president—building on his commander-in-chief power, his public image as *the* responsible political decision maker, and considerable precedent—has become too strong for serious challenge. The national government has become too large, and too many citizens are too dependent on it, to be stripped of all its authority and responsibility. "New federalism" proposals during the Nixon, Ford, and Reagan administrations have won only modest support, even from the governors and mayors who would receive new powers, if not money, under these schemes to reallocate authority from Washington to states and localities.

Few critics of the executive-dominance view have gone so far as to suggest that legislative supremacy is desirable or even workable. Even members of Congress, understandably unsympathetic to subordinating the legislature to any branch, do not seek to master the executive. Rather, those who favor a resurgent Congress have sought, and with some success, to redress the balance, to stem the historical flow of authority to the president. They have reasserted the need for congressional perspectives to be heard and to prevail when the nation supports them sufficiently. In short, the mainstream critics of executive force envision governmental decision making that is responsive to the sorts of interests only Congress is capable of representing adequately.

A Responsive Congress

The prolegislative reformers (most often conservatives in the pre-Reagan period and liberals after 1980) do not seek to subordinate the executive, but they do value both responsiveness and congressional power. Their intent is to make legislative participation in policy formation meaningful and to allow Congress to assert its own priorities, even over executive opposition, without resort to excessive centralization. Their ideas, including many of those implemented in the 1970s, lead to even more diffusion of authority and to intensified bargaining as the chief means of congressional conflict resolution.[17]

Proponents of legislative responsiveness and power have resisted efforts to reduce committee autonomy, to impose centralization by strengthening the political parties, or to foster both objectives through changes in the rules. Thus, they opposed altering the seniority system and the basic powers of committee leaders. Conceivably, election of committee chairpersons without regard to length of committee service could permit a disciplined majority to capture control of the panels. But such a result is unlikely unless selection of the chair is linked to centralization of legislative authority.[18] The record since modification of the seniority custom seems to suggest a further diffusion of power; party majorities have, and may use, the ability to replace or control autocratic chairpersons, and thus to promote responsiveness.

Recent changes in the committee assignment process have spread rather than concentrated influence in Congress. Extension of the "Johnson Rule" to the House and to subcommittees has guaranteed each member a major committee post before any colleague can receive a second prestige slot. House reforms of 1973 and 1975, especially those that promote subcommittee independence, go far to provide every member with an opportunity to influence important legislative business. Today members' personal preferences, rather than seniority or party loyalty, serve as the main criterion for committee assignments.[19] Although the job of assigning House Democrats to committees was transferred in 1975 from Ways and Means to the Steering and Policy Committee, party leaders have infrequently intervened in the assignment process.[20] In short, committee assignment practices seem to contribute to diffusion of legislative authority, and thus to make Congress a more responsive institution.

The pro-Congress reformers see ways to strengthen the committees, both in general and in relation to the executive, without impairing their autonomy. Many observers, including members of Congress, have decried the confusion and overlapping of committee jurisdictions. Efforts to realign committee jurisdictions, except for the modest 1977 Senate reforms, have accomplished little; too many members have vested interests in existing arrangements. The problem is compounded by the 1975 rule permitting the Speaker of the House to refer legislation to more than one committee. It is not unusual for two, three, or more panels to have jurisdiction over parts of particular pieces of legislation. While such a situation may enhance responsiveness in one sense—it permits more points of view to be heard—it also impedes congressional policy-making. Failure to enact sound programs may lead citizens, interest groups, and even members themselves to look to executive-supremacy as the only way to overcome policy inertia. Moreover, committee workloads are unevenly distributed; some panels have many major responsibilities while others have far less onerous burdens. Clarified and redrawn committee jurisdictions might help Congress capitalize on its members' energies and expertise. Realigned committees and subcommittees, especially if well staffed and supplied with information, might prove capable of initiating effective public policies.

Whether or not the system is restructured, congressional committees could benefit from improved procedures. More open, less carefully stage-managed hearings, increased opportunity for deliberation, and fewer constraints on the participation of rank-and-file and minority members should permit additional points of view to be aired. Improved hearings and extended consideration might produce more useful reports, which, if circulated to the full chamber well in advance of floor consideration, might help to raise the quality of debate. Some steps in these directions have been taken, but more could be done; wider participation and fuller discussion could make Congress more responsive and more effective in opposing the executive.

Along with the congressional supremacists' faith in open, autonomous committees goes a distrust of centralized political parties. Strengthened party caucuses or policy committees would reduce the chance for interests out of favor with party leaders to be heard; strong parties might run roughshod over minorities that deserve to have a say. Accordingly, the political parties in Congress should remain loose confederations that do little more than facilitate legislative organization. The Democratic Steering Committee in the Senate and the Democratic Steering and Policy Committee in the House—both of which assign Democrats to committees—could give the party leaders additional control. If these party panels responded regularly to leadership intervention in the assignment process—the party leader chairs each committee—centralization might follow.[21] If, on the other hand, larger bodies represent more points of view, without leadership domination, they could enhance responsiveness.

The pro-Congress forces seem as satisfied with the general procedural and structural organization of the legislature as they are with autonomous committees and weak political parties. To be sure, they would prefer longer and fuller debate in the House and greater opportunity to propose amendments without restriction; such reforms would permit a wider range of views to find expression. But they have resisted reforms that might alter the fundamental character of Congress. They opposed changes in the power of the House Rules Committee and in the Senate's rule of unlimited debate that might mute minority voices or minimize minority power. Decentralized authority, they believe, makes Congress more responsive.

Without making fundamental changes in legislative organization or procedure, the congressional supremacists seek to reassert legislative prerogatives in the face of what they see as a dramatic shift toward presidential domination of the policy-making process. Thus, they supported the passage of the War Powers Resolution and budget reform bills. Their expectations, however, have not been satisfied, The War Powers Resolution, as noted, has not had a clear restraining influence on presidential performance. The budget process, especially during Reagan's first term, worked to executive advantage, permitting the president to impose his fiscal priorities on Congress. During his second term the legislature had its financial way more readily, and this trend may continue if the process does not collapse altogether.

Reforms providing lawmakers with better staff resources, more information, and heightened analytic capacity were welcomed by pro-Congress proponents. In principle, these developments should improve congressional responsiveness. Increased staff can generate and analyze new data; lawmakers can secure careful research support based on reliable information. With its own independent staff the minority party can state its differences with the majority more clearly and persuasively. Beyond this, all members of the House might profitably use legislative assistants with specific policy responsibilities, comparable to those provided senators. In theory, more aid, data, and analysis should improve both the lawmakers' capacity and their ability to challenge executive branch specialists.

Yet enlarged staffs, however attractive they seem in the abstract, may not have strengthened the legislature's hand vis-à-vis the executive. Indeed, some skeptics believe that the larger personal and committee staffs have created new burdens rather than alleviated old ones. More employees highlight new areas for attention and, as a result, impose new demands on the already overcommitted time and energy of legislators. Moreover, large staffs risk converting the lawmaker into an office manager, to the detriment of policymaking and other tasks. Without proper supervision, staffers, especially investigators, may be tempted, for personal or ideological reasons, to engage in unrestrained partisanship and to neglect data gathering and idea generating.[22]

To the extent that greater staff support improves the quantity and quality of information that members of Congress actually use, it improves responsiveness. Insufficient and unreliable data, by contrast, make it difficult for legislators to oppose executive branch experts: poorly informed representatives may feel obliged to defer to bureaucratic specialists presumed to "know better." *Executive privilege*—a doctrine justifying the president's ability, in the "national interest," to withhold information from Congress (and the public)—and national defense requirements limit the data available to the assembly.[23] Interbranch competition and suspicion lead administrative branch personnel to withhold information. Moreover, the executive branch is often able to orchestrate events in a way that minimizes legislators' opportunity to advance alternative proposals. Administration sources brief the media in "off the record" or "not for attribution" sessions, releasing only selective information that they then interpret to suit their own purposes. In addition, news, appropriately structured, can be leaked to the news media.

Beyond these impediments to full disclosure imposed by the executive, Congress contributes to its own information deficit. A decentralized institution with numerous centers of independent power, each with lines to different information sources, leads to fragmented, uncoordinated data; information collected in one place for one set of purposes is often inaccessible to other legislators in other areas with other purposes in mind. The computer revolution has alleviated the problem to some degree; office consoles give members access to centralized data banks. But individual lawmakers still must make many decisions on complex and controversial issues with minimal information.[24]

To remedy this defect in congressional decision making, two types of reform have been recommended: one limiting executive privilege, the other expanding members' use of computerized storage and retrieval systems. Legislation has been proposed from time to time that would 1) require executive personnel to appear before legislative committees, if only to claim executive privilege; 2) require a formal, written statement by the president to invoke the privilege; and 3) enforce the request for information by mandating an automatic cutoff of funds for a noncomplying agency. If enacted, such a bill would force the executive to justify withholding information from Congress. Another means of tackling the information deficit would be to increase opportunities for members to learn; for example, more funds and time for foreign travel and reading, more on-site visits to federal installations. Other proposals include extended use of outside consultants or congressional task forces comparable to those that the president uses and the establishment of a "congressional institute of scholars" or some similar university-type organization.[25] Coupled with the growth of the General Accounting Office and the Congressional Research Service and the creation of the Congressional Budget Office and the Office of Technology Assessment, these steps should improve Congress's information resources.

Far more basic, and probably more promising in the long run, are proposals to improve computer access. While great strides have been made,[26] still more progress is possible. Desk-top terminals linked to central computers would permit lawmakers to retrieve information of interest to them. Legislators could choose what *they* want to know. Their freedom to specialize, to follow their own inclinations, would be enhanced and the risk of being overwhelmed by information of no use to them would be reduced. The information system would become the lawmakers' servant, not their master.

The often arduous task of discovering the existence, content, and location of bills of interest can be vastly simplified by improved computer facilities. The computer stores a legislative history; at any time lawmakers can get an up-to-date status report on any measure. By working out their own position before they have to vote, they can reduce their dependence on word-of-mouth assurances from experts, party colleagues, or House leaders, and avoid being caught off guard. Computers can help each legislator be in a far better position to interject personal views into congressional deliberations. Computerized information systems can also provide data on lobbyists (who they are, whom they represent, what legislation they support); on executive branch actions; on studies by congressional support agencies or various committee staffs; or on the content of present law. The ready information from these and other sources should enable members of Congress to make choices based on considerably more data than have traditionally entered their calculations.

In all these ways Congress can be strengthened relative to the executive. The War Powers Resolution positioned the legislature to assert some control over military commitments. The budget act did the same with respect to fiscal matters. In the long run, creation of new resources—expert staffs, better information, and a commitment to use them effectively—may prove more fundamental in permitting Congress to have its way, even in the face of stiff executive opposition. Increased legislative power, reflecting views that differ from those of the president, would obviously contribute to more responsive policy making.[27]

The legislative supremacists also have strong ideas about electoral politics. They stand firm against partisan redistricting and any effort to impose national, disciplined political parties. Indeed, the very "localism" deplored by believers in executive dominance—that greater concern for constituency views than national interests—is a positive virtue for those who back legislative power. Redistricting, even to reflect simple population equality, and party pressure to subscribe to a national party platform, would limit the representation of diverse interests, especially those geographically dispersed or otherwise incapable of representation on the basis of population alone.[28] Thus, an election system resembling the present one, in which candidates remain free to build their own organizations, raise their own funds, stake out their own issue positions, and appeal to whatever groups they deem appropriate, is highly desirable, according to legislative-dominance proponents.

Such arrangements allow the widest possible array of viewpoints to find expression in Congress. In short, they enlarge congressional responsiveness.

Pro-Congress reformers envision a decentralized, representative legislature capable of making its public policy choices stick against executive opposition. As a responsive institution, a resurgent Congress should be able to listen to a diversity of interests and blend the sentiments of numerous power holders into legislative programs that can compete on equal terms with executive proposals. Such competition, the interplay of roughly equal branches of government, should enhance the responsiveness of the entire policy process.

The more Congress is capable of frustrating the president, however, the greater the possibility of deadlock. The greater the need to reach agreements through bargaining, whether within the legislature or between Congress and the Executive, the less likely it is that policy will be bold or imaginative. Moreover, the greater the number of interests that any policy settlement must accommodate, the slower the decision will be in coming. Thus, a fully responsive legislature, open to all points of view and marked by multiple channels of communication, might produce policy of the "too little, too late" variety. It might find itself overtaken by events and outstripped by history. The price of responsiveness may be less responsibility.

An Accountable Congress

Regardless of whether executive or legislative supremacy seems preferable, accountability remains desirable; it serves to complement either responsibility or responsiveness. As noted earlier, accountability sustains responsibility in a straightforward fashion. The electorate chooses between two political parties and in so doing gives the winner both a mandate to govern and the majority to do so. In subsequent elections the voters decide, based on their assessment of the incumbent's performance, whether to renew that mandate or to place a new party in office. Retrospective evaluation by the electorate constitutes the chief check on the administration's behavior; unless the citizenry is prepared to hold its rulers accountable, the government's power would remain unlimited and unchecked.

For those who chiefly value a responsive Congress, accountability seems both more difficult and perhaps less critical. A decentralized system is certainly harder for voters to fathom. When things go badly, when fateful decisions emerge from elaborate bargaining among multiple participants at numerous stages of a complex process, it is difficult to know whom to blame. The voters must pay far more attention to pin down who did what. At the same time, however, the open channels of communication in a responsive Congress provide alternatives to accountability. Citizens can do more than judge ex post facto; they can, if they choose, use whatever access is available to them as individuals or group members to present their views in advance. Thus, accountability is another way by which the electorate can set national directions. Accountability provides a device by which the ruled can manage those whom they select to rule them.

A first condition for accountability is that citizens be aware of their representatives' records. Several steps seem likely to generate more information about Congress, although not all of them are within the power of the legislature to take. For one thing, the mass media can be encouraged to provide additional coverage. Admittedly, it is difficult to endow a 535-member, two-chamber institution with the aura and glamour of a single chief executive. Nevertheless television and the press could do a better job. They could give the kind of coverage usually reserved for dramatic events—for instance, the Senate Watergate hearings or the House Judiciary Committee's proceedings in the Nixon impeachment case—to important issues like national health insurance, social security reform, missile procurement, abortion and prayer, and the budget. As matters now stand, only the few events deemed newsworthy by the media receive extended treatment, and then only in the national press.[29]

Congress cannot compel media attention, but its "sunshine" reforms have simplified the media's task by exposing more of its activities to press investigation. Open hearings and committee meetings, recorded votes, and full disclosure of campaign and personal financial practices should help the citizenry discover where members of Congress stand with regard to public policy and perhaps why their actions were (or were not) taken.

Second, accountability requires informed, interested citizens capable of matching their own views with those of their representatives and judging them accordingly. Little direct reform is possible, but some current trends seem promising. Polls show that the better educated tend to be more knowledgeable about and interested in political affairs. As education levels rise across the nation, more citizens should hold Congress accountable. With better media coverage of the less secretive Congress, these voters could evaluate the legislature more carefully and more knowledgeably. At the very least, the extended coverage of the House on the C-SPAN cable television network will let interested people—a growing number if viewing statistics are accurate—watch one chamber in action. Coverage could easily be extended to the Senate, if the senators could be persuaded to let cameras in, and in 1986, the chamber seems prepared to do so, at least on an experimental basis.

Providing clear choices among candidates within single states or districts—the third prerequisite for effective accountability—is more problematic. Little can be done to guarantee that voters can select from ideologically distinct nominees. Under a responsible order, such a guarantee would be unnecessary. The individual candidates would be indebted to centralized parties, and the voter would merely have to evaluate the desirability of retaining the incumbent party. But under current electoral practices, which emphasize responsiveness more than responsibility, the parties remain decentralized. Whether the challenger is ideologically distinct from the incumbent depends on the uncertain operation of nominating politics in any given constituency.

Accountability, in short, will not be easily improved. As noted in Chapter 4, the reformers' goals have not been fully realized: the public has not, despite the increased potential to do so, become better informed about Congress. And reformers can do little to improve media attention to Congress or to increase citizens' interest in legislative politics. Congress has done what it can by making sure that those who wish to inform themselves are not thwarted by unnecessary secrecy in the legislative branch.[30] Greater numbers of interested citizens attuned to a more visible Congress give rise to the hope for greater accountability.

More accountability, however, is not without costs. Openness implies permeability, which in turn may inhibit both responsibility and responsiveness. The need to deliberate and decide in public, in the glare of the media spotlight, may deter decisive decision making. Political fears of antagonizing voters or supportive interest groups may breed congressional caution. Rather than jeopardizing their reelection prospects, career-oriented members may evade hard choices, deferring to the president or delegating to the bureaucracy. Responsibility would surely decline under these circumstances. Conversely, accessibility to outside forces may undercut responsiveness. To the degree that senators and representatives worry about charges of unethical dealings with special interests they may limit the access and influence of those interests. Here, too, efforts to maximize one value may interfere with realizing other values.

Majoritarian Democracy in Congress _____

The executive force and congressional supremacy visions of Congress are, in a sense, illusory. The proposals they entail are intended to

137

move Congress toward greater responsibility, responsiveness, and accountability, but they do not represent full-blown, widely shared statements of a "better" political order. Rather, they denote tendencies— toward a more powerful executive or a revived legislature—that seem most likely to improve the political system. Within these broad visions there remains considerable controversy about the wisdom and desirability of specific reforms. Those who advocate a more powerful president or a stronger Congress do not agree on the precise steps to achieve their goals. It is unlikely that widespread agreement on any package of fundamental reforms will develop. Reform is more likely to come as it has in the past: incrementally, in response to societal change, specific crises, or electoral developments.

This section offers a more pragmatic vision of a future Congress. The majoritarian democracy model builds on the reforms of the 1970s, using the best of them to obtain a workable trade-off between responsibility and responsiveness, deliberation and decisiveness. This modest proposal may satisfy no one; it may present a policy-making process too slow to be responsible, too centralized to be responsive. While both values have their assets, they are sufficiently exclusive that a gain in one is likely to bring about a loss in the other. The intent is to gain as much as possible of each value.

Such a mix is desirable because neither the executive dominance or the congressional supremacy position is entirely tenable. Advocacy of executive force apparently grew out of a misplaced, perhaps naive faith in the inherent goodness of the president, but the events and personalities of the 1960s and 1970s tarnished this view of executive nobility. Presidential domination of the nation's Indochina policy and the Watergate revelations about Richard Nixon (ironically demonstrating a thirst for power in a chief executive publicly committed to reducing the scope of federal government authority) made clear the extent to which presidential power had grown. Few liberals approved executive supremacy used in such fashion; it appears equally doubtful that conservatives would be eager to see such strength in the hands of a liberal in the White House. Thus, no matter whose ox is gored, there seems good reason to avoid an undue concentration of authority in the executive's hands.[31]

Yet the congressional supremacy arguments are no more promising or appealing. Neither a highly centralized Congress, independent of the president and capable of responsible action, nor a largely fragmented institution, totally responsive, presents a pleasing vision. The former possibility is both unrealistic (there are simply too many subjects to be handled with dispatch) and undesirable (the same arguments that apply to a powerful presidency militate against a concentration of authority in the legislature). Discontinuing federal programs to permit easier congressional dominance of those that remain seems impractical. There are too many programs, each with its own clientele, to allow easy termination. In addition, it is by no means certain that state and local governments could or would take up responsibility devolved from the federal level. The second formulation, the open institution with minorities protected at each stage of the decision-making process, invites paralysis. In short, there is little reason to expect beneficial results from converting Congress to either an exclusively responsible or exclusively responsive legislature.

The answer, clearly, is some combination of features that advances to some degree both responsibility and responsiveness. Majoritarian democracy would wed an open, responsive, deliberative stage of legislative policy making to a more decisive, responsible, decision-making phase. The former is democratic: it seeks open avenues of participation for all. The latter is majoritarian: it endeavors to permit majorities, given sufficient time for deliberation, to prevail at the point of decision.

This vision in no way discounts the importance of popular accountability. Accountability is highly desirable, and the steps, noted in the previous section, to make it more effective should be pursued. Admittedly, not all legislative activity can or should go on in public. "Open covenants, openly arrived at" is no more universally valid in Congress than in diplomacy. Topics such as national security demand secrecy. Compromise settlements on many matters may be worked out more easily in private. What is important is that the public be in a position to discover what has been done and who supported the actions taken. To the extent that Congress operates openly and the citizenry is attentive to the legislature, accountability is enhanced, the bond between rulers and ruled is tightened, and the prospect for popular control of government is improved.

Responsiveness in the Deliberative Stage

In the early stages of lawmaking, especially during committee consideration, the policy process should be most responsive. Citizens should have ample opportunity to present their views. (Later accountability operates, and citizens can render at the polls a verdict about whether their views were heard).[32] To foster responsiveness in Congress, the prolegislative reforms are intended to democratize Congress: to get responsive individuals into the legislature and to let them speak there for the widest possible diversity of interests.

In electoral terms this means continuation of the present arrangements. Current districting practice, which reflects population equality, is satisfactory; so is "localism," with its constituency-based, individualized campaigns. On the other hand, campaign reforms that favor incumbents are undesirable. With their vast campaign advantages (observers estimate that incumbents' congressional perquisites are worth more than a half-million dollars a year) they need little additional help. Some fear that the Federal Election Campaign Act and its amendments have made it harder for challengers to compete. The legislation permitted the rise of political action committees, which tend to support incumbents. Even though the Supreme Court struck down FECA limits on how much candidates can spend on their own behalf, challengers may simply be unable to raise sufficient funds to mount effective campaigns against entrenched members. Public financing of congressional elections, which would equalize the money available to incumbent and challenger, would have the same effect. The perquisites of office would still give incumbents an advantage, which challengers could not overcome by spending larger sums. In any case, the electoral process should operate to allow as wide a latitude as possible for candidates who speak for local interests and voice diverging concerns.

Inside Congress, majoritarian democracy calls for a moderately paced deliberative stage that promotes the expression of multiple points of view. At the committee level, members should be assigned to the panels that will enable them to serve their constituencies best. The changes in Senate and House committee assignment procedures and the limitations on holding subcommittee chairs diffuse power, giving junior legislators greater opportunities to achieve positions of significance. More important, perhaps, is the goal of the 1970 reorganization act that panel majorities firmly control the conduct of committee business. Under such conditions there would be less concern about the mode of selecting chairpersons. It is not seniority that has been at the root of most complaints, but rather the fact that the system automatically elevates the most senior majority member to a very powerful position. Now that the committee leaders are on notice that they may be removed for cause, requiring them to be sensitive to the rank-and-file members of the committee, the problem may be less acute. The real virtue of seniority—the automatic, impersonal, noncompetitive character of the choice of chairmen—is preserved when the committee leaders and their committee colleagues are more equal in power.

Such democratically governed legislative committees should be able to consider more fully the available options to each bill, especially given the greater information and research resources that Congress now possesses. Extra staff, but not so many that the members become office managers rather than policy makers, seem likely to help; enlarged minority staff should certainly help to air additional points of view. So, too, should the creation and use of computerized information systems that permit legislators to develop, promote, and sustain their own policy proposals. Finally, responsiveness might be better served if committees with clear jurisdictions scheduled open hearings well in advance, gave witnesses ample notice, and, perhaps most importantly, invited, encouraged, and perhaps subsidized the less well-organized interests to appear.

In short, majoritarian democracy envisions the survival of a fragmented Congress, featuring independent, specialized committees and subcommittees as the basis for the division of labor. The suggested reforms are designed to make sure that the widest possible range of opinion finds its way into legislative deliberations. Norms acknowledging specialization of, and reciprocity among, committees should continue to be observed. Likewise, political parties should retain their roles as nonideological facilitators of election and legislative organization. Under these conditions legislative committees—composed of expert lawmakers, adequately staffed, and open to the views of all interested parties—should generate responsible policy proposals.

Responsibility: Facilitating Policy Making

However responsible the process by which legislation is formulated, such bills must have a chance not only to pass Congress but also to survive executive branch opposition. Otherwise, of course, the legislative process is an exercise in futility. Unless the national legislature can act, and act in ways that resolve problems, it is not likely to serve as an effective counterweight to executive authority. Majoritarian democracy requires a decisive decision-making phase in which the legislature can approve or reject bills that address the nation's problems. Two needed reforms stand out: measures to help majorities to act and statutory restraints on presidential power.

With respect to the first requirement, reform should permit Congress to deal expeditiously with committee proposals, the product of the responsive deliberative phase. This requires removal of several procedural devices that protect minorities and slow down or block congressional action. The main focus here is on changing the rules to facilitate majoritarian action. Several reforms would help guarantee prompt dispatch of committee recommendations in the House. Extended panel consideration of proposals, often intended to bury the legislation permanently, could be prevented by a more usable discharge rule. After allowing sufficient time for full study and deliberation, say 90 or 120 days, a discharge petition bearing 150 signatures would enable bills to move to the floor for a vote.[33]

Although the Rules Committee has been tamed—it is largely under control of the party leadership—it remains capable of blocking legislation that a majority favors. The committee, in theory at least, might hold up, or impose unfavorable conditions on, a bill that the Speaker opposes but that an authorizing committee, or a bipartisan majority on the floor, wishes to see passed. To remedy this possibility, adoption of a variant of the 21-day-rule, twice enacted and then later rejected, would guarantee the full chamber the chance to act on reported legislation. If Rules imposes a three-week delay in getting the bill to the floor, the chair of the committee reporting the legislation could move to force Rules to act, and if supported by a majority of the full House, could in effect discharge that panel. Such a step would obviate the need to rely on party leaders to move legislation. Other minor changes aimed at eliminating the use of delaying tactics—excessive quorum calls or requiring the reading of the *Journal* in full—could make marginal improvements in the House's ability, already superior to that of the Senate, to deal decisively with pending bills.

As noted, the major target for reform in the Senate has been the filibuster. The new cloture rule—especially if coupled with changes eliminating the "morning hour," making debate germane and focused, and limiting the number of opportunities to filibuster—should move floor proceedings more quickly toward a decision point. Curbs on *holds*, the informal practice that permits a single senator to block consideration of legislation or executive nominations for extended periods, would also speed Senate action. So would rules that allow measures supported by majorities to reach the floor, even in the face of leadership opposition. Although it is not clear that they often use this tactic, Senate leaders can manipulate the chamber's schedule to thwart a majority of members. Although subject to possible abuse—easier access to the floor might clutter the agenda and prevent action—these changes could increase the likelihood that determined majorities carry the day on behalf of the bills they favor.[34]

Of course, these bills would have to be approved by the president, who could still veto measures and prevail unless Congress mustered a two-thirds majority in each house to override the veto. Some reforms already enacted may eventually enhance Congress's competitive position. Despite all the uncertainties and problems with the revised budget process, Congress can, if it is determined, use it to assert its own fiscal priorities. The imposition by Congress of a spending ceiling in line with anticipated revenue, and allocation of that sum to various budgetary categories, could make legislative budget decisions serious competitors with those the executive proposes. In addition, the Congress might reconsider a proposal by David R. Obey (D-Wis.) of an "omnibus budget" that would merge all authorizations, appropriations, and revenue measures in a single bill. The plan would speed up the process and give the budget the force of law; it would centralize budget making and, if used independently of the executive, might increase the efficiency of financial decision making by the legislature.[35] Putting budgeting on a two-year cycle, as some have proposed, might serve the same purposes. Finally, the anti-impoundment features of the 1974 budget act, requiring the president to release funds unless the legislature agrees to his action, have enabled congressional fiscal priorities to prevail more often.

Legislation defining and regularizing the claim of executive privilege and requiring agencies to divulge information would reduce the information deficit under which Congress continues to operate. The War Powers Resolution has the potential, again if Congress demonstrates the determination to use or threaten to use it, to make the executive take congressional sentiments seriously in decisions about the use of military forces in "undeclared wars" or "police actions"; it can restore congressional influence in the determination of foreign policy. All these steps could redress in favor of Congress the executive-legislative imbalance of power; all could contribute to a policy process in which both branches are forces to reckon with. From Congress's perspective, renewed strength would enable the legislature to make effective and efficient policy decisions.

Needed: A New Congressional Image

Statutory and structural changes, however much they would strengthen Congress against the president, are not enough to create an effective majoritarian institution. Subtler change, more difficult to achieve, is necessary. Congress must enhance its reputation as a body committed to placing national interests above local concerns. It must become an institution whose integrity is beyond suspicion and that can rise above "politics as usual" to make contributions to the national welfare that are equal, if not superior, to those of the executive. Congress suffers in this regard, for the public seems to assess it more as an appendage than as a rival of the president. When the citizenry holds the chief executive in high esteem, it usually values the legislature as well: when the president's prestige falls, so does that of Congress.[36] Congress's public image also suffers whenever it appears to thwart presidential leadership.

Competing for public respect with the unitary executive is not easy for the plural legislature. Yet some of the reforms proposed and adopted may enhance Congress's reputation. More media attention, less internal secrecy, and greater assertiveness in policy making may help citizens realize that the legislature is an important feature of the political landscape. A major cause of their skepticism is a sense that lawmakers are not entirely ethical. Doubts about the detachment of legislators have prompted efforts to ensure that they are as free as possible from conflicts of interest and seek to promote the public good, not their own financial positions. The reputation of Congress and popular support for its views are eroded by persistent fears that legislators are still not entirely free from self-serving behavior.

Members' illegal or unethical actions over the past two decades, even after the House and Senate ethics codes were adopted in 1977, have sustained the public's concern over congressional ethics. The pressures of legislative life also keep ethics at issue. On the one hand, public expectations are high; citizens want their elected representatives to be beyond reproach. On the other hand, to put it bluntly, legislators need money. They must engage in virtually nonstop campaigning, which is costly. Some maintain residences both in their constituency and in Washington. Some are caught up in the expensive and demanding social life of the capital. In addition, the nature of the lawmaking task creates difficulties. The notion that Congress should be responsive and stay in touch with the populace requires that lawmakers listen to the requests and petitions of many groups and organizations. It is not surprising that some with policy concerns exploit their access to legislators to further their own goals; in so doing they may offer inducements that sometimes fall between corruption—graft and bribery—and legitimate campaign contributions.

In recent years criminal indictments against several legislators—in the Abscam affair, for instance—have made the headlines. Far more pervasive than these dramatic events, however, are conflict-of-interest situations where lawmakers render judgments in which they have a personal stake. How is the public to regard Congress when, to cite only one case, Sen. Russell Long of Louisiana, senior Democrat on the Finance Committee, which writes the tax laws for the oil industry, derives substantial income from oil and gas holdings? What should citizens make of the lawmakers who accept sizable sums from political action committees with major interests in programs whose contents the legislators determine? The frequent posing of such questions has led to sunshine statutes and financial disclosure laws currently on the books. Each chamber, in addition, has an ethics committee charged with policing the ethical conduct of its members. According to critics, however, neither has accomplished much; both incentive and enforcement powers have been lacking.

Some reformers proposed to do even more to promote congressional ethics. They want more stringent codes of ethics, more thoroughly enforced. Others recommend expanded conflict of interest statutes with broad self-denying ordinances and an extension of the prohibition on receiving direct payment for representing an interest in any proceeding before Congress. They would extend the prohibition to cover indirect payment in the form of bonuses and stock options as well.[37] Others go beyond this: they would raise members' base salary—perhaps even double it—to a level adequate to cover all reasonable living costs and bar entirely the receipt of outside income. These reformers find Congress's current self-policing reforms inadequate, and they are unwilling to rely exclusively on the electorate to punish transgressors. It is extremely difficult to establish when genuine conflict of interest exists; legislators may share viewpoints with constituents and act on behalf of those interests without engaging in improper conduct. In other words, the line between public and private interest is not easy to draw, and the reformers want to do more to ensure that senators and representatives avoid, or at least reveal, any stakes in the issues that they must decide.

In short, if Congress is to compete with the executive, and to make its policy determinations prevail, it must have the support of the public; it must be recognized as a nonself-serving body whose priorities are not suspect. To this end, strong and well-enforced codes of conduct, conflict of interest statutes, and disclosure laws should help convince the citizenry that the legislature has nothing to hide and thereby raise the popular esteem so necessary for an effective Congress.

A last, and perhaps most important, requisite for a Congress capable of independent policy making is the will and determination to assert its preferences. Critics often charge, and with some justice, that many lawmakers are unwilling to run the political risks of serious commitment to policy making. They prefer, so the argument runs, to concern themselves with local interests and to let the president define the legislative' workload. Congress has often been less than forceful in promoting its own initiatives. Until recently at least, Congress tolerated internal norms of reciprocity and courtesy that placed minority power and inaction above majority rule and decisiveness. Congress has stressed self-protection: it can take credit for what goes right and avoid the blame for unsuccessful policies. If the legislature is to move toward more effective policy making, it must overcome its tendency to dodge risk and defer to the executive or other experts rather than to stand and fight for its own preferences.

What is required is a Congress coequal, in more than just a theoretical sense, with the president, a legislature willing to assert its views and to accept the consequences when its actions prove unsuccessful. This necessitates more political courage; legislators must be prepared to adopt publicly a national posture on issues even when local conditions might suggest some other course of action. They must eschew a legislative culture that puts a premium on something for everyone and seeks this goal through reciprocity and logrolling; rather they must be prepared to say "no" to a colleague and, more difficult, hear "no" said to them. Members of Congress must be willing to match their best efforts against the ideas of the executive and to stand or fall on the quality of those efforts. Such a show of determination will not come easily, and there will unquestionably be electoral casualties along the way. Yet only if such an exercise of will is made can Congress hope to achieve parity with a powerful executive.

Summary

Majoritarian democracy envisions an operative system of checks and balances. More precisely, it projects a system of separate institutions, legislative and executive, sharing overlapping powers. This view assumes that the older, now seemingly naive faith in the beneficence of the president is untenable and that some executive-legislative partnership in policy making is desirable. Such cooperation, from the legislative point of view, includes three major components:

1) *A responsive deliberative phase of policy making.* Policy formulation would reflect a democratic, participatory process. A strengthened and more accessible legislature, with better staff and information resources, would sift proposals and come up with legislation designed to serve the nation's needs. Such a careful, reflective, and open deliberative stage would take time and would create intervals during which problems might intensify or opportunities for solutions might be lost. Yet such a price must be paid if politics are to be responsive, if solutions are to reflect citizens' wants, needs, and desires. Moreover, the costs can be minimized if the deliberative stage is not allowed to drag on beyond all reasonable necessity.

2) *A responsible decision-making phase of policy making.* The deliberative stage, during which committees produced legislation to be considered by the full chamber, would be followed by a decisive, action phase of decision making. At this point Congress should be organized, in majoritarian fashion, to make decisions. Easier discharge from com-

mittees; simpler access to the floor; more germane debate, especially in the Senate; elimination of delaying tactics, most particularly the Senate filibuster, could permit simple majorities to act. After due deliberation and careful formulation, bills should be judged on their merits and voted up or down without delay.

Costs are incurred at this stage as well. To move legislation with dispatch means foreclosing opportunities for minorities to stall. Minorities can and should have a full say during the deliberative stage, but at the point of action they must not be permitted to make policy by blocking decision making. At this stage the need to be responsible must override the need to represent, to be responsive. Congress must first listen carefully and then act decisively.

3) *A strengthened Congress relative to the executive.* Congressional policy making, reflecting a satisfactory mix of responsiveness and responsibility, must produce decisions that have a reasonable chance of prevailing against presidential power. Majoritarian democracy envisages a Congress with increased statutory authority, a better public reputation, and a stronger will to make legislative priorities competitive. Continued reform in these directions would go far toward demonstrating such determination on Congress's part.

Even though these proposals can be adopted incrementally, without changing the Constitution, the prospects for additional reform are uncertain. The executive will resist such changes and some in the legislature may be reluctant to yield powers they presently possess. Majoritarian democracy presents one vision of Congress and the presidency—each with its own constituency and independent power base—working together to make responsible and responsive public policy. With greater access to and information about Congress, citizens would be better prepared to hold their elected representatives accountable. If this picture is attractive, Congress can continue to build on the reforms of the 1970s and early 1980s. The essential reinvigoration of the legislature depends on such action.

Conclusion

During the 1950s and 1960s numerous critics of Congress found the institution wanting. When conditions were conducive, in the 1970-77 period particularly, they enacted a broad series of reforms designed to promote legislative responsiblity, responsiveness, and accountability. Although reformers then and now seldom advance "pure," philosophic visions of an ideal Congress, their proposals tend to reflect two contrasting and often incompatible perspectives. For the most part, those who put a premium on prompt, efficient solutions to policy problems (that is, who favor responsibility) favor a centralized Congress, a feature of the executive force and responsible parties models. They are prepared to sacrifice openness and multiple channels of communication—that is, responsiveness—for effective resolution of policy issues. They propose additional reforms to enhance the executive's policy-making position, and they are prepared to rely on citizen-enforced accountability to keep the powerful presidency in check.

On the other side are those, equally committed to reform, who value most a free and open deliberative process. As the price for responsiveness, they are ready to endure a decentralized scheme of things that the prolegislative (literary and "Whig") theories find so attractive. They view favorably a legislature, however irresponsible, that reaches decisions slowly and only after considerable negotiation and compromise. They, too, propose a variety of reforms to achieve their goals. These reforms rely less on accountability after the fact at the polls than on the ability of individual citizens or organized groups to present their views prior to policy formulation. Prolegislative reformers promote a Congress ready to restrain, even to impose its own views on, the president and executive branch.

There is, of course, no right way to choose between these alternative visions of Congress and its future, either on definitive evaluation criteria or on empirical grounds. The choice ultimately rests on normative values, on the relative weight assigned to the competing values of responsibility and responsiveness. Indeed, in the real world neither perspective has dominated the reform movement, although decentralization and fragmentation seem more powerful during the 1980s than in the previous decade. Because reforms were adopted piecemeal over a period of years—the same way that Congress makes substantive policy—there was no overall consistency in the pattern of reform; proponents of each posture won some victories and suffered some setbacks. Realistically, this is all reformers should reasonably expect, but neither side is satisfied, and each continues to advance its particular reform agenda. Others, less philosophically inclined, look for some middle ground, some optimum mix of responsibility, responsiveness, and accountability that will permit Congress and the president to play their respective parts in the policy-making process. Majoritarian democracy is one, but only one, manifestation of this search for a better legislature.

There are clear limits, however, to what reform can accomplish. One moral of the reform story is that broader societal change—events and elections—may stir the reform impulse; without such outside pressures reform may wither. A second lesson is that reforms reflect different values and motivations, and in consequence, fail to meet fully some of their proponent's goals. Reformers should not expect that short-term success will inevitably endure over the long haul. As the world around Congress changes, and the people who serve there enter and leave, reformed structures and processes may cease to produce acceptable results and may require additional adjustment. Incremental solutions, the institutional tinkering so attractive to pragmatic reformers, may help, at least temporarily, but they are likely to prove impermanent as broader change impinges on them.[38]

In the absence of any widely shared vision of what the legislature should be, reform is likely to be episodic and incremental. Congress remains fundamentally a representative institution attuned to political pressures and public preferences. When there is consensus in the country, Congress is likely to reflect it; no institutional structures or processes can keep a determined majority of members from acting. When agreement is lacking, as it often is on controversial matters, reform cannot induce action; conventional congressional politics—decision through bargaining and compromise—is likely to emerge.

Barring a major policy disaster or constitutional crisis, reform will remain problematic. Congress, for lack of a viable alternative, may well continue to "muddle through" as part of the classic pattern of American politics and policy making. The reformed Congress of the 1990s will most probably be different from the legislature of the 1980s, which is unquestionably quite distinct from that of the 1970s, but it is not clear in what particular ways. It is in this context that the quest, perhaps quixotic, for the quintessential Congress will continue.

NOTES

1. In the 40 years between 1946, when the Republicans won control of the Senate and House while Harry S Truman was president, and 1986, divided government prevailed for 22 years.
2. (Solon was an Athenian statesman of the late seventh and early sixth centuries B.C. who instituted legal reforms.) For arguments supporting a strong presidency, see Robert A. Dahl, *Congress and Foreign Policy* (New York: Harcourt, Brace & World, 1950); James M. Burns, *Congress on Trial* (New York: Harper, 1949), and *The Deadlock of Democracy* (Englewood Cliffs, N.J.: Prentice-Hall, 1963); Walter Lippmann, *The Public Philosophy* (Boston: Little, Brown, 1954); and Clinton Rossiter, *The American Presidency*, rev. ed. (New York: Harcourt, Brace & World, 1960). On the contemporary manifestation of the propresident position in the proposals of the Committee on the Constitutional System, see Dom Bonafede, "Reform of U.S. System of

Government Is on the Minds and Agendas of Many," *National Journal*, June 29, 1985, 1521-24.

3. See American Political Science Association, Committee on Political Parties, *Toward a More Responsible Two-Party System* (New York: Rinehart, 1950); E. E. Schattschneider, *Party Government* (New York: Rinehart, 1942); Austin Ranney, *The Doctrine of Responsible Party Government* (Urbana, Ill.: University of Illinois Press, 1962); David S. Broder, *The Party's Over: The Failure of Politics in America* (New York: Harper & Row, 1972); Evron M. Kirkpatrick, "Toward a More Responsible Two-Party System: Political Science, Policy Science or Pseudo-Science?" *American Political Science Review* 65 (1971): 965-90; and Gerald M. Pomper, "Toward a More Responsible Two-Party System: What Again?" *Journal of Politics* 33 (1971): 916-40.

4. In reality, British parties scarcely resemble the image of them held by the responsible parties school. See David Butler, "American Myths about British Political Parties," *Virginia Quarterly Review* 31 (1955): 45-56; and Robert T. McKenzie, *British Political Parties* (New York: Praeger, 1964).

5. The propresident reformers, of course, are less than enchanted by the devolution of full committee powers to subcommittees. This additional decentralization makes it all the more difficult to induce Congress to act; more participants must be mobilized to support presidential policy proposals.

6. See Barbara Hinckley, "Seniority 1975: Old Theories Confront New Facts," *British Journal of Political Science* 6 (1976): 383-99; and Glenn R. Parker, "The Selection of Committee Leaders in the House of Representatives," *American Politics Quarterly* 7 (1979): 71-93.

7. On minority exercise of "blocking power" in Congress, see Roberta Herzberg, "Blocking Coalitions and Policy Change," in *Policy Change in Congress*, ed. Gerald C. Wright, Jr., Leroy N. Rieselbach, and Lawrence C. Dodd (New York: Agathon, 1986).

8. The Speaker's control over Rules and the Democratic Caucus's ability to instruct the committee have reduced the need to reintroduce the 21-day-rule, under which the Speaker could, over committee objection, call up measures for floor consideration after the bill had been in the Rules Committee's hands for more than 21 days. The rule was adopted on two occasions—most recently in the 89th Congress (1965-67)—and did facilitate the movement of legislation to the floor. But in each instance it did not survive renewed conservative strength in the subsequent Congress and was stricken from the rules.

9. For instance, new rules might eliminate or restrict 1) the morning hour, when senators make short speeches and handle miscellaneous chores not immediately related to lawmaking; 2) the practice of insisting that the *Journal* be read in full; and 3) the dilatory use of repeated quorum calls.

10. Filibusters can begin at numerous points: on the motion to take up a bill, on amendments, on passage, and on accepting a conference report. Reformers have proposed making the motion to take up a bill nondebatable, thus removing one opportunity to talk a bill to death.

11. In 1985 Congress used this strategy when it joined the Gramm-Rudman-Hollings deficit reduction scheme to essential legislation to increase the federal debt ceiling. Congress, in effect, forced the Reagan administration to risk substantial reductions in its defense budget to win approval of enlarged

borrowing authority necessary to keep the government operating. The strategy worked: the president signed the bill, with reluctance and reservations.

12. The item veto fight neatly illustrates the interplay of politics and principle in reform proposals. On the one hand, some reformers, recognizing that they could not muster a two-thirds vote to amend the Constitution, proposed to give the president the item veto for a two-year trial period. The experiment would expire before the end of the Reagan administration, permitting its supporters, mainly Republicans, to reassess their position should the Democrats win the presidency in 1988. On the other hand, some item veto supporters saw the issue as a matter of principle. Sen. Edward Kennedy (D-Mass.), hardly a close ally of the Reagan administration, supported the proposal, arguing that "the fundamental issue ... is fiscal responsibility, and it has little to do with the partisan politics of the moment.... A larger principle and a long perspective are at stake" (Quoted in the Boston Globe, July 24, 1985, 3).

13. See Bonafede, "Reform of U.S. System," 1523.

14. Of course, this system requires that the electorate have command of the political issues in presidential (and congressional) campaigns, and there is some doubt that, as presently constituted, the system is capable of rendering the sort of policy mandates that this level of accountability requires. See Norman H. Nie, Sidney Verba, and John R. Petrocik, *The Changing American Voter*, enlarged ed. (Cambridge, Mass.: Harvard University Press, 1979); Morris P. Fiorina, *Retrospective Voting in American National Elections* (New Haven, Conn.: Yale University Press, 1981); and Paul R. Abramson, John H. Aldrich, and David W. Rohde, *Continuity and Change in the 1980 Elections*, rev. ed. (Washington, D.C.: CQ Press, 1982).

15. James Burnham, *Congress and the American Tradition* (Chicago: Regnery, 1959); and Alfred de Grazia, *Republic in Crisis: Congress against the Executive Force* (New York: Federal Legal Publications, 1965).

16. Burnham, *Congress and the American Tradition*.

17. Diffusion of authority, as noted, is highly compatible with legislators' career aspirations. In a stable institution such as Congress, many lawmakers aspire to long-term congressional service. Thus, structural and procedural reforms that serve to open avenues to influence, even over small segments of legislative business, have been attractive. They have allowed legislators to make a mark and to find a niche for themselves early in their congressional careers.

18. In the 94th Congress, when seniority ceased to be binding, there was no centralization. The House Democratic leaders—Speaker Carl Albert (Okla.) and Majority Leader Thomas P. O'Neill, Jr. (Mass.)—recommended that the senior member of each committee be given the chair. The Steering and Policy Committee recommended ousting two senior chairmen: Wright Patman (Texas) and Wayne Hays (Ohio). The caucus restored Hays but deprived W. R. Poage (Texas) and F. Edward Hébert (La.), as well as Patman, of their chairs. This was scarcely a centralized process; nor has subsequent selection of chairs been particularly centralized.

19. See also Kenneth Shepsle, *The Giant Jigsaw Puzzle: Democratic Committee Assignments in the Modern House* (Chicago: University of Chicago Press, 1973); Irwin N. Gertzog, "The Routinization of Committee Assignments in the U.S.

House of Representatives," *American Journal of Political Science* 20 (1976): 693-712; and Steven S. Smith and Christopher J. Deering, *Committees in Congress* (Washington D.C.: CQ Press, 1984).

20. Party leaders are more likely to dominate the committee assignment process when the same party controls the White House and both houses of Congress. Under such circumstances the leaders might be tempted to try to place presidential loyalists in important posts. Leaders capable of controlling committee action through manipulating panel membership would, of course, tend to centralize power.

21. In 1973 the newly enlarged Senate Democratic Steering Committee seemingly manipulated the membership of the Finance Committee, adding liberals in what appeared to be an effort to weaken the position of the committee's chairperson, Russell Long (La.). Two years later the Steering Committee placed two more liberals on Finance, three on Armed Services, and, in a head-to-head confrontation, James Abourezk (S.D.) rather than conservative James B. Allen (Ala.) on Judiciary. These incidents suggest that the Steering Committee may support the party leaders, but it has not, over the past decade, been noticeably inclined to do so in such overt fashion.

22. See Michael J. Malbin, *Unelected Representatives: Congressional Staff and the Future of Representative Government* (New York: Basic Books, 1980).

23. In *U.S. v. Nixon* (1974), the Supreme Court required the defendant to turn over to a special prosecutor Watergate tapes that Nixon asserted were protected by executive privilege. While not applicable in instances involving possible criminal misconduct, executive privilege did have many useful purposes, the Court seemed to say. The implication was that the doctrine might well apply in other, more ordinary circumstances.

24. On the information problem in general, see John S. Saloma III, *Congress and the New Politics* (Boston: Little, Brown, 1969). For recent developments, see Joseph Cooper and G. Calvin Mackenzie, eds., *The House at Work* (Austin, Texas: University of Texas Press, 1981); and *Congressional Quarterly Weekly Report*, July 13, 1985, 1379-82.

25. On these suggestions, see Charles R. Dechert, "Availability of Information for Congressional Operations," and James A. Robinson, "Decision-Making in Congress," in *Congress: The First Branch of Government*, coord. Alfred de Grazia (Washington, D.C.: American Enterprise Institute, 1966), 167-211 and 259-94.

26. See Stephen E. Frantzich, *Compuors in Congress* (Beverly Hills, Calif.: Sage, 1982).

27. Increased information resources will be of little value if members do not use them or use them unproductively. Some observers fear that the use of computers to win reelection—to answer the mail or solicit campaign funds rather than to promote programs or to conduct oversight—will detract from Congress's capacity to be responsive in policy terms. Legislators remain free to use data as they see fit, for their personal purposes, political or programmatic; if they decide to pursue "undesirable" (from the observer's standpoint) goals, no amount of data will improve responsiveness to public interests.

28. When the Supreme Court in *Baker v. Carr* (1962) and *Wesberry v. Sanders* (1964) mandated population equality for House districts, there was a fear that reapportionment would cause conservative rural areas to lose represen-

tation to the liberal urban areas. In fact, the dozen or so seats that rural areas lost in the redistricting process that these decisions triggered in the 1960s and 1970s wound up controlled by suburban conservatives rather than by big-city liberals (the cities also lost population). More recent shifts have seen the seats redistributed regionally. The industrial Frost Belt (the Northeast and Midwest) has yielded seats to the southwestern Sun Belt. Overall, the effect of court-enforced reapportionment has been minimal. See Richard Born, "Partisan Intentions and Election Day Realities in the Congressional Redistricting Process," *American Political Science Review* 79 (1985): 305-19; and Peverill Squire, "Results of Partisan Redistricting in Seven U.S. States during the 1970s," *Legislative Studies Quarterly* 10 (1985): 259-66. See also Bruce E. Cain, "Assessing the Partisan Effects of Redistricting," *American Political Science Review* 79 (1985): 320-33. However, should the courts reapportion districts to ensure minority representation—of blacks in central cities, for example—or to impose some standard of proportional representation—a party winning a particular proportion of votes should get that same proportion of seats—the fears of the pro-Congress reformers might be realized. While the Court has been asked to rule on both issues, it has yet to do so.

29. On the media and Congress, see Robert Blanchard, ed., *Congress and the News Media* (New York: Hastings House, 1974); Stephen Hess, *The Washington Reporters* (Washington, D.C.: Brookings Institution, 1981); Susan Miller, "News Coverage of Congress: The Search for the Ultimate Spokesman," *Journalism Quarterly* 54 (1977): 459-65; Michael J. Robinson and Kevin Appel, "Network News Coverage of Congress," *Political Science Quarterly* 94 (1979): 407-18; Charles M. Tidmarch and John J. Pitney, Jr., "Covering Congress," *Polity* 17 (1985): 464-83; and Peter Clarke and Susan H. Evans, *Covering Campaigns: Journalism in Congressional Elections* (Stanford, Calif.: Stanford University Press, 1983).

30. A few changes in financial disclosure requirements might make a difference at the margins. For instance, at present members are required to specify their various holdings only in broad categories; the top net worth bracket is $250,000 and above. Many senators have assets well above that figure, and more precise categories covering a broader range would help interested citizens assess legislators' finances more accurately.

31. As a practical matter, the reforms necessary to implement a presidential-dominance arrangement, especially with responsible parties, would require amending the Constitution and making numerous statutory revisions. Congress can hardly be expected to enact the dissolution of its own claims to policy-making influence.

32. In this section voting is treated as a means of transmitting views on political issues. Voting simultaneously fosters accountability and responsiveness. As a retrospective judgment, it holds incumbents to account for their past performance. Looking ahead, it offers suggestions about what should be done in the future; at least it does so if policy sentiments shape voters' choices.

33. One of the chief reasons for the relative infrequency with which discharge petitions (requiring 218 signatures, a majority of the full House) are signed is the reluctance of rank-and-file representatives to risk the wrath of powerful committee leaders and experts. Easier discharge require-

ments coupled with a relaxation of the chairperson's control over the committee should increase the prospect of getting legislation to the floor. On the other hand, these changes would make it possible for a minority to force floor consideration of bills unacceptable to the majority. While such legislation presumably would not pass, the tactic could complicate the schedule and, in delaying action on priority bills, retard congressional responsibility.

34. These majorities would, in all probability, continue to be similar to those found at present—shifting from issue to issue and created as a result of a negotiation process.

35. *Congressional Quarterly Weekly Report*, November 24, 1984, 2983-84. The Democratic Caucus rejected the Obey proposal at the start of the 99th Congress (1985-87); see *Congressional Quarterly Weekly Report*, December 8, 1984, 2054-55.

36. Glenn R. Parker, "Some Themes in Congressional Unpopularity," *American Journal of Political Science* 21 (1977): 93-110; and Jack Dennis, "Public Support for Congress," *Political Behavior* 3 (1981): 319-50.

37. See the New York City Bar Association, Report of the Special Committee on Congessional Ethics, *Congress and the Public Trust* (New York, Atheneum, 1970). The New York bar has proposed to prohibit, effective six years after election, the practice of law by sitting legislators and to bar members' law firms from representing the clients that the members cannot serve. Other reformers seek a postemployment ban, like that imposed on former executive branch employees, on former legislators' dealings with the federal government. On ethics in general, see Robert S. Getz, *Congressional Ethics* (New York: Van Nostrand, 1966); Robert Sherrill, "Why We Can't Depend on Congress to Keep Congress Honest," *New York Times Magazine*, July 19, 1970, 5ff.; Task Force on Broadcasting and the Legislature, *Openly Arrived At* (New York: Twentieth Century Fund, 1974); and Edmund Beard and Stephen Horn, *Congressional Ethics: The View from the House* (Washington, D.C.: Brookings Institution, 1975).

38. For a major theoretical effort to explain congressional change and reform, see Lawrence C. Dodd, "A Theory of Congressional Cycles: Solving the Puzzle of Change," in *Policy Change in Congress*, ed. Wright, Rieselbach, and Dodd.

Appendix: Major Congressional Reforms, 1970-85

Reforms Promoting Responsiveness

Redistributing Committee Power

1970   If a House Democratic committee chair declines to call a committee meeting, a majority can vote to meet anyway, with the ranking majority member presiding.

Any House committee member with support of a committee majority can move floor consideration of a bill if the chair fails to do so within seven days after a rule is granted.

1971   House Democratic and Republican committees on committees need not follow seniority in nominating committee chairs.

Ten House Democrats can force a vote in the party caucus on the Committee on Committees' nominations for committee chairs.

1973   In the House Democratic Caucus, one-fifth of those present and voting can force a vote on each nominee for committee chair.

Senate Republicans on each committee can elect their ranking member without regard to seniority.

1975   Senate Democrats can vote in caucus for committee chairs without regard to seniority.

The House Democratic Caucus can select Appropriations subcommittee chairs by the same procedures used to pick full committee chairs.

Strengthening the Subcommittees

1973   House Democrats designate their members on each full committee as the committee caucus with power to choose subcommittee chairs and to set subcommittee budgets.

The House "Subcommittee Bill of Rights" mandates that legislation be referred to subcommittees; that subcommittees be able to meet, hold hearings, and report legislation; and that each have adequate staff and budget.

1973-75 House Democrats establish a "bidding" procedure, reflecting seniority, for determining subcommittee assignments.

1974   Each House full committee (Rules and Budget committees excepted) is required to have at least four subcommittees.

| 1976 | The committee caucus of each House full committee is empowered to determine the number of its subcommittees and to define their jurisdictions. |
| 1977 | House subcommittee chairs are selected by secret ballot. |

Democratizing Reforms

1970	Senators are limited to service on two major and one minor committee.
	No senator can chair more than one full committee or more than one subcommittee of a major committee.
1971	Each House subcommittee chair is entitled to hire the subcommittee staff.
	No House Democrat can serve on more than two legislative committees or chair more than one legislative subcommittee.
1973	No House Democrat can serve on more than one exclusive, one major, or two nonmajor committees. Each member is entitled to one exclusive or major committee assignment.
1975	The chair of an exclusive or major House committee is barred from chairing any other committee or serving on any other exclusive, major, or nonmajor committee.
1977	House Democrats cannot chair more than one subcommittee.
	The House Speaker is obligated to appoint conferees from among those with basic responsibility for the legislation and to include supporters of the bill's major provisions to the greatest extent possible.
1978	House members can attend any committee or subcommittee meeting (except of the Ethics Committee) even if it is a closed session.
	House Democrats who chair a full committee can chair a subcommittee only on that committee.
1979	House Democrats are limited to service on five subcommittees of standing committees.

Other Reforms

1970	The minority party in the House is guaranteed a minimum of 10 minutes of debate on any amendment printed in the *Congressional Record* at least one day prior to the debate.
	The minority party in the House is entitled to call its own witnesses on at least one day of committee hearings on a bill.
	The minority party in the House is given at least three days to file minority views on committee reports.
1971	One-half of a Democratic state delegation in the House can nominate candidates for committee assignments in opposition to the choice of the Committee on Committees.
1975	The minority party in the House can hire one-third of committee staff.
	Floor debate in House on conference reports must be divided equally between majority and minority members.
1977	The House Democratic Caucus can elect the chair of the Democratic Congressional Campaign Committee. Previously, the chair was elected by the committee itself.

Reforms Promoting Accountability

"Sunshine" Reforms

1970 Television and radio coverage of House committee hearings is authorized.

House teller votes are recorded.

House and Senate committee votes are recorded and made available to the public.

1973 All House committee sessions are open to the public. A separate roll call vote is required to close sessions.

1975 House committee sessions can be closed only with a separate roll call vote each day.

All Senate committee sessions are open to the public.

1977 Only the full House, by recorded roll call vote, can close a conference committee meeting.

1978 Television coverage of House floor sessions is permitted.

Campaign Reforms

1974 Federal Election Campaign Act (FECA) amendments limit individual and organization contributions to congressional campaigns.

FECA amendments require congressional candidates to report source and use of campaign funds.

Ethics Reforms

1977 House limits use of franked mail.

1977-78 Senate and House adopt codes of ethics requiring disclosure of members' income and financial holdings, barring unofficial office accounts, and limiting outside income.

1985 Senate raises permissible level of outside income to 40 percent of congressional salary.

Reforms Promoting Responsibility

Challenging the Executive

1970 The Congressional Research Service of the Library of Congress is enlarged.

1970, 1974 The General Accounting office is enlarged and strengthened.

1972 The Office of Technology Assessment is created.

1973 The War Powers Resolution is enacted.

1974 The Congressional Budget and Impoundment Control Act is passed, creating the Congressional Budget Office.

Strengthening the Political Parties

1973 House Democratic leaders—Speaker, majority leader, and whip—are made members of the party Committee on Committees.

House Democrats establish the Steering and Policy Committee, with the Speaker as chair.

1974   House enacts a modest revision and clarification of committee jurisdictions.

House Speaker is empowered to refer bills to committees jointly and sequentially and to create ad hoc committees to expedite treatment of legislation.

1975   House Democratic Steering and Policy Committee is given the party's Committee on Committees' powers.

House Speaker is empowered to nominate Democratic members of the Rules Committee.

1977   House Speaker is empowered to set time limits on joint and sequential committee consideration of legislation.

Senate leaders are given enlarged powers over bill referrals and scheduling.

Senate significantly revises its committee jurisdictions.

Changing the Rules

1970   House committees are permitted to meet while House is in session, except under special circumstances.

House establishes an electronic voting system.

House is allowed to dispense with reading of the *Journal*.

1970,   The use of quorum calls in House for dilatory purposes is limited.
1977,
1979

1975   Senate revises cloture rule: 60 senators can cut off debate.

1977,   House can cluster roll call votes to expedite voting. Subsequent votes.
1979   in a series are limited to a five-minute period.

1979   Twenty-five, rather than 20, House members are required to demand a roll call in the Committee of the Whole House.

Senate is required to vote on a bill within 100 hours after cloture is invoked.

Selected Bibliography

General Views, Reviews, and Overviews

Theoretical Orientations and Perspectives

American Political Science Association, Committee on Political Parties. *Toward a More Responsible Two-Party System.* New York: Rinehart, 1950.

Bolling, R. *House Out of Order.* New York: Dutton, 1965.

Burnham, J. *Congress and the American Tradition.* Chicago, Ill.: Regnery, 1969.

Burns, J. M. *The Deadlock of Democracy.* Englewood Cliffs, N.J.: Prentice-Hall, 1963.

Cooper, J. "Strengthening the Congress: An Organizational Analysis." *Harvard Journal on Legislation* 2 (1975): 301-68.

Davidson, R. H., D. M. Kovenock, and M. K. O'Leary. *Congress in Crisis: Politics and Congressional Reform.* Belmont, Calif.: Wadsworth, 1966.

Davidson, R. H., and W. J. Oleszek. "Adaptation and Consolidation: Structural Innovation in the House of Representatives." *Legislative Studies Quarterly* 1 (1976): 37-65.

de Grazia, A. "Toward a New Model of Congress." In *Congress: The First Branch of Government*, coordinated by A. de Grazia, 1-22. Washington D.C.: American Enterprise Institute.

Dexter, L. A. "Undesigned Consequences of Purposive Legislative Action." *Journal of Public Policy* 1 (1981): 413-31.

Dodd, L. C. "Understanding Legislative Change: Perspectives on the U.S. Congress." Paper presented at the Annual Meeting of the Social Science History Association, 1982.

Jones, C. O. "How Reform Changes Congress." In *Legislative Reform and Public Policy*, edited by S. Welch and J. G. Peters, 11-29. New York: Praeger, 1977.

———. "Will Reform Change Congress?" In *Congress Reconsidered*, edited by L. C. Dodd and B. I. Oppenheimer, 247-60. New York: Praeger, 1977.

Oleszek, W. J. "A Perspective on Congressional Reform." In *Legislative Reform and Public Policy*, edited by S. Welch and J. G. Peters, 3-10. New York: Praeger, 1977.

———. "Integration and Fragmentation: Key Themes of Congressional Change." *Annals* 466 (1983): 193-205.

Patterson, S. C. "Conclusions: On the Study of Legislative Reform." In *Legislative Reform and Public Policy*, edited by S. Welch and J. G. Peters, 214-22. New York: Praeger, 1977.

Rohde, D. W., and K. A. Shepsle. "Thinking about Legislative Reform." In *Legislative Reform: The Policy Impact*, edited by L. N. Rieselbach, 9-21. Lexington, Mass.: Lexington Books, 1978.

Saloma, J. S., III. *Congress and the New Politics.* Boston, Mass.: Little, Brown, 1969.

Change and Reform in the 1970s and 1980s

Congressional Quarterly. "Inside Congress." In *Congress and the Nation*, vol. 4, 743-94. Washington, D.C.: Congressional Quarterly, 1977.

Democratic Study Group. *Special Report: Reform in the House of Representatives.* No. 94-28. Washington, D.C.

Dodd, L. C., and B. I. Oppenheimer. "The House in Transition: Partisanship and Opposition." In *Congress Reconsidered*, 3d ed., edited by L. C. Dodd and B. I. Oppenheimer, 34-64. Washington, D.C.: CQ Press, 1985.

Dumbrell, J. "Strengthening the Legislative Power of the Purse: The Origins of the 1974 Budgetary Reforms in the U.S. Congress." *Public Administration* 57 (1980): 479-96.

Huntington, S. P. "Congressional Responses to the Twentieth Century." In *The Congress and America's Future*, 2d ed., edited by D. B. Truman, 6-38. Englewood Cliffs, N.J.: Prentice-Hall, 1973.

Lowe, D. E. "The Bolling Committee and the Politics of Reorganization." *Capitol Studies* 6 (1978): 39-61.

Ornstein, N. J. "The Democrats Reform Power in the House of Representatives, 1969-1975." In *America in the Seventies*, edited by A. Sindler, 1-48. Boston, Mass.: Little, Brown, 1976.

———. "The House and the Senate in a New Congress." In *The New Congress*, edited by T. E. Mann and N. J. Ornstein, 363-83. Washington, D.C.: American Enterprise Institute, 1981.

Ornstein, N. J., R. L. Peabody, and D. W. Rohde. "The Senate through the 1980s: Cycles of Change." In *Congress Reconsidered*, 3d ed., edited by L. C. Dodd and B. I. Oppenheimer, 13-33. Washington, D.C.: CQ Press, 1985.

Patterson, S. C. "The Semi-Sovereign Congress." In *The New American Political System*, edited by A. King, 127-77. Washington, D.C.: American Enterprise Institute, 1978.

Rieselbach, L. N. *Congressional Reform in the Seventies.* Morristown, N.J.: General Learning Press, 1977.

Shaw, M. "Congress in the 1970s: A Decade of Reform." *Parliamentary Affairs* 34 (1981): 253-90.

Sheppard, B. D. *Rethinking Congressional Reform: The Reform Roots of the Special Interest Congress.* Cambridge, Mass.: Schenkman Books, 1985.

Sundquist, J. L. *The Decline and Resurgence of Congress.* Washington, D.C.: The Brookings Institution, 1981.

Collections

de Grazia, A., coord. *Congress: The First Branch of Government.* Washington, D.C.: American Enterprise Institute, 1966.

Ornstein, N. J., ed. *Congress in Change: Evolution and Reform.* New York: Praeger, 1975.

Rieselbach, L. N., ed. "Symposium on Legislative Reform." *Policy Studies Journal* 5 (1977): 394-497.

———. *Congressional Reform: The Policy Impact.* Lexington, Mass.: Lexington Books, 1978.

Welch, S., and J. G. Peters, eds. *Legislative Reform and Public Policy.* New York: Praeger, 1977.

Congressional Documents

U.S. Congress. House. Select Committee on Committees. *Hearings on the Subject of Committee Organization in the House.* 3 vols. Washington, D.C.: Government Printing Office, 1973.

———. Commission on Administrative Review. *Final Report.* 2 vols. Washington, D.C.: Government Printing Office, 1977.

———. Select Committee on Committees. *Final Report.* Washington, D.C.: Government Printing Office, 1980.

U.S. Congress. Senate. Commission on the Operation of the Senate. *Toward a Modern Senate: Final Report.* Washington, D.C.: Government Printing Office, 1976.

———. Study Group on Senate Practices and Procedures. *Report of the Study Group on Senate Practices and Procedures to the Committee on Rules and Administration.* Washington, D.C.: Government Printing Office, 1984.

———. Temporary Select Committee to Study the Senate Committee System. *Final Report.* Washington, D.C.: Government Printing Office, 1984.

Structural Change and Reform

Political Parties

Crook, S. B., and J. R. Hibbing. "Congressional Reform and Party Discipline: The Effects of Changes in the Seniority System on Party Loyalty in the U.S. House of Representatives." *British Journal of Political Science* 15 (1985): 207-26.

Davidson, R. H. "Congressional Leaders as Agents of Change." In *Understanding Congressional Leadership,* edited by F. H. Mackaman, 135-56. Washington, D.C.: CQ Press, 1981.

Deering, C. J., and S. S. Smith. "Majority Party Leadership and the New House Subcommittee System." In *Understanding Congressional Leadership,* edited by F. H. Mackaman, 261-92. Washington, D.C.: CQ Press, 1981.

Jones, C. O. "Can Our Parties Survive Our Politics?" In *The Role of the Legislature in Western Democracies,* edited by N. J. Ornstein, 20-36. Washington, D.C.: American Enterprise Institute, 1981.

———. "House Leadership in an Age of Reform." In *Understanding Congressional Leadership,* edited by F. H. Mackaman, 117-34. Washington, D.C.: CQ Press, 1981.

Oppenheimer, B. I. "The Changing Relationship between House Leadership and the Committee on Rules." In *Understanding Congressional Leadership,* edited by F. H. Mackaman, 207-26. Washington, D.C.: CQ Press, 1981.

Ornstein, N. J., and D. W. Rohde. "Political Parties and Congressional Reform." In *Parties and Elections in an Anti-Party Age,* edited by J. Fishel, 280-94. Bloomington: Indiana University Press, 1978.

Peabody, R. L. *Leadership in Congress: Stability, Succession and Change.* Boston, Mass.: Little, Brown, 1976.

Sinclair, B. "The Speaker's Task Force in the Post-Reform House of Representatives." *American Political Science Review* 75 (1980): 397-410.

Waldman, S. "Majority Leadership in the House of Representatives." *Political Science Quarterly* 95 (1980): 373-93.

Committees

Bach, S. "Committee and Subcommittee Change in the House of Representatives." Paper presented to the Annual Meeting of the American Political Science Association, 1984.

Davidson, R. H. "Two Avenues of Change: House and Senate Committee Reorganization. In *Congress Reconsidered*, 2d ed., edited by L. C. Dodd and B. I. Oppenheimer, 107-33. Washington D.C.: CQ Press, 1981.

Davidson, R. H., and W. J. Oleszek. *Congress against Itself*. Bloomington: Indiana University Press, 1977.

Deering, C. J. "Subcommittee Government in the U.S. House: An Analysis of Bill Management." *Legislative Studies Quarterly* 7 (1982): 533-46.

Fenno, R. F., Jr. *Congressmen in Committees*. Boston, Mass.: Little, Brown, 1973.

Haeberle, S. H. "The Institutionalization of the Subcommittee in the U.S. House of Representatives." *Journal of Politics* 40 (1978): 1054-65.

Ornstein, N. J. "Causes and Consequences of Congressional Change: Subcommittee Reforms in the House of Representatives, 1970-1973." In *Congress in Change: Evolution and Reform*, edited by N. J. Ornstein, 88-114. New York: Praeger, 1975.

Ornstein, N. J., and D. W. Rohde. "Seniority and Future Power in Congress." In *Congress in Change: Evolution and Reform*, edited by N. J. Ornstein, 72-87. New York: Praeger, 1975.

Parris, J. H. "The Senate Reorganizes Its Committees, 1977." *Political Science Quarterly* 94 (1979): 319-37.

Rieselbach, L. N., and J. K. Unekis. "Ousting the Oligarchs: Assessing the Consequences of Reform and Change on Four House Committees." *Congress and the Presidency* 9 (1981-82): 83-117.

Rudder, C. E. "Committee Reform and the Revenue Process." In *Congress Reconsidered*, edited by L. C. Dodd and B. I. Oppenheimer, 117-39. New York: Praeger, 1977.

Stanga, J. E., and D. N. Farnsworth. "Seniority and Democratic Reforms in the House of Representatives: Committees and Subcommittees." In *Legislative Reform: The Policy Impact*, edited by L. N. Rieselbach, 35-47. Lexington, Mass.: Lexington Books, 1978.

Smith, S. S., and B. A. Ray. "The Impact of Congressional Reform: House Democratic Committee Assignments." *Congress and the Presidency* 10 (1983): 219-40.

Smith, S. S., and C. J. Deering. *Committees in Congress*. Washington, D.C.: CQ Press, 1984.

Unekis, J. K. "The Impact of Congressional Reform on Decision-Making in the Standing Committees of the House of Representatives." *Congressional Studies* 7 (1980): 53-62.

Unekis, J. K., and L. N. Rieselbach. "Congressional Committee Leadership: Continuity and Change, 1971-1978." *Legislative Studies Quarterly* 8 (1983): 251-70.

_____. *Congressional Committee Politics: Continuity and Change.* New York: Praeger, 1984.

Staff and Information Resources

Frantzich, S. E. *Computers in Congress: The Politics of Information.* Beverly Hills, Calif.: Sage, 1982.

Hammond, S. W. "Congressional Change and Reform: Staffing the Congress." In *Legislative Reform: The Policy Impact,* edited by L. N. Rieselbach, 183-93. Lexington, Mass.: Lexington Books, 1978.

Jones, C. O. "Why Congress Can't Do Policy Analysis (or words to that effect)." *Policy Analysis* 2 (1976): 215-64.

Malbin, M. J. *Unelected Representatives: Congressional Staff and the Future of Representative Government.* New York: Basic Books, 1980.

Schick, A. "The Supply and Demand for Analysis on Capitol Hill." *Policy Analysis* 2 (1976): 215-34.

Worthley, J. A. "Legislative Information Systems: A Review and Analysis of Recent Experience." *Western Political Quarterly* 30 (1977): 418-30.

Rules and Informal Norms

Bach, S. "The Structure of Choice in the House of Representatives: Recent Use of Special Rules." Paper presented to the Annual Meeting of the American Political Science Association, 1980.

Loomis, B. A., and J. Fishel. "New Members in a Changing Congress: Norms, Actions and Satisfaction." *Congressional Studies* 8 (1981): 81-94.

Oleszek, W. J. *Congressional Procedures and the Policy Process.* 2d ed. Washington, D.C.: CQ Press, 1984.

Oppenheimer, B. I. "Changing Time Constraints on Congress: Historical Perspectives on the Use of Cloture." In *Congress Reconsidered,* 3d ed., edited by L. C. Dodd and B. I. Oppenheimer, 393-413. Washington, D.C.: CQ Press, 1985.

Ornstein, N. J., and D. W. Rohde. "The Strategy of Reform: Recorded Teller Voting in the House of Representatives." Paper presented to the Annual Meeting of the Midwest Political Science Association, 1974.

Renfrow, P. D. "The Senate Filibuster System, 1917-1979: Changes and Consequences." Paper presented to the Annual Meeting of the American Political Science Association, 1980.

Rohde, D. W., N. J. Ornstein, and R. L. Peabody. "Political Change and Legislative Norms in the United States Senate, 1957-1974." In *Studies of Congress,* edited by G. R. Parker, 147-88. Washington, D.C.: CQ Press, 1985.

Wolanin, T. R. "The View from the Trench: Reforming Congressional Procedures." In *The United States Congress: Proceedings of the Thomas P. O'Neill, Jr., Symposium,* edited by Dennis Hale, 209-28. Chestnut Hill, Mass.: Boston College, 1982.

Change, Reform, and the Legislative Environment

Redistricting, Elections, Turnover

Alexander, H. E. *Financing Politics: Money, Elections and Political Reform,* 3d ed., Washington, D.C.: CQ Press, 1984.

Bullock, C. S., III. "Redistricting and Congressional Stability, 1962-1972." *Journal of Politics* 37 (1975): 569-75.

Cover, A. D., and D. R. Mayhew. "Congressional Dynamics and the Decline of Competitive Congressional Elections." In *Congress Reconsidered*, 2d ed., edited by L. C. Dodd and B. I. Oppenheimer, 62-82. Washington, D.C.: CQ Press, 1981.

Fenno, R. F., Jr., "If, as Ralph Nader Says, Congress is 'the Broken Branch,' How Come We Love Our Congressmen So Much?" In *Congress in Change: Evolution and Reform*, edited by N. J. Ornstein, 277-87. New York: Praeger, 1975.

Ferejohn, J. A. "On the Decline of Competition in Congressional Elections." *American Political Science Review* 71 (1977): 166-76.

Fiorina, M. P. *Congress: Keystone of the Washington Establishment.* New Haven, Conn.: Yale University Press, 1977.

Hacker, A. *Congressional Districting*, rev. ed. Washington, D.C.: The Brookings Institution, 1964.

Jacobson, G. C. *Money in Congressional Elections.* New Haven, Conn.: Yale University Press, 1980.

Mann, T. E., and R. E. Wolfinger. "Candidates and Parties in Congressional Elections." *American Political Science Review* 74 (1980): 617-32.

Parker, G. R., and R. H. Davidson. "Why Do Americans Love Their Congressmen So Much More Than Their Congress?" *Legislative Studies Quarterly* 4 (1979): 53-61.

Legislative-Executive Relations

Aberbach, J. D. "Changes in Congressional Oversight." *American Behavioral Scientist* 22 (1979): 493-515.

Cohen, R. E. "Congress Steps Up Use of the Legislative Veto." *National Journal* 12 (1980): 1473-77.

Cooper, J. "Postscript on the Congressional Veto: Is There Life after Chadha?" *Political Science Quarterly* 98 (1983): 427-29.

Davidson, R. H. "Breaking Up Those 'Cozy Triangles': An Impossible Dream?" In *Legislative Reform and Public Policy*, edited by S. Welch and J. G. Peters, 30-53. New York: Praeger, 1977.

Davis, E. L. "Legislative Reform and the Decline of Presidential Influence on Capitol Hill." *British Journal of Political Science* 9 (1979): 465-79.

Dodd, L. C., and R. L. Schott. *Congress and the Administrative State.* New York: Wiley, 1979.

Ellwood, J. W., and J. A. Thurber. "The Politics of the Congressional Budget Process Re-examined." In *Congress Reconsidered*, 2d ed., edited by L. C. Dodd and B. I. Oppenheimer, 246-71. Washington, D.C.: CQ Press, 1981.

Franck, T. M., and E. Weisband. *Foreign Policy by Congress.* New York: Oxford University Press, 1979.

Gilmour, R. S. "The New Congressional Oversight and Administrative Leadership." Paper presented to the Everett McKinley Dirksen Congressional Leadership Research Center-Sam Rayburn Library Conference, Understanding Congressional Leadership: The State of the Art, 1980.

Ippolito, D. S. *Congressional Spending.* Ithaca, N.Y.: Cornell University Press, 1981.

LeLoup, L. T. "Budgeting in the U.S. Senate: Old Ways of Doing New Things." Paper presented to the Annual Meeting of the Midwest Political Science Association, 1979.

———. "Process versus Policy: The U.S. House Budget Committee." *Legislative Studies Quarterly* 4 (1979): 227-54.

Rudder, C. "The Impact of the Budget and Impoundment Control Act of 1974 on the Revenue Committees of the U.S. Congress." Paper presented to the Annual Meeting of the American Political Science Association, 1977.

Schaefer, W. P., and J. A. Thurber. "The Causes, Characteristics and Political Consequences of the Legislative Veto." Paper presented to the Annual Meeting of the Southern Political Science Association, 1980.

Schick, A. *Congress and Money: Budgeting, Spending, and Taxing.* Washington, D.C.: Urban Institute, 1980.

Shuman, H. E. *Politics and the Budget: The Struggle between the President and the Congress.* Englewood Cliffs, N.J.: Prentice-Hall, 1984.

Wander, W. T., F. T. Herbert, and G. W. Copeland, eds. *Congressional Budgeting: Politics, Process and Power.* Baltimore: Johns Hopkins University Press, 1984.

Wildavsky, A. *The Politics of the Budgetary Process.* 4th ed. Boston, Mass.: Little, Brown, 1984.

Zeidenstein, H. G. "The Reassertion of Congressional Power: New Curbs on the President." *Political Science Quarterly* 93 (1978): 393-409.

Public Scrutiny: Ethics

Beard, E., and S. Horn. *Congressional Ethics: The View from the House.* Washington, D.C.: The Brookings Institution, 1975.

Bullock, C. S., III. "Congress in the Sunshine." In *Legislative Reform: The Policy Impact,* edited by L. N. Rieselbach, 209-21. Lexington, Mass.: Lexington Books, 1978.

Congressional Quarterly. *Congressional Ethics.* Washington, D.C.: Congressional Quarterly, 1977.

Twentieth Century Fund. *Openly Arrived at: Report of the Twentieth Century Fund Task Force on Broadcasting and the Legislature.* New York: Twentieth Century Fund, 1974.

The Impact of Change and Reform on Public Policy

Asher, H. B., and H. F. Weisberg. "Voting Change in Congress: Some Dynamic Perspectives on an Evolutionary Process." *American Journal of Political Science* 22 (1978): 391-425.

Berg, J. "The Effects of Seniority Reform on Three House Committees." In *Legislative Reform: The Policy Impact,* edited by L. N. Rieselbach, 49-59. Lexington, Mass.: Lexington Books, 1978.

Clausen, A. R., and C. E. Van Horn. "The Congressional Response to a Decade of Change, 1963-1972." *Journal of Politics* 39 (1977): 624-66.

Dodd, L. C. "Congress, the Presidency, and the Cycles of Power." In *The Post-Imperial Presidency,* edited by V. Davis, 71-99. New Brunswick, N.J.: Transaction Books, 1980.

———. "Congress, the Constitution, and the Crisis of Legitimation." In *Congress Reconsidered,* 2d ed., edited by L. C. Dodd and B. I. Oppenheimer, 21-53. Washington, D.C.: CQ Press, 1981.

_____. "A Theory of Congressional Cycles: Solving the Puzzle of Change." In *Policy Change in Congress*, edited by G. C. Wright, Jr., L. N. Rieselbach, and L. C. Dodd. New York: Agathon Press, 1986.

Hammond, S. W., and L. I. Langbein. "The Impact of Complexity and Reform on Congressional Committee Output." *Political Behavior* 4 (1982): 237-63.

Huddleston, M. W. "Thraining Lobsters to Fly: Assessing the Impacts of the 1974 Congressional Budget Reform." Paper presented to the Annual Meeting of the Midwest Political Science Association, 1979.

Johnson, L. K. "Legislative Reform of Intelligence Policy." *Polity* 17 (1985): 549-73.

Kaiser, F. M. "Congressional Change and Foreign Policy: The House Committee on International Relations." In *Legislative Reform: The Policy Impact*, edited by L. N. Rieselbach, 61-71. Lexington, Mass.: Lexington Books, 1978.

Malbin, M. J. "The Bolling Committee Revisited: Energy Oversight on an Investigative Subcommittee." Paper presented to the Annual Meeting of the American Political Science Association, 1978.

Oppenheimer, B. I. "Policy Implications of Rules Committee Reforms." In *Legislative Reform: The Policy Impact*, edited by L. N. Rieselbach, 91-104. Lexington, Mass.: Lexington Books, 1978.

_____. "Policy Effects of U.S. House Reform: Decentralization and the Capacity to Resolve Energy Issues." *Legislative Studies Quarterly* 5 (1980): 5-30.

Ornstein, N. J., and D. W. Rohde. "Shifting Forces, Changing Rules and Political Outcomes." In *New Perspectives on the House of Representatives*, 3d ed., edited by R. L. Peabody and N. W. Polsby, 186-269. Chicago, Ill.: Rand McNally, 1977.

Price, D. E. "The Impact of Reform: The House Subcommittee on Oversight and Investigation." In *Legislative Reform: The Policy Impact*, edited by L. N. Rieselbach, 133-57. Lexington, Mass.: Lexington Books, 1978.

Rieselbach, L. N. "Congressional Reform: Some Policy Impiications." *Policy Studies Journal* 4 (1975): 180-88.

Rudder, C. E. "The Policy Impact of Reform of the Committee on Ways and Means." In *Legislative Reform: The Policy Impact*, edited by L. N. Rieselbach, 73-89. Lexington, Mass.: Lexington Books, 1978.

Index

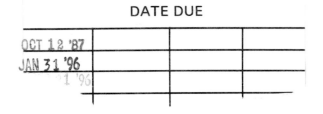